CANON
AND
THEOLOGY

OVERTURES TO BIBLICAL THEOLOGY

The Land
by Walter Brueggemann

God and the Rhetoric of Sexuality
by Phyllis Trible

The Ten Commandments and Human Rights
by Walter Harrelson

A Whirlpool of Torment
by James L. Crenshaw

Texts of Terror
by Phyllis Trible

The Suffering of God
by Terence E. Fretheim

New Testament Hospitality
by John Koenig

Jesus, Liberation, and the Biblical Jubilee
by Sharon H. Ringe

The Economy of the Kingdom
by Halvor Moxnes

Holiness in Israel
by John G. Gammie

The Feminine Unconventional
by André LaCocque

A Theology of the Cross
by Charles B. Cousar

Reading Isaiah
by Edgar W. Conrad

The Old Testament of the Old Testament
by R. W. L. Moberly

Prayer in the Hebrew Bible
by Samuel E. Balentine

Canon and Theology
by Rolf Rendtorff

Ministry in the New Testament
by David L. Bartlett

Editors

WALTER BRUEGGEMANN, McPheeder Professor of Old Testament at Columbia Theological Seminary, Decatur, Georgia

JOHN R. DONAHUE, S.J., Professor of New Testament, Jesuit School of Theology at Berkeley, California

SHARYN DOWD, Professor of New Testament at Lexington Theological Seminary, Lexington, Kentucky

CHRISTOPHER R. SEITZ, Associate Professor of Old Testament, Yale Divinity School, New Haven, Connecticut

Overtures
to an
Old Testament
Theology

CANON
AND
THEOLOGY

Rolf Rendtorff

**Translated and edited
by Margaret Kohl**

**With a Foreword
by Walter Brueggemann**

 FORTRESS PRESS   Minneapolis

CANON AND THEOLOGY
Overtures to an Old Testament Theology

First English-language edition published by Fortress Press in 1993.

These essays were published in German as *Kanon und Theologie: Vorarbeiten zu einer Theologie des Alten Testaments* by Neukirchener Verlag in 1991.

Library of Congress Cataloging-in-Publication Data

Rendtorff, Rolf, 1925–
    [Kanon und Theologie. English]
    Canon and theology : overtures to an Old Testament theology / Rolf
Rendtorff ; translated and edited by Margaret Kohl. — 1st North
American ed.
        p.   cm. — (Overtures to biblical theology)
    Translation of: Kanon und Theologie.
    Includes bibliographical references and indexes.
    ISBN 0-8006-2665-6 (alk. paper)
    1. Bible. O.T.—Criticism, interpretation, etc.   I. Kohl,
Margaret.   II. Title.   III. Series.
BS1192.4313   1993
230—dc20   93-22408
                                                               CIP

The paper used in this publication meets the minimum requirements of American National Standard for Information Sciences—Permanence of Paper for Printed Library Materials, ANSI Z329.48-1984   ∞ ™

Manufactured in the U.S.A.   AF 1–2665

97   96   95   94   93   1   2   3   4   5   6   7   8   9   10

Contents

Foreword

Rolf Rendtorff (University of Heidelberg) has emerged as one of the pivotal and most seminal Old Testament interpreters of this generation. On the one hand, he is one of the heirs and practitioners of that interpretive tradition embodied in that peculiar generation of German interpreters of the postwar generation, including not only Gerhard von Rad, but also Martin Noth, Walther Zimmerli, Hans Walter Wolff, Claus Westermann, Karl Elliger, and Hans-Joachim Kraus. That generation of interpreters, whose work came to fruition in the *Biblischer Kommentar* series, established categories of theological interpretation that have since dominated Old Testament studies. As a student of von Rad, Rendtorff has long worked from these magisterial paradigms of interpretation.

On the other hand, Rendtorff, more than anyone on the German scene, has seen that the models of interpretation generated by that galaxy of scholars, brilliant as they were, are, in large ways, context-determined, and that it is now necessary to move beyond those categories in response to the new contexts in which scholarship now finds itself. In important ways, Rendtorff has broken with the conventional, classical modes of historical criticism in order to move on to other modes of criticism and interpretation.

In two ways, Rendtorff has become a pivotal figure for the next wave of Old Testament scholarship. First, he has moved away from German methods that have long dominated the field, methods that seek to understand the text developmentally and genetically. In place of such an approach, Rendtorff has moved in ways that are enormously daring and quite unconventional. Second, within the last generation, it is correct to say that most of the fresh impetus in scholarship is now operative in the United States, and not in Germany as heretofore. Rendtorff has become active and influential in current U.S. discussions, with particular reference to canonical, literary, and sociological studies. He has become an active, contributing member of the U.S. Society of Biblical Literature, and in important ways mediates between U.S. and European studies. He has been able to take the lead in fashioning new questions and perspectives for international study.

These essays evidence the rich and broad agenda to which Rendtorff has addressed himself over time, and the sensitive and compelling way in which he is able to do specific textual work in the service of that agenda. While his work has decisively reshaped many areas to which he has addressed himself, we may identify three areas in which his contributions are especially important.

First, he has written a series of definitive studies concerning the book of Isaiah. Rendtorff is not the only one who has worked on the canonical shape and intention of the book of Isaiah, but no other scholar has done such sustained, close textual work as he. He stands among those scholars who have redefined what it means to study the book of Isaiah.

Second, Rendtorff has committed himself to the theological task of interpreting the Old Testament, with particular attention to a canonical reading. He has entered into a discussion that has been heretofore largely a U.S. conversation, with reference to the work of Brevard Childs, James Sanders, and Joseph Blenkinsopp. His work runs parallel to that of Childs, but moves in very different ways. Whereas Childs is concerned to do a church reading of the text, or as Rendtorff says of Childs, his work is "systematic rather than canonical," Rendtorff pays primary attention to the canonical shape of the literature itself, without reference to dogmatic traditions. His work takes on importance as it reflects both continuity with and a break from the older categories of von Rad.

Third and most important, Rendtorff has addressed himself to the difficult issue of Jewish-Christian readings of the Old Testament/Hebrew Scriptures. Here he parts company decisively with Childs. The scandalous preemption of Scripture by Christians to the exclusion of Jews, most blatant and advanced in Germany but everywhere operative among Christians, has turned out to be a dead end, both theologically and in terms of colleagueship that is prepared to do serious study. The patterns of exclusionary Christian interpretation, however, run very old and very deep.

Thus it has taken courage and imagination on the part of Rendtorff to think through in such a compelling way the problems he (and all of us) have inherited, a way beyond our conventional exclusionary commitments. Rendtorff has insisted, however, that a community of Jewish and Christian reading must be genuinely theological, and must not erode into a safer history of religions approach. It is obvious that for a German scholar to take up this task means a break with practices that are culturally thick, as well as intellectually well entrenched.

On all these counts, Rendtorff is enormously important for our future shared work. Not a great deal of his writing has been translated into English, and therefore the offer of these essays is a cause of celebration for us. Because Rendtorff is constantly and restlessly moving toward new categories, it is correct to say that his work in its specific parts and in its impressive sum total is a powerful "Overture" for our coming work in theological interpretation of Scripture. He is as precise and technical in his exegetical work as one can be, but keeps his eye on the larger issues that entail nothing less than a reversal of a practice of interpretation that has sustained failed and dangerous social practice. Rendtorff is peculiarly well equipped to do both the technical and the larger hermeneutical work that reinforce each other. As interpreters along with him, we are enormously in his debt as he continues to generate new possibilities for our common work.

Walter Brueggemann

Translator's Note

The essays in the present volume have been taken from a number of different sources. Some have been translated from German for the first time. Some were originally papers read in English, and have been revised for publication here. Two contributions are reprinted here in the form in which they stand in the periodicals where they were first published. The provenance of each essay is given in the footnotes and the acknowledgments.

Biblical quotations have been taken from the Revised Standard Version, except where changes of wording were required in order to bring out the nuance of the German text.

I should like to express my sincere thanks to Professor Rendtorff for his kindness in answering questions, considering particular problems of translation, and offering helpful solutions to points of difficulty.

Margaret Kohl

Abbreviations

AB	Anchor Bible
ABD	Anchor Bible Dictionary
ASTI	*Annual of the Swedish Theological Institute,* Leiden
ATD	Das Alte Testament Deutsch, Göttingen
BBB	Bonner Biblische Beiträge, Bonn
BETL	Bibliotheca ephemeridum theologicarum lovaniensium
BEvT	Beiträge zur Evangelischen Theologie, Munich
BKAT	Biblischer Kommentar: Altes Testament, Neukirchen-Vluyn
BWANT	Beiträge zur Wissenschaft vom Alten und Neuen Testament, Leipzig
BZAW	Beihefte zur Zeitschrift für die alttestamentliche Wissenschaft, Berlin
BZ NF	*Biblische Zeitschrift,* Neue Folge, Freiburg
EvT	*Evangelische Theologie,* Munich
GAT	Grundrisse zum Alten Testament, Göttingen
HBT	*Horizons in Biblical Theology,* Pittsburgh
IB	*Interpreter's Bible*
Int	*Interpretation: A Journal of Bible and Theology,* Richmond, Va.
JBL	*Journal of Biblical Literature,* Philadelphia
JBTh	*Jahrbuch für Biblische Theologie,* Neukirchen
JQR	*Jewish Quarterly Review,* London and Philadelphia
JSOT	*Journal for the Study of the Old Testament,* Sheffield
JSOTSup	*Journal for the Study of the Old Testament,* Supplement Series, Sheffield
JSS	*Journal of Semitic Studies,* Manchester
KHC	Kurzer Hand-Commentar zum Alten Testament, K. Marti, ed., Freiburg, 1879–1905

OTL	Old Testament Library
RGG[2]	*Die Religion in Geschichte und Gegenwart,* Tübingen
SAT	Die Schriften des Alten Testaments, Göttingen
SBS	Stuttgarter Bibelstudien, Stuttgart
Semeia	*Semeia: An Experimental Journal for Biblical Criticism,* Chico, Calif., Decatur, Ga.
TBl	*Theologische Blätter,* Leipzig
TBü	Theologische Bücherei, Munich
THAT	*Theologisches Handwörterbuch zum Alten Testament,* Munich etc., 1971–
TLZ	*Theologische Literaturzeitung,* Leipzig
TRE	*Theologische Realenzyklopädie,* Berlin and New York, 1977–
TRu	*Theologische Rundschau,* Tübingen
VF	*Verkündigung und Forschung,* Munich
VT	*Vetus Testamentum*
VTSup	*Vetus Testamentum,* Supplements, Leiden
WMANT	Wissenschaftliche Monographien zum Alten und Neuen Testament, Neukirchen-Vluyn
ZAW	*Zeitschrift für die alttestamentliche Wissenschaft,* Berlin
ZTK	*Zeitschrift für Theologie und Kirche,* Tübingen

CHAPTER 1

Old Testament Theology:
Some Ideas for a
New Approach

INTRODUCTION

It is more than thirty years since the appearance of Gerhard Von Rad's *Old Testament Theology* (vol. 1, 1957; vol. 2, 1960). Its publication is often considered to have marked an epoch in the history of research.[1] And yet people often quote one of H. Wheeler Robinson's sayings: that a new theology of the Old Testament has to be written in every generation. Von Rad himself would emphatically have supported this demand, for he was highly conscious of the degree to which his own design was molded by particular constellations in the Old Testament scholarship of his time. In the preface to the first volume of his *Theology* he wrote: "The characteristic thing in today's situation, in my opinion, is the surprising convergence—indeed the mutual intersection—which has come about during the last twenty or thirty years between introductory studies and Biblical theology."[2]

Von Rad himself cites a whole series of important preconditions and presuppositions which made possible and shaped his own work. In his

---

1. Cf., for example, W. H. Schmidt, " 'Theologie des Alten Testaments' vor und nach Gerhard von Rad," *VF* 17 (1972): 1–25; J. H. Hayes and F. C. Prussner, *Old Testament Theology: Its History and Development* (Atlanta: John Knox Press; London: SCM Press, 1985), 233: "In his theology . . . von Rad . . . inaugurated a new epoch in the study of Old Testament theology."

2. G. von Rad, *Old Testament Theology*, vol. 1, trans. G. M. Stalker (Edinburgh: Oliver & Boyd; New York: Harper, 1962), v. This is a remarkable contrast to Hugo Gressmann's assertion, made in 1924, that this connection "may be considered as having been for the most part surmounted" (see n. 8 below).

preface he already describes how scholars inspired by Gunkel's investigation of literary genres had come upon forms of sacral law, all kinds of cultic texts, rituals, liturgies, "and, in particular, very ancient credal formulae." Moreover, "the history of tradition has taught us in a new way to see in the three gigantic works of the Hexateuch, the Deuteronomistic history, and the Chronicler's history, the most varied forms of the presentation of God's history with Israel in its different strata." The structure of his book, especially the first volume, then shows at every step other premises derived from the scholarship of the immediately preceding decades: the God of the patriarchs, the settlement of the promised land, amphictyony, the feast of the renewal of the covenant, apodictic law, charismatic "judges," the holy war, and much else.

Many of these premises, which thirty years ago were shared by most Old Testament scholars (at least in the German-speaking countries), are now disputed. Some of them have been abandoned altogether. Consequently we are enjoined in the light of von Rad's own methodological approach to work out a new outline. In doing so—apart from the change in the presuppositions—we have once more to consider what structure a survey of this kind ought to have. The debate about "the center" of the Old Testament which followed von Rad's *Theology* contributed many different slants and aspects here. Of special interest too are the books by Walther Zimmerli (1972) and Claus Westermann (1978) which, published after von Rad's *Theology,* belonged to the same context theologically and in the history of research. But in order to discover criteria for the layout of a new study, it is useful first to look again at the history of the discipline.

THE HISTORY OF RESEARCH

The history of Old Testament theology as a scholarly discipline begins with Johann Philipp Gabler's "proper distinction" between biblical and dogmatic theology (1787).[3] If we survey the models presented since that time, we shall be able to distinguish four main types:

1. GENERAL PHILOSOPHICAL AND THEOLOGICAL SURVEYS

The nineteenth century produced two great but very different surveys, each of which tried to translate an already existing holistic philosophical

---

3. J. P. Gabler, "Oratio de justo discrimine theologiae biblicae et dogmaticae regundisque recte utriusque finibus" (1787).

or theological concept into a "biblical theology" or an "Old Testament theology," as the case might be.

Wilhelm Vatke

In 1835 Wilhelm Vatke presented an account entitled (if we translate it into English) "The Religion of the Old Testament, Developed according to the Canonical Books." (His general heading was "Biblical Theology Scientifically Presented, Vol. 1.") This is a comprehensive and consistent exposition of Hegel's concept of the philosophy of religion, applied to the religion of the Old Testament. Vatke justifies this approach as follows:

> The all-important thing is hence to assume from the very outset a standpoint which itself, by virtue of its concepts, has the utmost generality. It must not, therefore, be derived from any particular point of view. This higher objectivity can be engendered only by philosophy, as the science of sciences; for philosophy abolishes the limitations of every individual science and every particular viewpoint, turning them into the fluid moment of a higher Whole, truth itself; and thus, in this very way, in the contemplation of history gathers together the Spirit's different forms of appearance into the Idea of Spirit itself. (p. 16)

This approach will then determine the structure and development of the account:

> The true classification of the Whole must be already given in the concept and idea of religion, and it is from that point that the arrangement of the empirically given material must necessarily be deduced. (p. 171)

Even its critics have not been able to escape the powerful impact made by this self-contained outline, especially since the "rediscovery" of Vatke by Rudolf Smend, Jr., and Lothar Perlitt. Even in 1960, von Rad wrote in the preface to the second volume of his *Theology:* "Vatke, the publication of whose *Religion des Alten Testaments* in 1835 marked the first full-scale appearance of this branch of Biblical scholarship, wished to handle Israel's spiritual and religious development as a unit, that is to say, as a coherent evolution." In a later assessment, Walther Zimmerli wrote: "In him, historical grasp and valid inward interpretation were welded into an indissoluble unity in his view of the process of the coming-to-itself of the Spirit, a process which embraced the whole of the Old Testament testimonies and which arrived at its fulfilment in Christianity. Here 'true' and 'pure' theology are fused into one" (*TRE* 6:432).

Gustav Friedrich Oehler

Gustav Friedrich Oehler developed his *Theology of the Old Testament* from a completely different angle. His book was published posthumously, being based on the final version of the lectures he gave in the winter semester of 1870/71. He is especially indebted to Johann Christian Konrad von Hofmann, whose two main works, *Weissagung und Erfüllung im alten und neuen Testamente* (Prophecy and fulfillment in the Old and New Testaments [1841]) and *Der Schriftbeweis* (Scriptural evidence [1852–55]), seemed to him to provide a fruitful approach for solving the still "unaccomplished task of delineating the whole course of the Old Testament history of salvation in its organic continuity, and with due regard to the progressive reciprocity between the word of revelation and the events of history."[4] He describes his own concept as follows:

> What is here unfolded is one great divine economy of salvation—*unum continuum systema,* as Bengel puts it—an organism of divine deeds and testimonies, which, beginning in Genesis with the act of creation, advances progressively to its completion in the person and work of Christ, and will find its close in the new heaven and earth predicted in the Apocalypse; and only in the context of this whole can details be rightly estimated.... Now, to introduce men and women to the organically historical knowledge of the Old Testament is the very business of the discipline to which these lectures are to be devoted. (p. 2)

In the consistency of its implementation Oehler's survey can hardly be compared with Vatke's, not least because of its considerable borrowings from dogmatics. Thus sections headed "History" or "Development" alternate with sections on "Doctrine" or "Theology," and didactic digressions (he calls them *Lehrstücke*) are continually introduced into the latter without any detectable system. Nevertheless, this account deserves to be set over against Vatke's philosophical design as a competing and contrasting model of an overall theological outline.

The succeeding period produced no comparable general surveys. In the latter years of the nineteenth century and the first years of the twentieth this was hardly to be expected, in view of the theological development. But it is remarkable that no such design emerged from dialectical theology either, although here overriding concepts such as "revelation" and "Word of God" were available. Here apparently approaches found within Old Testament scholarship itself proved more potent (see above on G. von Rad). For an Old Testament theology as it has to be written today, this model would hardly be a possible one, simply because a corresponding overriding theological concept is not at present in sight.

---

4. G. F. Oehler, *Theology of the Old Testament,* trans. E. D. Smith and S. Taylor (Edinburgh: T. & T. Clark, 1874–93), 61. (The translation here and in the following passage has been slightly altered.)

2. SURVEYS IN THE FRAMEWORK OF THE HISTORY OF RELIGION

According to Gabler's definition, biblical theology is historical in kind (*e genere historico*). He goes on to differentiate between "true"—that is, exegetical and historical—biblical theology and "pure" biblical theology, which has to work out the fundamental religious ideas.[5] Many writers of Old Testament theologies, however, have restricted themselves essentially to the first part of this task (Vatke being an exception; see above).

This restriction is already evident in the first great outline of an Old Testament theology, which was written by Georg Lorenz Bauer (1796); and it also applies to many after him.[6] In some of these theologies we also find marked elements of a systematic presentation, for example in Hermann Schultz's influential and several times revised Old Testament theology (1869, 5th ed. 1896).[7] It is especially true of the final German edition (published after the English translation), in which the last major section is headed: "The Religious World View of the Congregation of the Second Temple" (pp. 385–643). Nonetheless, the layout as a whole remains determined by the historical question. Incidentally, in Schultz's last two editions we also find the term "history of religion," as the heading for section 3 of the introduction: "The Religion of the Old Testament in the Context of the History of Religion."

As far as the succeeding period is concerned, it may be sufficient to quote Zimmerli: "The pendulum swings violently towards the side of (historically) 'true theology'—the question about 'pure theology' recedes into the background" (*TRE* 6:437). In this connection it is striking that the term "history of religion" continued to be used in the more general sense of the term, whereas no overall account of the theology or religious history of the Old Testament, or Israel, emerged from the orbit of the history of religions school at all.[8] Other writers of accounts

---

5. Cf. here now above all, as well as work by R. Smend (esp. "Johann Philipp Gablers Begründung der biblischen Theologie," *EvT* 22 [1962]: 345–57), D. Ritschl, " 'Wahre,' 'reine' or 'neue' biblische Theologie? Einige Anfragen zur neueren Diskussion um 'Biblische Theologie,' " *JBTh* 1 (1986): 135–50 (=his *Konzepte, Ökumene, Medizin, Ethik: Gesammelte Aufsätze* [Munich 1986], 111–30).

6. For details see the excellent summary account by W. Zimmerli in *TRE* 6:426–55. An extract from Bauer's work, translated into English by Philip Harwood, was published in 1838 (London: Charles Fox) under the title *The Theology of the Old Testament*.

7. H. Schultz, *Old Testament Theology*, trans. J. A. Paterson (Edinburgh: T. & T. Clark, 1892).

8. In his great essay "Die Aufgaben der alttestamentlichen Forschung," *ZAW* 42 (1924): 1–33, Hugo Gressmann proclaimed: "The age of literary criticism was followed by the Near East age" (pp. 8f.), and further declared: "The old liaison between 'biblical theology'

of Israel's religious history, such as Bernhard Stade (1905) and Gustav Hölscher (1922), seem to have been almost completely untouched by the questions raised by the history of religions school.[9]

3. SYSTEMATIC SURVEYS

The revival of Old Testament theology in the 1930s was marked by a whole series of surveys all laid out according to a systematic concept. Apart from Ernst Sellin, who really belonged to an older generation (b. 1867),[10] we must mention Ludwig Köhler, who "borrowed from elsewhere" the outline of his Old Testament theology (1945),[11] and therefore chose "a very simple scheme... theology, anthropology, soteriology" (preface to the first edition). Possible connections between this scheme and traditional Christian dogmatics are not mentioned.

Walther Eichrodt and Otto Procksch

The most distinctive new design for an Old Testament theology was published by Walther Eichrodt between 1933 and 1939.[12] The three volumes are entitled "God and People" (1933), "God and the World" (1935),

---

on the one hand and, on the other, literary criticism and introductory scholarship in general... may be considered as having been for the most part surmounted, now that the concept 'history of religion' has victoriously prevailed" (p. 31). The question of a total survey is not suggested here, however.

Interesting in this connection are the comments made by Otto Eissfeldt in 1930 about the tensions between the history of religion school and dialectical theology: "The fact that several representatives of this new theology started off in the history of religion school shows that the systematics of that school has not always done justice to the special character of Christianity or, to be more precise, the Protestant Christianity of the Reformation." But he himself pleads primarily for openness toward the world of religions (RGG^2 4, 1904).

9. The tradition of presenting the history of Israel's religion was taken up again in the 1960s—by Helmer Ringgren (1963) and Georg Fohrer (1969) among others. Neither shows how he intends his outline to be understood in the field of tension between "theology" and the "history of religion." Conversely, in his *Theologische Grundstrukturen des Alten Testaments* (Berlin and New York: de Gruyter, 1972) Fohrer does not mention the existence of his *Geschichte der israelitischen Religion,* published three years previously (1969; Eng. trans., *History of Israelite Religion,* trans. D. E. Green [London: SPCK; New York and Nashville: Abingdon, 1973]). The contrast to Sellin (cf. n. 10, following) is striking.

10. Sellin tried to divide "true" and "pure" theology by publishing his *Alttestamentliche Theologie auf religionsgeschichtlicher Grundlage* (Leipzig, 1933) in two parts: part 1, "Israelitisch-jüdische Religionsgeschichte" (The history of Israelite-Jewish religion) and Part 2, "Theologie des Alten Testaments" (The theology of the Old Testament).

11. L. Köhler, *Old Testament Theology,* trans. A. S. Todd (London: Lutterworth Press; Philadelphia: Westminster Press, 1957).

12. W. Eichrodt, *Theology of the Old Testament,* trans. J. A. Baker from the 6th ed. (London: SCM Press; Philadelphia: Westminster Press, 1961).

and "God and Man" (1939). This threefold division was taken from Otto Procksch, who had made it the basis of his lectures. Procksch's own account was only published posthumously, in 1950.

There is a fundamental distinction between the two accounts, however. In Eichrodt, the first two parts are in reverse order, compared with Procksch's book, the section on "God and People" being moved to the beginning. God in his relations to Israel is therefore discussed first of all, and creation is considered only after that. In other words, the second article of the creed is treated before the first. Here the influence of Karl Barth's theology is unmistakable. It is made even clearer when, as guiding concept for the first volume, Eichrodt chooses the word "covenant," presenting all the varied aspects of YHWH's relation to Israel as a development of the covenant idea. (The covenant concept is not given the same prominence in Procksch.)

All in all, Eichrodt's outline has a strongly static character. He talks about the covenant relationship, the statutes of the covenant, the organs of the covenant, and so forth, but not about God's acts with Israel in history. The exodus is only mentioned quite by the way. Procksch evidently felt the deficiency of a merely systematic account, and therefore preceded his systematic section (B. "The World of Ideas") by a historical one (A. "The Historical World"). Here too, however, the exodus as a separate theme is missing. "Moses' real arena" is Sinai (German ed., pp. 71, 82ff.).

Other Surveys

Most of the theologies that still have to be considered[13] also follow some particular systematic structure. Most of them are less stringently arranged than those of Procksch and Eichrodt, however, and also frequently lean more heavily on traditional patterns of systematic theology. J. H. Hayes and F. C. Prussner make the same point: "In many works which we have surveyed, we have noted the use of a dogmatic scheme borrowed from Christian dogmatics or systematic theology, a scheme which organizes the material according to the broad topics of Theology, Anthropology, and Soteriology (God, Man, and Salvation)" (p. 246). This may also be said of outlines published "before and after Gerhard von Rad" (cf. n. 1 above).

13. I am restricting myself here largely speaking to the accounts which have exerted a recognizable influence in the context of the present-day German-speaking discussion, or which can play a part in my own reflections about a new outline of an Old Testament theology. In the American context the picture is somewhat different in some respects; cf. here Hayes and Prussner, *Old Testament Theology*.

It is especially noticeable that the accounts all begin by talking about God. This is true, with certain variations, for the theologies of Köhler (see above), Theodorus Christiaan Vriezen (Dutch, 1949; Eng. trans., 1958), Edmond Jacob (French, 1955; Eng. trans., 1958), Walther Zimmerli (1972),[14] and Claus Westermann (1978).[15] At the same time, if we look at these books more closely we shall find that the differences in the development are more important than the consensus in the way they begin.

Köhler opens his account with a paragraph about "God's existence." His first sentence is: "The assumption that God exists is the Old Testament's greatest gift to mankind." Vriezen begins the development of section 7, "God," with a first subsection headed "God Is a Holy God." He expounds this by saying: "*Qados* is God as *the Wholly Other.*"[16] Jacob heads his first section: "The Living God, Center of Revelation and Faith." Zimmerli begins with the paragraph "The Revealed Name," after he has previously explained that "the Old Testament firmly maintains its faith in the sameness of the God it knows by the name of Yahweh," and that this must be seen as "the central focus where alone we find the inner continuity acknowledged by the faith of Israel itself" (p. 14). Westermann starts with the question: "What Does the Old Testament Say about God?" (the heading for part 1), which he then develops in "The Saving God and History" (part 2), and "The God Who Blesses, and Creation" (part 3).

Even this first, basic example shows how varied the development of approaches which at first sight seem comparable can be, and how much these differences are determined and molded by the theological presuppositions of the particular author. Further observation also shows the fundamental difference of the theological approaches "before and after Gerhard von Rad." We have already seen that in Eichrodt and Procksch the exodus is not treated as a separate theme. The same is true of Köhler, and can still be said even of Vriezen and Jacob. In Zimmerli and Westermann it is very different. Zimmerli heads his second section "Yahweh, God of Israel since Egypt." In Westermann, part 2, "The Saving God and History," begins with a section on the exodus. Here a fundamentally new

14. W. Zimmerli, *Old Testament Theology in Outline,* trans. D. E. Green (Edinburgh: T. & T. Clark; Atlanta: John Knox Press, 1978).

15. C. Westermann, *Elements of Old Testament Theology,* trans. D. W. Stott (Atlanta: John Knox Press, 1982). Georg Fohrer's book, *Theologische Grundstrukturen* (see n. 9 above), can for the most part hardly be compared with the others, and I shall not consider it here.

16. In what follows I am not proposing to assign the books to particular "theologies," since that will be in any case clear to the informed reader.

theological approach emerges, whose scholarly inception is marked by von Rad's "creed" thesis of 1938, the theological results of which began to win general acceptance during the 1950s.

The comparison could be profitably prolonged and would bring to light, as well as much common ground, important theological differences, for example in the question of soteriology, the law, the cult, prophecy, wisdom, and so forth. Here we must take into account didactic and to some degree practical reasons for the arrangement of the material. All this shows that the layout of a systematically determined plan depends to a great extent on the individual presuppositions of the authors concerned—their theological premises, historical-critical premises, didactic premises, and many others. This is by no means intended as criticism. Still less is it a value judgment. On the contrary, it is meant to serve as an indication that in this context the question about what is "right" and what is "wrong" can have only highly limited validity.

4. A CANON-RELATED SURVEY (GERHARD VON RAD)

Gerhard Von Rad's *Theology* cannot be fitted into any of the groups we have hitherto described. It is often presented under the catchword "history of tradition," which is obvious and correct in more than one respect. And yet the catchword fails to delineate the fundamental idea behind the survey as a whole. For here the decisive point is the requirement that "we must submit ourselves to the sequence of events as the faith of Israel saw them."[17]

As a consequence, von Rad begins with "the theology of the Hexateuch." This shows particularly clearly how important he found a presentation which takes its bearings from the canonical form of the texts. For contrary to his own viewpoint (according to which the ancient "creed" formulations show the exodus to be the fundamental historical saving event), and contrary to his opinion about the relatively late development in Israel of belief in creation and its fundamental subordination to faith in salvation, he begins with the primeval history. And his account of the "Hexateuch" as a whole follows "the time-division of the canonical saving history" which underlies the "Hexateuch's" structure.

Here, therefore, we can talk about a "canon-related" survey.[18] This is also shown by the fact that for the books that follow the "Hexateuch,"

17. Von Rad, *Theology,* 1:120.

18. This expression is an anachronism inasmuch as the discussion about the theological significance of "the canon" only started very much later, and since von Rad himself was not thinking here about the "final canonical form" of the texts, as is the case in the most recent discussion.

which are not dependent on a "canonical" scheme in the same way, von Rad no longer follows the presentation of the biblical texts themselves, but chooses a thematic arrangement of the material under the overall heading of "Israel's Anointed." This clearly brings out his own main interest with regard to the history of the period of the judges and especially the monarchy. The orientation toward "the canon" in the second volume has different consequences again. On the one hand, the account here is based on a historical plan, which views prophecy as a changing phenomenon in Israel's history. But on the other hand the prophets are treated individually, according to the prophetic books of the Old Testament canon. So as a whole the canonical biblical books provide the guideline for this outline of an Old Testament theology.

SOME IDEAS ABOUT A NEW APPROACH

My own new approach is intended to take its bearings from von Rad's outline in several ways.

1. OVERALL STRUCTURE

Fundamentally speaking, the basis of the overall structure is to be the theological concept which can be perceived in the books of the Old Testament itself. Here the word "fundamentally" includes the proviso that (at least at the moment) we cannot always detect a concept underlying the order and arrangement of the individual books—or the arrangement has not always been made according to theological criteria. Consequently the "canonical" aspect must not be unduly pressed, but should be considered and taken into account in the context of the theological viewpoint.

Here the question about "theology *in* the Old Testament" proves fruitful.[19] Thus in what von Rad calls "the time-division of the canonical saving history," for example, we can see the blueprint and exposition of a holistic theological view of God's history with the world and with Israel, from creation to the beginning of the handing over of the promised land.[20] Within this total design, both the time-division as a whole and the

19. R. Smend, "Theologie im Alten Testament," in *Verifikationen: Festschrift für G. Ebeling* (Tübingen, 1982), 11–26 (= "Die Mitte des Alten Testaments," in his *Gesammelte Studien,* BEvT 99 [Munich 1986], 1:104–17).

20. The "canonical" settlement begins in East Jordan. The events reported in Numbers 21 also return in the recapitulations of the fundamental saving events of the early period which von Rad called "free adaptations of the creed in cultic lyric" (e.g., Pss. 135:11; 136:19f.; Neh. 9:22). This shows that it is the Pentateuch, not the "Hexateuch," which is molded by this canonical scheme.

theological profiles of the great individual eras (primeval history; history of the patriarchs; exodus and Sinai; the settlement of the promised land) bring out very clearly the theological work which has been accomplished here. The same is true, given the appropriate modifications, for the two other great historical outlines, the Deuteronomistic and the Chronicler's histories.

Where the prophetic books are concerned, we have to keep in mind two fundamental considerations. On the one hand, the special profiles of the individual prophets or prophetic books must be evident. Consequently the books should be treated and viewed as individual units, on von Rad's model. The query about the prophet's actual words in any given case is the subject of highly controversial discussion among scholars today, so that here great caution is enjoined. Nevertheless the question about the "profile" of the message of individual prophets must certainly be asked, and an answer attempted. But we also have to ask in each case whether there is a recognizable trend as a whole in the prophetic book as we have it, especially since we may presume that here again "theology in the Old Testament" will become evident. Yet on the other hand the prophets (or prophetic books) must not be isolated from the cohesion of the historical outlines, especially since the books themselves always give the historical framework in which they are to be read and understood—at least in the heading. "The silence about the prophets" in the Deuteronomistic history[21] must not, in its turn, be passed over in silence, the more so since recent research has offered some important clues here.

The way we should treat the other books in the Old Testament canon must be decided from case to case, in accordance with their varying character. The principles established for the prophetic books must be observed here too: on the one hand the particular character and theological profile of the individual books have to be worked out in each case; on the other hand they must be fitted as far as possible into the historical scheme presented by the "first" books of the Hebrew canon.

As a whole, we can see that here again von Rad's methodological ideas provide bearings. For he talked about the "surprising convergence, indeed the mutual intersection, between introductory studies and Biblical theology." Our own scheme will now have to pick up the more modern discussion, which takes into account the final form of the texts—

---

21. The phrase is K. Koch's ("Das Profetenschweigen des deuteronomistischen Geschichtswerk," in *Die Botschaft und die Boten: Festschrift für H. W. Wolff* [Neukirchen-Vluyn, 1981], 115–28) and was evidently coined in reminiscence of Lothar Perlitt's phrase about the "silence over the covenant" among the prophets (L. Perlitt, *Bundestheologie im Alten Testament*, WMANT 36 [Neukirchen-Vluyn, 1969], 129ff.).

whether in the light of redaction history, composition history, or "canon criticism"—and inquires about their theological intention. Here we are concerned initially and above all with the final form as a literary and theological phenomenon—that is, as the final stage in the history of an editorial or composition process.[22] In this context the "diachronic" aspect of the earlier stages and forms of the text must continually be kept in mind.[23] At the same time, in view of the fact that in the Old Testament "theology is historically speaking a relatively late product,"[24] it is this "relatively late" stage particularly which must be given the greatest possible attention in any theology *of* the Old Testament which aspires to be more than a history of the Israelite religion or changing forms of belief.[25] The "dogmatic" question about the theological "validity" of the final form is not in the forefront of interest here.[26]

2. SYSTEMATIC ASPECTS

All the various outlines of an Old Testament theology have to struggle with the problem of how a historical account, or a presentation oriented toward the canonical form of the text, can be combined with the summary, systematic treatment of individual themes, ideas, terms, and so forth. It was Procksch who made this dilemma particularly evident, and he tried to solve it by dividing his book into two sections, one on "the historical world" of the Old Testament and one on its "world of ideas." This bipartite division has found no successors, however.[27] Most modern

22. It is true of these processes as it is for "theology" in the Old Testament in general that they are "not merely anonymous (or at most pseudonymous) but are as a rule the creation of schools" (Smend, "Theologie," 115 n. 69).

23. Cf. here chapter 3 below.

24. Smend, "Theologie," 116.

25. This includes the explicit recognition of the justification and necessity of an account of the history of Israelite religion and faith, and even implies the hope that such an account will be written in a less theologically "distanced" attitude than is generally the case in books of this kind. (An exception is W. H. Schmidt's *The Faith of the Old Testament*, trans. J. Sturdy [Philadelphia: Westminster Press; Oxford: Basil Blackwell, 1983], a valuable book whose original German edition [Neukirchen-Vluyn, 1968] has been continually reissued and revised [6th ed. 1987].)

26. Some remarks of Childs's, which tend in this direction, have evoked the vehement protest of James Barr among others, especially in *Holy Scripture: Canon, Authority, Criticism* (Philadelphia: Westminster Press; Oxford: Clarendon Press, 1983).

27. Von Rad's first heading is: "A History of Yahwism and of the Sacral Institutions in Israel in Outline," and in the task he sets himself he differs from Procksch, his purpose being to reconcile to some degree the "two pictures of Israel's history [which] lie before us—that of modern critical scholarship and that which the faith of Israel constructed" (*Old Testament Theology*, 1:107).

Old Testament theologies have a systematic general plan (see the section "Systematic Surveys," above) and then treat the individual themes or concepts from case to case, in longitudinal historical sections. This certainly allows the historical aspect to be considered and also, at various points, the "canonical" concept of certain Old Testament writings or "works," although these things are not made an explicit theme.

Von Rad chooses the reverse method. He takes into account the need for a systematic presentation of particular elements by treating them at appropriate points in the form of excursuses (although it is only occasionally that he describes them as such). He devotes detailed digressions, for example, to the subjects creation, commandments, sacrifice, "the angel of Yahweh," the covenant with David, righteousness, the word of God, "the Day of Yahweh," and many others. So with the help of the table of contents and the index, the reader can elicit and put together all the multifarious things which the book has to say about individual theological questions.

My own thinking has led me to make a clear distinction between these two aspects or paths of access to the texts and their content, though without wrenching these aspects apart. Consequently my own proposed outline is to consist of two main parts: a first section which will follow the "canonical" plan of the Old Testament books or collections (see the section "Overall Structure," above) and a second which will consider individual themes and concepts—perhaps also individual theological outlines, and so on, within the Old Testament. The choice here will be determined by the necessities suggested by the history of research. The two parts will be linked by way of cross references, so that readers can themselves relate the two aspects, both of which are indispensable for a proper understanding of the Old Testament.[28]

BIBLICAL THEOLOGY?

Old Testament theology has issued from Christian dogmatics. Consequently it has always basically remained a discipline of Christian theology, even if awareness of this fact has sometimes become dimmed or has even been completely lost. In most presentations the connection is evident, if only because Christian theologumena or concepts are used as yardsticks, often merely quite by the way; but this very lack of delibera-

---

28. In the framework of the presentation, I propose to establish this relationship from case to case by inserting individual thematic chapters into the account, in the form of excursuses.

tion betrays how much a matter of course this presupposition is. Where the link was meant to be deliberately abandoned, a possible way out was to label the account "history of religion."

The fact that there is no Jewish "theology of the Tanach" has to do with this genesis. The lack of such a theology is initially due to the wholly different way of dealing with the Bible which has developed in the post-biblical Jewish tradition, where the Bible is fundamentally viewed as a unity, and is made the object of a halachistic or haggadistic interpretation which is largely thematically determined. But the way modern biblical studies developed has also played a part; for here Jewish scholars could work on the biblical texts only as orientalists or historians, the "theology" remaining the monopoly of the specifically Christian theological faculties.[29]

What conclusions must we draw today from the history of this development? Jewish biblical scholars will wish to give their own answers to this question.[30] For the Christian Old Testament scholar the question has two fundamentally different aspects. On the one hand before he begins to concern himself with the Old Testament as a scholar at all, he has it before him as a component part of the Christian Bible, and hence in a certain relation to the New Testament. On the other hand he very soon learns that the Old Testament already existed as Holy "Scripture" before the Christian community came into being at all—that is to say: as Jewish Holy Scripture. He therefore has to render an account of what this fact means for his own theological interpretation of the Old Testament.

The multiplicity of the possible answers, and those given in the course of the history of Christian interpretation, can initially be reduced to the question: Does the interpreter consider the pre-Christian (i.e., Jewish) meaning of the text to be theologically relevant or not? If he does not, his task is relatively simple, because the New Testament provides him with a secure standard of judgment by which to evaluate and classify the Old Testament theologically. Even then, many interpretative variants are open to him, both positive and negative. He can see the Old Testament as a preliminary stage, as a pointer or path leading to the New (for example

29. Cf. here M. H. Goshen-Gottstein, "Christianity, Judaism, and Modern Bible Study," VTSup 28 (1975): 69–88.

30. Approaches for a discussion about this may be found in M. Klopfenstein et al., eds., *Mitte der Schrift? Ein jüdisch-christliches Gespräch: Texte des Berner Symposions vom 6.-12. Januar 1985* (Bern, 1987). A book on this subject by Moshe Goshen-Gottstein is to be expected in the immediate future; it will contain a first outline of a Jewish "theology of the Tanach" and will thereby deliberately break through the limitation of Jewish biblical scholars to nontheological aspects of interpretation.

typologically, christologically, by way of salvation history, and so forth); or he can view it as superseded; or as a necessary counterpart or antitype to the New Testament; or as the testimony of an alien religion; and so on. If the relation is seen in a positive light, this can raise the question of a "biblical theology as a whole." This is what has been meant in germ ever since Gabler, and the question about its possibility or impossibility has recently once again become the subject of more intensive discussion.[31]

But if the Christian interpreter considers the pre-Christian, Jewish sense of the text to be relevant even apart from its subsequent inclusion in the newly developed Christian theology, then his task is a different one. He must first view the Old Testament texts in their "canonical" context, that is to say as a component part of the pre-Christian Jewish biblical canon,[32] and he must also interpret them theologically in that context. This leads to new hermeneutical tasks for which the previous history of Christian biblical interpretation offers no models and but few guidelines; for this is in general a new theological approach, which takes the Jewish religion seriously as an independent entity and according to its own self-understanding.

From the angle of this approach, two fundamental questions present themselves. First, when a Christian scholar tries to interpret the Old Testament texts in the light of their Jewish context, how is this attempt related to Jewish interpretation? Here matters are in a state of flux because, as I have already indicated, the question about a Jewish theological interpretation of the Tanach is today the subject of discussion among Jewish scholars themselves. At this point there could be a fruitful exchange in both directions, although here the Christian interpreter must always remain aware of his limited competence.

Second, a new answer must be found for the question: What is the theological significance of the fact that the Jewish Bible has been made one of the two component parts of the Christian Bible, thus being set in a new context? Here too, entirely new hermeneutical questions arise, provided that it is not simply assumed that the texts have received a new "Christian" meaning which is now the only one that is binding for the Christian interpreter, and for Christian theology and the church. Here above all we shall have to ask in an entirely new way about the common ground and the reciprocal relations between Jewish and Christian reli-

31. Among other things, the appearance of the *Jahrbuch für Biblische Theologie* (vol. 1, 1986; vol. 2, 1987; vol. 3, 1988) may be judged as a sign of this.

32. Here the question about the precise time of the final closure of the Jewish canon is of secondary importance, since at the time of the New Testament an authoritative "Scripture" certainly existed, and is frequently expressly cited as such.

gion and theology; for it emerges that this is by no means a question of mutually exclusive alternatives.

This is no more than a bare sketch; but it is in this briefly outlined context that I hope to develop a new design for a theology of the Old Testament.

CHAPTER 2

Rabbinic Exegesis
and the Modern Christian
Bible Scholar

It is a great honor for me as a Christian scholar to participate in this symposium. When I say "as a Christian scholar" this first of all points to a deficit: that I am not a Jew. The great history of Jewish exegesis of the Bible is not part of my own history, whether this be seen from a religious, national, or social point of view. Nonetheless, for me as a biblical scholar Jewish exegesis is of special importance. Perhaps I should say: it could be, or should be, of importance—and that is just the point where my specific involvement with the subject begins. Modern Christian biblical scholarship has almost totally ignored the very existence of Jewish exegetical tradition. If we go back to the prehistory of modern biblical studies, at the time of the Renaissance, humanism, and the Reformation, we realize that Christian theologians acquired their knowledge of the Hebrew language from Jewish rabbis—while at the same time they refused to share with their Jewish teachers in the study of Jewish exegesis.[1]

This rejection had a double effect. On the one hand the Jews were ousted from the development of modern biblical exegesis. On the other hand Christians lost their link with the tradition of interpreting the Hebrew Bible, and as a consequence lost even their mere knowledge of the language of this tradition, namely postbiblical Hebrew. However, they made a virtue of necessity and declared Hebrew to

Paper read in English at the Eighth World Congress of Jewish Studies, Jerusalem, 1981, panel sessions. The paper has undergone some stylistic revision.
1. See here M. Goshen-Gottstein, "Christianity, Judaism and Modern Bible Study," VTSup 28 (1975): 69–88.

be a dead language which had to be studied like other ancient languages. At the beginning of the nineteenth century, W. M. L. de Wette and others called for a renewal and intensification of Hebrew studies, but they argued that those studies would actually be hindered rather than helped by a consideration of rabbinic Hebrew. So by the beginning of modern biblical studies in the strict sense, traditional Jewish exegesis had fallen completely into oblivion among Christian scholars.

This is the case even today. The vast majority of Christian biblical scholars have never so much as glanced at a rabbinic text—and if they did, they would not understand a word, because they have never learned rabbinic Hebrew. The consequences of this situation are far-reaching. They begin with lexicography. Ever since the emergence of modern Christian Hebrew lexicography, it has been usual and permissible to explain biblical words by parallels—either existing or constructed—from any Semitic language, ancient or modern, except postbiblical Hebrew. In Gesenius's dictionary, which has been the standard German dictionary for biblical Hebrew for more than a hundred and sixty years, there is almost no hint that postbiblical Hebrew exists. In the first edition of Koehler-Baumgartner the situation is even worse, and only the third edition shows a slight improvement—and then only because a Jewish scholar had been co-opted.

I have to admit that the picture I have drawn results from my personal experience in the framework of German Protestant scholarship. Perhaps the situation looks different elsewhere, although the international literature on Old Testament subjects makes me doubt it.

The main consequence of this disregard of the Jewish exegetic tradition is to be found in the attitude of Christian scholars, who proceed as if the interpretation of the Bible had begun only in the nineteenth or at best in the eighteenth century. They handle the biblical texts like scrolls or clay tablets recently found in excavations or desert caves. They generally show no awareness of the continuity of biblical tradition, neither its development from its beginnings to its final canonical form, nor the further tradition of the Bible as the Holy Scripture of the Jewish community, and later of the Christian community as well. As a general rule, Christian scholars try to ascertain the earliest stages of the tradition embodied in a certain text, and only reluctantly proceed to trace its further development.

It would be beyond the scope of this paper to discuss the hermeneutical and theological implications of this exegetical approach, and I can only refer to the extremely exciting discussion aroused by Brevard Childs's book, *Introduction to the Old Testament as Scripture* (1979).[2] But I would draw attention to the interrelations between this modern Christian approach to the Bible and the disregard of the Jewish exegetical tradition. It is true that Christian biblical scholars used to ignore *all* exegetical traditions prior to the Enlightenment (which does not necessarily mean that they were enlightened!). But between traditional Jewish exegesis and *any* Christian tradition of interpreting the Bible there is a fundamental difference.

First, there was almost no Christian interpretation at all of the Hebrew text of the Bible. I need not develop this well-known fact here, but I do wish to stress this lack of continuity in the Christian relationship to the Hebrew text. Second, from the very beginning Christian interpretation of the Bible tried to prove that the texts had a new sense, different from their original meaning. It is not my purpose here to discuss the legitimacy and necessity of this procedure. But it is only in recent times that Christian scholars have begun to realize that there is a difference between the interpretation of the Bible itself and its adoption by, and adaptation to, the Christian faith. (They have only just begun to make this distinction, and even today many of them really deny any such difference—but that again is beyond the scope of this paper.)

Of course I am far from maintaining that the aim of rabbinic exegesis was to explain the original historical meaning of the biblical texts. But at least it was not the intention of these exegetes to alter the sense of the text, for they tried to understand and to explain the Bible as a whole, and as the Holy Scripture of the Jewish community. They thus preserved the continuity with the biblical tradition itself, even though their interpretation was entirely and wholly bound up with the development of Jewish life and thinking throughout the centuries. Consequently rabbinic exegesis is also a fundamental source for a knowledge of the Judaism of the period concerned. But this does not diminish its significance for an understanding of the Bible itself.

On the contrary, in my view it is precisely this double aspect of rabbinic exegesis which makes it extremely important for the Christian scholar. There can be no doubt that there is an anti-Jewish element in the ignoring of the Jewish exegetical tradition by Christian scholars. Regardless of whether the individual scholar is aware of this, and irrespective of whether he or she personally agrees with this viewpoint or disapproves of it, the existence of this interrelation is indisputable. In recent years,

2. B. Childs, *Introduction to the Old Testament as Scripture* (Philadelphia: Fortress Press, 1979).

however, an increasing number of Christian theologians, among them biblical scholars, have begun to try to overcome this dreadful tradition. I think that German Christians should be among the first to join in such a movement.

One of the first steps in this direction could be to devote some attention and some scholarly effort to the Jewish interpretation of our common Bible. For me personally this is one of the "issues central to my existence and to my scholarship,"[3] and I try to introduce students and younger scholars to this field. But I have to confess that there are considerable difficulties in the way of a non-Jewish scholar who has neither a Jewish education nor a scholarly training in Jewish studies, if he or she wishes to enter this field. I may leave aside the obvious need to acquire an adequate knowledge of rabbinic Hebrew, although I must admit that the means available for these studies are not precisely impressive. Perhaps at this point we are coming up against the difficulties our Jewish colleagues have to face when they try to "forge new links with rabbinic studies."[4] A modern, scholarly dictionary of rabbinic Hebrew would be a wonderful thing, and could make access to rabbinic literature very much easier.

The difficulties about the next step are more serious. I might continue with complaints about the lack of introductory literature, and of course it would be very useful to have something comparable to Albeck's introductions to the Mishnah and the Talmudim for the Midrashic literature as well, and not only in Hebrew. But one can take refuge in the good old Strack, whose German edition was reprinted a few years ago. And with the help of W. Bacher's eighty-year-old book on exegetical terminology (also reprinted in the 1960s) one can find one's way through the texts.

The real problem, however, is not the "technical" or even the philological access to the texts but, to use a rather high-flown term, the hermeneutical question: What are the guidelines for studying the Midrashim? What use can we make of those studies? This is obviously a special problem for the non-Jewish scholar. Jewish scholars can use rabbinic literature as part of their own tradition without feeling the need for any hermeneutical justification or for an elaborate methodological concept. (I am leaving aside the question of the extent to which Jewish biblical scholars actually make use of this tradition, although I believe that this is a question which should be discussed.) Christian scholars who wish to break through the disregard and ignorance of rabbinic exegesis

---

3. Goshen-Gottstein, "Christianity," 88.
4. Ibid., 87.

have to account to themselves (and to their colleagues as well) about their purpose in doing so, and the means they are going to use.

Earlier I mentioned the double aspect of rabbinic exegetical literature, and I should like to come back to this point. For me, interest in rabbinic exegesis is first of all an interest in Judaism. I cannot discuss this point here, but I have to mention it for a twofold reason. On the one hand the practical usefulness of rabbinic studies for modern exegesis is not the only justification for such studies, and for me personally it is not the main one. On the other hand it would be difficult to convince Christian scholars who themselves have no specific interest in Judaism about the need for and even the usefulness of rabbinic studies unless we could demonstrate usable results. But for the moment the latter point is not my concern. We should concentrate on the first aspect.

It is from this point of view that the subject of this symposium has particular relevance for the Christian scholar: "Modern Study of the Bible in the Framework of Jewish Studies." That means looking at the Bible as a Jewish document and studying the interpretation of the Bible as it is found within the continuum of Jewish history. This is undoubtedly a far-reaching and almost an all-embracing conception, for in a certain sense all rabbinic literature is an interpretation of the Bible. But for my own part I would prefer to restrict myself to the Midrashic literature.

I think there are good reasons for such a restriction. For Christian scholars, the starting point is the text of the Bible in its present form. The Midrashic literature enables them to follow the interpretation verse by verse, unlike Mishnah and Gemarah. Needless to say, this should not exclude the study of Talmudic references to particular verses, phrases, and words, especially since for the German reader these are easily accessible by way of the indexes of the Goldschmidt edition. But what I have in mind is the continuous study of rabbinic texts.

Before coming back to the hermeneutical problem, I should like to make some remarks about the question of editions, because I feel that this is the very point at which new relationships between biblical and Jewish studies could lead to fruitful results. I must emphasize that I am not an expert in this field; I should like only to pass on a few observations and reflections. For example, no critical edition of Sifra exists. It might be objected that we have Weiss's 1862 edition; but this is only the marvelously printed edition of a single manuscript from the Bodleian Library, without any reference to other manuscripts or editions. What I should like to point out, however, is the fact that in his extremely useful *Tora Shlema,* Menachem Kasher uses an uncritical nineteenth-century edition. This shows many divergences from the Weiss edition, as well as from the reprint of the Venice edition of 1545, not to speak of Finkel-stein's facsimile edition of the Assemani manuscript. What the reader is given here is far removed from the original text of Sifra.

I am well aware that Sifra is a bad example, because there are critical editions of Sifrei Bemidbar and Sifrei Devarim, and of some other Midrashim. But this brings me to another point. Horovitz's edition of Sifrei Bemidbar includes an introduction in German, whereas the edition of Sifrei Devarim completed by Finkelstein is entirely in Hebrew. This may be said of most (if not all) other critical editions. I know that this is a delicate point but I do not hesitate to touch on it. The question is: For whom are these editions intended? This seems to me to be one of the most important aspects of our topic.

The problem has two interrelated sides. The one is how to bring Jewish studies closer to modern biblical studies; the other is how to enable biblical scholars to make use of the results of Jewish studies. Modern biblical studies are an international and interdenominational field, and we must ask ourselves whether we wish to build up two classes of scholars. Of course scholars are not a homogeneous group, but nevertheless we should not make the barriers higher than necessary. I am convinced that there are a considerable number of non-Jewish biblical scholars who would be ready to study rabbinic texts provided they could be given some guidance; and we should encourage them. Many of them are studying Akkadian, Sumerian, hieroglyphic Egyptian—why not rabbinic Hebrew? One reason could be that all the other languages are accessible to them in the wrappings of a modern language which they have to know anyway, if it is not even their own. Let us make rabbinic texts readable without compelling scholars to learn the subtleties of modern Hebrew as well. Perhaps some of them will be inspired to learn that also!

Let me come back to the hermeneutical problem. The study of rabbinic exegesis can show us how Jewish interpreters in the classical period read their Bible. As I have already mentioned, these insights are on the one hand an important source for an understanding of the Judaism of that particular period. This is of great importance in itself. But what could be the results for an understanding of the biblical texts themselves? Modern scholars would usually say that the uncritical and unhistorical approach to the texts makes the rabbinic interpretation more or less irrelevant for modern exegesis. One of the principal objections is that rabbinic exegesis, like every other premodern exegesis, takes the Bible as a whole, disregarding the different sources, levels, redactions, and so forth. But it could even be that this very feature is one of the strengths of rabbinic exegesis, if only we understood how to use it.

Let me give a single example. At the beginning of the book of Leviticus we read: ויקרא אל־משה וידבר יהוה אליו מאהל מועד. Modern scholars take it for granted that either the entire verse or at least the reference to the 'ohel mo'ed is to be ascribed to the redactor, and that this also applies in particular to the unusual position of the Divine Name as subject in the middle of the verse. Interpretation of the text can therefore only begin after the original text has been purged of the secondary additions. In the Midrashic literature, however, we find an extensive discussion of this verse in its given wording.

The aggadic tradition understands the reference to the 'ohel mo'ed as a pointer to Moses' building of the mishkan. Now the Lord calls him to enter. Why had he not entered before? Tanchuma says: שהיה מתיירא לבוא; Yalqut Shimoni adds: ה' על המשבן כי ענן; Midrash Haggadol: לא בא הכתוב אלא להודיע ענותנותו וצניעותו של משה.

All of them discuss at length the extraordinary position Moses has before God, even going as far as Tanchuma does in comparing the ויקרא spoken by God to Moses with that spoken in the creation story: גדול היה משה, ראה מה כתיב, ויקרא אלהים לאור יום. וכאן ויקרא אל משה. זו קריה וזו קריה. There are libraries full of literature dealing with the different views of Moses in the Bible. The Midrashic literature could add some very significant aspects to this discussion.

In the halachic tradition there is a discussion about another aspect of this verse, namely the relationship between ויקרא and וידבר. Sifra opens thus: הקדים קריאה לדבור. A very interesting discussion follows in which God's speech to Moses in Leviticus 1 is compared with that in Exodus 3, Exodus 24, and elsewhere, the question being argued as to whether the precedence of קריאה is limited to דברות or extends to אמירות and צוויים as well. Rashi sums up this discussion: לכל דברות ולכל אמירות ולכל צוויים קדמה קריאה. It is obvious that in this discussion quotations from quite different strata of biblical texts are being compared with each other. The question is whether this is legitimate. I am convinced that it could be very useful to study the results of this seemingly uncritical method, and to see whether in the process observations can be made which modern interpreters are not as a rule in a position to make, because of the preceding critical separation of the texts. I must confess that I am highly allergic to the method of using the concordance selectively according to literary-critical prejudices or—to mention a particularly horrifying example—to the writing of books about Deuteronomy in which the first four chapters are not even mentioned, because they are "Deuteronomistic."

All too often such a sophisticated critical method demonstrates its own absurdity.

Of course I am in no way pleading for the adoption of the Midrashic exegetical method instead of the historical-critical one. But I do wish to point out that under certain aspects the weakness of the Midrashic exegesis could actually be its strength, in that it takes the Bible as it is, and asks about interrelationships between different texts without taking note of their probable age and prehistory. Needless to say we cannot and should not disregard the results of modern biblical studies in general. But perhaps the study of rabbinic literature particularly can help us to be aware of the completely hypothetical character of all our critical theories and keep our minds open for unexpected insights into the meaning of biblical texts.

In this way a highly fruitful interaction between modern biblical studies and rabbinic exegesis could come into being. I should like to use the opportunity provided by this symposium to stimulate a discussion among biblical scholars, Jews and non-Jews, about the possibility of establishing cooperation and an exchange of ideas and experiences in this field. As a utopian long-term project, I would suggest something akin to Strack-Billerbeck's renowned *Kommentar zum Neuen Testament aus Talmud und Midrasch,* although the two could not be comparable in a number of aspects.

But we would probably do better to leave ambitious projects of this kind to the next generation, and confine ourselves to some cautious first steps in the exploration of this almost unknown territory.

CHAPTER 3

Between Historical Criticism and Holistic Interpretation: New Trends in Old Testament Exegesis

Having been invited to speak about "Recent Trends and Major Developments in Modern Biblical Research," I asked myself how to understand the word "recent." Of course, many different definitions and delimitations are possible. Yet because the word appears in relation to the word "developments," I found it useful not to take it in too restricted a sense. Being no longer so young myself, I decided to choose as a starting point for my considerations the time, about forty years ago, when I began to study the Hebrew Bible.

I

In Old Testament scholarship the late 1940s and particularly the 1950s were the time of the great "schools": the two main schools, the Albright school and the Alt school, and in addition to them the British-Scandinavian cultic schools: the Myth and Ritual school and the Uppsala school. There is no need before this audience to go into details about these schools. Rather I want to focus on their respective relations to exegesis.

The Albright school wanted primarily to know what had happened. By means of the biblical texts, in whose historical truth they had confidence, they tried to reconstruct the history of biblical times. The historical reliability of the texts had to be proved by "external evidence," mainly

Paper read in English at the Congress of the International Organization for the Study of the Old Testament, Jerusalem, 1986.

by archaeology. One could say that they focused on something that lies behind the texts.

At first glance, the intention of the Alt school was entirely different or even contradictory. Their main concern was with the texts themselves. But they, too, had the intention of finding something behind the texts, in this case, the *traditions* which found expression in the texts. They also tried to reconstruct history, namely the history of traditions, their origins, their *Sitz im Leben* in certain institutions, mainly cultic ones, and the way these traditions reached written form. One could say that these scholars were primarily interested in the prehistory of the texts.

The cultic schools, finally, focused on the religious background of the Hebrew Bible, seeing Israel only in terms of the ancient Near Eastern world. In their search for religious and cultic patterns they took the biblical texts, so to speak, as pieces of a lost mosaic which they tried to reconstruct. Some of them did it explicitly *against* the given meaning of the texts, claiming that only a later theological redaction had changed the original meaning, which modern scholarship had to restore.

To be sure, this characterization is far too rough to do justice to the intentions of these schools, let alone of the individual scholars working within the framework of one of them. My point is that, in spite of the obvious fundamental divergences and even contradictions among the schools, they had in common a certain approach to the biblical texts, taking them, within the respective paradigms, mainly as a means, sometimes even as tools, for discovering something assumed to lie behind the texts.

With regard to the two main schools another common ground must be added: all these scholars were strict Wellhausenians. For them *Literarkritik* according to the rules of the "Newer Documentary Hypothesis" was self-evident. It belonged to the undisputed prerequisites of their scholarship as the larger, embracing paradigm within which both schools worked. Certainly, this approach to the biblical texts was not restricted to the Pentateuch or Hexateuch but was an overall attitude: not to take the given text as a starting point for interpretation and as a basis for the reconstruction of history, but first of all to analyze the text according to the rules of *Literarkritik*. For, according to the commonly accepted methodological principles, only the "original" text, freed from "redactional" additions and from "secondary" linking to other texts, could be used as a reliable means for reconstructing history or the history of traditions.

Thus within mainstream Old Testament scholarship of the period under discussion, *the given text* of the Hebrew Bible is rarely taken as the subject of interpretation or as material for historical exploration, and so on. Instead, texts have been used that existed only as a result of critical destruction and reconstruction by modern scholars.

To repeat: the description is too rough. Many scholars, time and again, have dealt with certain biblical texts in their given form and have tried to interpret them in their own right and not simply as a means to something that lies behind the text. Actually there is, and always has been, a plurality of method. Nevertheless, my main point is a double one: (1) Old Testament scholarship in its various forms very often has used the biblical text for divergent purposes and, at the same time, has neglected the interpretation of the text itself. (2) Bible scholars often constructed their own texts and took those texts as a basis for interpretation and historical reconstruction.

Both of these aspects clearly show that the whole concept of exegesis was mainly diachronic.

I am far from denying the necessity and usefulness of efforts to reconstruct Israelite history, including the history of traditions and the history of religion. On the contrary, one has to appreciate all the work which has been done in this field, and one hopes that certain new fields such as, for example, social history, will make further progress. Yet one should distinguish those investigations from *exegesis* or *interpretation* of biblical texts themselves. I am, however, highly distrustful of the traditional *Literarkritik* so far as it leads to a production of texts. The subject of any interpretation has to be first and foremost the given text of the Hebrew Bible.

II

This brings me to the second part of my paper. In the last one or two decades the situation of Old Testament scholarship has changed remarkably. At the same time, it has become much more complicated. I dare not judge whether the "schools" still exist and to what extent scholars consider themselves associated with them. But there remain many who are still working along the lines described above, particularly in Europe.

There is, however, a growing number of scholars who question the exclusive validity of these rules, or even their usefulness at all; there are those who have already left the framework of these paradigms or never even entered it. Of course, their approaches and methods are quite different, and sometimes it seems almost impossible to relate them to one another. Nevertheless, I think they share a common denominator: they are interested in the text itself, and that implies: in the text as it stands.

This interest in the final form of the text reflects a fundamental shift

28   *CANON AND THEOLOGY*

in priorities. In many handbooks and introductions to exegetical method, the student is told first of all to look for tensions and inconsistencies in the text and to analyze it accordingly. In contrast, the new approaches aim to understand the text as readers have it before them. Therefore, in spite of the differences in details and also in the underlying theoretical conceptions, one has to emphasize strongly the common interest in the given text in its integrity as opposed to the hitherto dominating analytical approach.

The limited scope of this paper does not allow a detailed description and analysis of the different approaches, nor is this necessary before this audience.[1] Instead, I want to focus on one aspect that to my mind is crucial: the question of continuity and discontinuity in Old Testament exegesis. For this purpose let me try a very rough grouping of the new methods.

Of course, the main impact comes from modern "literary criticism" and its predecessors in different kinds of *Literaturwissenschaft*.[2] The concepts of these new approaches are mainly synchronic. Their interest is directed to the *literary* aspects of the biblical text, to art, style, techniques, narrative strategies, and the like. In this field great progress has been achieved during the last ten years, and although many of the studies are still in an experimental stage, our understanding of the Hebrew Bible has been remarkably enriched by them. Among the practitioners of these new approaches one finds many scholars who obviously are not interested in the traditional methods of biblical studies. Some of them, coming themselves from literary studies, have probably never dealt with those methods; others turned to the new approaches leaving behind them not only the old methods but also the questions those methods tried to answer.

This seems to me to be a crucial point: the use of new methods does not make the old questions disappear. We have to ask whether or to what extent the questions posed by traditional Old Testament scholarship have been legitimate and of what relevance they are in a changed framework. This brings me to the other main approach that emphasizes the importance of the text as it stands: the canonical approach. Many similarities

---

1. A useful survey and critical evaluation of the new approaches is given by J. Barton, *Reading the Old Testament: Method in Biblical Study* (Philadelphia: Westminster Press; London: Darton, Longman and Todd, 1984).

2. It should be mentioned that there have been some important forerunners of these new developments, among them James Muilenburg, Meir Weiss, and Luis Alonso Schökel. There is also a strong influence by Hermann Gunkel and, last but not least, by Martin Buber and Franz Rosenzweig.

exist between the "literary" and the "canonical" approaches: both stress the primary importance of the text as it stands, denying the supremacy of analytical methods and historical questions.

Yet there is one basic difference. Scholars working in the framework of a canonical approach are fully aware of the fact that the text we have before us represents the final stage of what is sometimes a long historical process. They take into account the possibility of changes in the original narrative or poetic form; they recognize the "depth dimension" of the text before us and even think that to distinguish different sources or layers "often allows the interpreter to hear the combined texts with new precision."[3]

Here the diachronic aspect belongs to the concept itself. The final form of the text is taken as something composed from different, and sometimes divergent, parts. Its unity is not primarily understood as a literary one, but as the deliberate result of a "canonical process" of composing and shaping according to certain theological guidelines.[4] This does not diminish the significance of the final text. On the contrary, this text has its theological relevance for the "community of faith" for whom it possessed "divine authority."[5]

This is not the place to enter into a theological discussion of the concept of canonicity. But I believe that there could be a fruitful interrelation between the different approaches of a renewed "close reading" of the biblical text in its now given form, whether one prefers to call it reading the Bible "as literature" or "as canon." It seems to me to be the strength of the canonical approach that it is concerned with larger units, such as biblical books, and even with the canon as a whole. Thus the holistic reading of the Bible, which is often neglected when only smaller literary units are studied, receives the attention it deserves.[6] None of the smaller units exists independently of the larger composition of which it is part, and an appropriate understanding of those larger compositions often demands an insight into diachronic developments.

One final word: there is much discussion about a "change of paradigm." Certainly, the paradigm within which Old Testament scholarship

---

3. B. S. Childs, *Introduction to the Old Testament as Scripture* (Philadelphia: Fortress Press; London: SCM Press, 1979), 76.

4. For observations on "canon conscious redactions" see G. Sheppard, "Canonization: Hearing the Voice of the Same God through Historically Dissimilar Traditions," *Int* 36 (1982): 21–33.

5. Childs, *Introduction*, 74.

6. For a holistic interpretation of a whole biblical book see M. Greenberg, *Ezekiel, 1–20*, AB 22 (Garden City, N.Y.: Doubleday, 1983).

has worked for more than a century, namely the old German *Literarkritik*, has lost its general acceptance. It is no longer possible to maintain that serious Old Testament scholarship has to be indispensably tied to this set of methodological principles. So far there is no alternative concept that has been generally accepted. According to Thomas Kuhn, one could say that there are different models used by certain groups of scholars, but none of them has won general acceptance.[7] Old Testament scholarship now is in a stage of transition, and we cannot know whether there will be a new paradigm or if the near future will be characterized by a plurality of approaches and methods.

Therefore, it makes no sense for some scholars or groups to claim that their own method, as time-honored or even brand-new, is the only correct one. At the same time, it would not be wise of those working with new approaches to ignore completely the questions posed by former generations of scholars without scrutinizing their legitimacy and their usefulness in highlighting certain aspects or solving certain problems in the given text. Surely, continuity as such is of no value. But a loss of communication among Old Testament scholars by mere discontinuity of approaches could do much harm to international and interreligious endeavors toward a mutual understanding of our common Hebrew Bible. That is the reason we need congresses like this one in order to reestablish and to strengthen the relationships among those committed to this task.[8]

---

7. T. Kuhn, *The Structure of Scientific Revolutions* (Chicago: Univ. of Chicago Press, 1962).
8. I am grateful to Cheryl Exum for improving my English.

CHAPTER 4

Toward a Common
Jewish-Christian Reading
of the Hebrew Bible

Recently, Jon D. Levenson published an article entitled "Why Jews Are Not Interested in Biblical Theology."[1] Having read his article, one can only agree with him. If biblical theology really is as Levenson has portrayed it, there would indeed be no reason why Jews should be interested in it. And there can be no doubt that there is a lot of truth in his depiction of Christian biblical theology past and present. However, the reader is left with a question as to whether this could really be the last word on the issue. He or she wonders whether it would not be more apt to say that Jews are not interested in *Christian* (in particular Protestant) biblical theology because of its biases and because of "the failure of the biblical theologians to recognize the limitation of the context of their enterprise."[2]

Levenson's readers were soon rescued from uncertainty. Only one year after his article had appeared, he published a book that could hardly be deemed anything other than a piece of biblical theology—*Jewish* biblical theology, of course. The author states clearly in the preface that one of the main motivations for him to write this book was "the lack of sophisticated

Lecture delivered in English at the 1989 University of Notre Dame Conference on "Hebrew Bible or Old Testament? Studying the Bible in Judaism and Christianity." The text has undergone some stylistic revision.

1. J. D. Levenson, "Why Jews Are Not Interested in Biblical Theology," in J. Neusner, B. A. Levine, and E. S. Frerichs, eds., *Judaic Perspectives on Ancient Israel* (Philadelphia: Fortress Press, 1987), 281–307.
2. Ibid., 304.

theological reflection upon even such central and overworked aspects of the religion of Israel as creation and covenant," and that the book is to be understood as "a theological study."[3] This teaches us that not being interested in biblical theology does not mean, or at least need not mean, not being interested in a theological interpretation of biblical texts.

So we can leave aside the question of biblical theology as an established theological discipline and turn to the more general and more fundamental question of a theological reading of the Hebrew Bible. Because our main topic is a common reading of the Bible, let us try to find out what the aim of such a venture could be, what possibilities and chances we can discover for carrying it out, what obstacles we shall have to face, and how we can hope to overcome them.

Before doing so it would be useful to realize that in many fields of Old Testament scholarship (and here I am deliberately using the internationally established term "Old Testament") there is a seemingly unproblematic cooperation between Jewish and Christian scholars. The more remote the fields of research are from theological or even religious problems, the easier the cooperation seems to be. Yet it would be interesting to look more closely at the different fields of biblical research in order to find out how unproblematic the cooperation really is.

Let me give a few examples. Archaeology is one of the preferred fields of cooperation between Jews and Christians. The evolution of methods and techniques is to a high degree a common endeavor. Of course there is a certain competition and rivalry between different schools, but in many cases this is not mainly an issue between Christians and Jews; the division is rather between conservatives and liberals, for example—or however one wants to define the different groups or schools. Here the frontiers often cut across religious affiliations. To a certain degree this is also true with regard to the interpretation of the findings. But because this interpretation is linked with more general historical views, including the history of religion, at certain points specific Jewish interests are inevitably at stake. I need only mention the far-reaching problems we now face with regard to the early history of Israel: the questions of nomadism, conquest, social revolt; the question of the origins of Yahwistic monotheism, and the like. All these problems have their implications for Israelite—and that ultimately means Jewish—historical identity. Conversely, Christian identity is not directly affected by these problems. The question is: To

---

3. J. D. Levenson, *Creation and the Persistence of Evil: The Jewish Drama of Divine Omnipotence* (San Francisco: Harper & Row, 1988), xiv.

what degree are scholars conscious of these implications? Or are they motivated by more or less unconscious preconceived opinions? Let me take another example from the field of philology or linguistics. Learned Jewish biblical scholars now utilize sophisticated means to try to prove that P, the so-called Priestly Code, is of preexilic origin.[4] This would appear to be a purely linguistic question, or at most a historical one. But the discussion is obviously motivated by the old and still enduring fight against Julius Wellhausen's notion of the decline of ancient Israelite culture marked by priestly leadership. The interesting fact is that Wellhausen openly and explicitly used his arguments as anti-Jewish weapons; the modern linguists, in contrast, allege—surely bona fide— purely scholarly interests. In my view it would be much more useful to discuss problems related to Wellhausen's views (and those of his successors) on postexilic Israel in their complexity, and with an open and clear explanation of the interests involved.

The third field I should like to mention is the modern literary approach to the Hebrew Bible. Here we find Jewish and Christian biblical scholars working along the same lines, sometimes in explicit dissociation from the traditional *Literarkritik* (source criticism and the like), but mainly without mentioning those previously generally accepted methods at all. In my view, it is in this field that there are the fewest differences between Jewish and Christian scholars. But at the same time, many of those working in this field are not interested in theology, but explicitly claim their method of interpretation to be purely literary. I appreciate this seemingly unbiased cooperation, but I do not believe that it will be very helpful for a theological understanding of the Hebrew Bible.[5]

Finally, if one examines the programs of international Bible congresses, one finds very few contributions that could be deemed to be theological in a strict sense. There is evidently something like a "historicist evasion," to use the term coined by Levenson.[6]

---

4. I am thinking especially of A. Hurvitz, *A Linguistic Study of the Relationship between the Priestly Source and the Book of Ezechiel* (Paris, 1982), and a number of articles by the same author.

5. As regards the specific situation in North America, with its "recent emergence of scholars and academic departments that are not beholden to any religious perspective," see J. D. Levenson, "The Hebrew Bible, the Old Testament, and Historical Criticism," in R. E. Friedman and H. G. M. Williamson, eds., *The Future of Biblical Studies: The Hebrew Scriptures* (Atlanta: Scholars Press, 1987), 19–59, quotation from p. 52.

6. J. D. Levenson, "Theological Consensus or Historicist Evasion? Jews and Christians in Biblical Studies," in R. Brooks and J. J. Collins, eds., *Hebrew Bible or Old Testament? Studying the Bible in Judaism and Christianity* (Notre Dame, Ind.: Univ. of Notre Dame Press, 1990).

THE NEED FOR A COMMON BIBLICAL THEOLOGY

Let me return to the question of the rationale behind the endeavor for a common theological reading of the Bible by Jews and Christians. My first step toward an answer is to declare that in my opinion a common reading is an irrefutable necessity. The simple fact is that for both Jews and Christians the Hebrew Bible or Old Testament is Holy Scripture. If each group lived separate from the other in a world without any relation to the world of the other, there would be no need to take note of divergent readings and interpretations of their respective Holy Scriptures. But this is not the case. On the contrary, ever since Christians and Jews began to have a separate history—that is, ever since Christianity emerged from Judaism—the two communities have been closely and, it seems, indissolubly linked with one another, for better or for worse. This makes it virtually impossible simply to ignore the use of the Bible made by the other religious community.

From the fourth century onward, the situation was determined by Christian dominance over the Jews. The Christian interpretation of what now came to be called the Old Testament was therefore the officially accepted one. There was no chance for a mutual exchange of views and opinions, and most Christians never heard about Jewish interpretation of the Bible except from polemics and the mostly incorrect details that were used for anti-Jewish purposes. I suspect that on the Jewish side, knowledge of Christian interpretation of the Bible was not much better and not unbiased. This situation did not change substantially until the last century when, after Enlightenment and emancipation, the Jews in Europe began to live under less oppression and to participate to some degree in the life of their Christian environment.

But even then there was no real exchange between Jewish and Christian interpretations of the Bible. The reasons are manifold. First, Jewish and Christian communities lived without any relationship to each other, and mainly without taking note of one another at all. Second, in the academic area Jews had no access to the field of biblical studies because it was the domain of Christian theological faculties.[7] Third, theology as a discipline was generally understood as something particularly Christian, and this view was shared by many, if not most, Jews as well. Thus on both sides, even those who were interested in a certain exchange were convinced that no Jewish equivalent to Christian theology existed.[8]

7. See M. H. Goshen-Gottstein, "Christianity, Judaism and Modern Bible Study," VTSup 28 (1975): 69–88.
8. Levenson tells the story of a European biblical scholar who in Israel was unable to

One could argue that this situation still exists even today, and generally speaking this might be true. But the mere fact of symposia and meetings, as well as a number of publications by Jewish and Christian authors within the last few years, indicates a change, or at least the beginning of something new.[9] It is the first time in history that Jews and Christians have had the opportunity to meet on an equal level, without being dependent on any political or religious institution or authority, and to meet as individuals, each with his or her own commitment to a religious tradition and community. I have to add that, regrettably, this only became possible after the *Shoah* (the Holocaust), and only forty years after that event. (Perhaps this has something to do with the forty years several times mentioned in the Bible.)

THE RELEVANCE OF JEWISH INTERPRETATION

The immediate question is whether we are ready and able to begin a dialogue that should have begun almost two thousand years ago but is now starting under fundamentally different conditions. I believe that we have no alternative. As a Christian, I should like to say that it is high time for Christians to begin to appreciate the Jewish interpretation of our common Bible. The main precondition is, from the outset, to refrain from taking traditional Christian interpretation as a yardstick for the meaning and relevance of Jewish interpretation.

Let me try to analyze the implications of such a claim. With regard to the Hebrew Bible or Old Testament, the first precondition is the theological acknowledgment of the fact that this book is the Holy Scripture of the Jews. Of course, historically speaking this is a mere truism. But as a Christian theological statement it is of fundamental importance. In Christian theological tradition, the Jews are usually talked about in the past tense, in relation to Old and New Testament times. Jews belonging to the present time are mainly subjects of political and social consideration. In the theological field, they appear first of all in the chapter on "mission." There is a wide variety of opinion as to whether the Jews are just to be deemed the same as any other non-Christians (in accordance with Paul's words that "there is neither Jew nor Greek" [Gal. 3:28]), or as

---

find anyone who was interested in Old Testament theology (see "Why Jews Are Not Interested," 281).

9. I may point here especially to a symposium held in Bern, Switzerland, in January 1985. The papers are published in M. Klopfenstein et al., eds., *Mitte der Schrift? Ein jüdisch-christliches Gespräch: Texte des Berner Symposions vom 6.-12. Januar 1985* (1987).

something special—perhaps still as God's chosen people (according to another statement of Paul's: "They are Israelites, and to them belong the sonship, the glory, the covenant" [Rom. 9:4-5]). In any case, the common Christian view of the Jews is that they should have acknowledged Jesus as the Messiah, and that there is still hope that one day they will do so (again according to a statement of Paul's that at the end "all Israel will be saved" [Rom. 11:26], which is interpreted—wrongly in my opinion—as the expectation of a final conversion of the Jewish people to Jesus Christ).

My claim that we should acknowledge without any qualification the fact that the Hebrew Bible is the Holy Scripture of the Jews presupposes acceptance of the dignity and the independent value of the Jewish religion. This has a whole series of implications; and ultimately what is at stake is the question about the Christian church's sole possession of the truth, or Christianity's claim to absoluteness. I am fully aware of that, but I feel obliged to make it quite clear that in my opinion the first and most important precondition for a serious and meaningful theological dialogue between Jewish and Christian biblical scholars is the theological acceptance of the Jewish religion on its own terms by its Christian partners.

In order not to be misunderstood, I have to add that this does not at all mean simply turning things upside down and claiming that Judaism is the only legitimate successor of biblical Israel. The fact is that both Judaism *and* Christianity are successor religions of biblical Israel. Our task will be to acknowledge this fact and to define sensitively and clearly the theological meaning of this "and." I believe that a responsible mutual discussion of our respective relations to the Hebrew Bible could be of great value for the definition of this theological problem as a whole.

THE BIBLE AS A WHOLE AND IN ITS SEPARATE PARTS

This leads to the problem of the canon. Since the emergence of a new debate about the significance of the canon of the Hebrew Bible or Old Testament—a debate inaugurated particularly by Brevard Childs and James A. Sanders—a wealth of literature on this topic has appeared.[10] I need not enter into this discussion here. I will confine myself to a few remarks. Whatever the history of the settling of the canon in its final form may have been, the fact is that both religious communities, Judaism and Christianity, have structured their religious traditions on the basis of the

10. For the most recent discussion in Germany see I. Baldermann et al., "Zum Problem des biblischen Kanons," *JBTh* 3 (1988).

canon in its given form, Hebrew or Greek. I do not believe it to be of great theological importance whether and when there was a decision by any authority with regard to the canon, its content, its religious status, and so forth. From a certain time onward, from the second or third century or whenever, both communities of faith took the collection of scriptures which we now know as the Hebrew or the Greek Bible as their Holy Scripture. This means that the number of books belonging to each collection, as well as the wording, was fixed at a certain time by decision or custom. (Of course I do not deny that the investigation of the history of the canonization can be a very interesting scholarly field, but I doubt whether the results will be able to contribute to the *theological* question of the canon.)

This actual definition of the Bible as Holy Scripture implied a clear-cut distinction between the Bible itself and any other religious tradition, be it written or otherwise. Jewish tradition established a distinction between תּוֹרָה שֶׁבִּכְתָב and תּוֹרָה שֶׁבְּעַל־פֶּה. On the one hand this declares the Torah to be incomplete if not taken in both of its forms; on the other hand it does not allow us to mix the two up: הַכָּתוּב is only the Bible itself, and nothing else.

In Christianity's earliest stage we find the same language. The New Testament regularly speaks of "the Scripture" (ἡ γραφή) or "the Scriptures" (αἱ γραφαί) when referring to the Jewish Scripture(s), Hebrew or Greek (*which*, is itself a matter of dispute among scholars). Later, another collection of books was added, this eventually becoming the New Testament. So from a certain point of view the situation seems comparable with that in Judaism: the Bible, supplemented by other religious writings. But in fact the development unfolded very differently, in two respects especially. In the first place, Christians took both collections together to be the one Bible. The original distinction between the two sets of books was therefore abandoned, and with it the authoritative character of the original Scripture(s). The canon or Bible was the whole two-part collection of holy writings. Second, within this Bible virtually only the New Testament had theological authority. The Old Testament was interpreted as supporting the New Testament, or as pointing toward it, or as a mere forerunner that sometimes did not yet see and understand things clearly enough. Of course there were many hermeneutical variants in the course of the centuries; but what is important in our present context is the fact that in the Christian tradition the Old Testament lost its independent value and authority, if not its independent meaning altogether.

THE REFORMATION AND MODERN CHRISTIAN THEOLOGY

If this denigration of Old Testament authority were still the state of affairs today, we should have no reason and no basis for discussing the topic of a common biblical theology. But it is not. In the meantime two events have taken place that are related to each other in certain respects: the Reformation and the Enlightenment. It would go far beyond the scope of this paper to unfold the different aspects of these two fundamental events in their bearing on my topic, so I shall be very brief.

The Reformation brought to the consciousness of educated Christian people the existence of the Hebrew Old Testament as distinct from the Greek New Testament. At the same moment, at least at the margins of consciousness, the Jewish character of the Old Testament emerged. (Luther himself was fully aware of this, with all the uneasiness that the insight caused him.) But first of all, a new awareness of the distinction and difference between the two parts of the Christian Bible arose. It was therefore almost unavoidable that at the very moment when, two and a half centuries later, the theologians of the Enlightenment began to discover the Bible as something in its own right (and not only as a source of *dicta probantia*–proof texts for dogmatics) they should have made a distinction between the two parts of the Christian Bible. The day when biblical theology was born[11] was at the same time the birthday of Old Testament theology, as distinct from New Testament theology. At the same time scholars became conscious of the Jewish character of the Old Testament, or Hebrew Bible. Georg Lorenz Bauer equated "biblical theology of the Old Testament" with "the theory of the religion of the ancient Hebrews," which he also called "the history of Jewish dogmatics" (*jüdische Dogmengeschichte*).[12]

I think that this is the point in the history of the interpretation of the Bible at which our reflections should and could start. From then on, the Hebrew Bible became a distinct and more or less independent subject of theological research. I say "more or less independent" because on the one hand Old Testament theology was declared to be the first part of a complete biblical theology, but on the other hand hardly anyone actually wrote about both parts. The main interest was concentrated on the Old

---

11. I am referring here to Johann Philipp Gabler's famous lecture: "Oratio de justo discrimine theologiae biblicae et dogmaticae regundisque recte utriusque finibus" (1787).

12. G. L. Bauer, *Theologie des Alten Testaments oder Abriss der religiösen Begriffe der alten Hebräer: Von den ältesten Zeiten bis auf den Anfang der christlichen Epoche. Zum Gebrauch akademischer Vorlesungen* (Leipzig, 1796); Eng. trans., *The Theology of the Old Testament*, trans. P. Harwood (London: Charles Fox, 1838).

Testament, and it was only half a century later that the first elaborated New Testament theology appeared.[13]

Yet with regard to our topic, one fundamental point did not change: the study of the Old Testament continued to be part and parcel of Christian theology. It therefore shared the vicissitudes of theological trends and quarrels. During the nineteenth century Old Testament studies to a large extent lost their relationship to theology and turned toward becoming a purely historical and philological matter. But Old Testament studies always remained part of Christian tradition, even though disputed and denounced, until in 1921 Adolf von Harnack called for the elimination of the Old Testament from the Christian church.[14] In any case, Christian theologians believed that *they* had to decide what to do with the Old Testament. And now I switch from the past tense to the present, because even today the situation is unchanged for the majority of Christian theologians, in particular for Old Testament scholars: the Old Testament is, at least theologically speaking, only relevant, if not even only existent, as a part of the Christian tradition.

In the decades after the Second World War, Old Testament scholarship in Germany underwent a fundamental change toward a more explicit theological commitment, mainly as a consequence of the dialectical theology of Karl Barth and others, and intensified by the challenge of Nazi ideology, which had compelled German theologians to defend the Old Testament as a legitimate component of Christian theology.[15] I believe that some of the present inconsistencies are based on the situation of the postwar years; since then, many Old Testament scholars have felt obliged to justify the use of the Old Testament within the Christian church and theology, but they have never been trained for that undertaking. They therefore try to carry it out with their own homemade theological and hermeneutical instruments. I shall come back to this later.

SOME PROPOSITIONS FOR A COMMON BIBLICAL THEOLOGY

I claimed above that Christians must acknowledge without any qualification the fact that the Hebrew Bible is the Holy Scripture of the Jews.

13. F. C. Baur, *Vorlesungen über neutestamentliche Theologie* (Leipzig, 1864).

14. A. von Harnack, *Marcion* (Leipzig, 1921, 2d ed. 1924).

15. For an insider it is therefore surprising to see Wellhausen (who explicitly denied being a theologian) depicted as being in the same boat as Eichrodt, von Rad, and others, who explicitly wrote as Christian theologians (see Levenson, "Hebrew Bible, the Old Testament, and Historical Criticism"), but the parallelism is indeed striking. On the Nazi challenge to Christian use of the Old Testament, see chapter 8 below.

I added that this claim presupposes the acceptance of the dignity, independence, and value of the Jewish religion. I am convinced that it is both simple and evident that Christian biblical scholars must first of all realize and accept the fact that they are dealing with a book that is part and parcel of another living religious tradition as well, and that they must face the challenge to their traditional handling of the Old Testament.

Let me switch my usage once more, this time from the third person plural to the first person singular. From this point on, I wish neither to attack nor to defend anyone. In other words, I want to leave the field of the history of Old Testament interpretation and research, and enter the field of reflections about the possibilities and chances for a future common theological reading of our common Hebrew Bible. (I hope it will not merely remain a path to Utopia.)

At the outset, let me state some of my presuppositions for the following remarks (without discussing or justifying them):

1. The Hebrew Bible is a collection of Israelite (or Jewish) Scriptures which de facto acquired its final form before either rabbinic Judaism or Christianity came into being. Consequently neither a rabbinic nor a Christian interpretation of the Hebrew Bible can be historical.[16]

2. Both for (rabbinic) Jews and for Christians, the Hebrew Bible (or Greek Old Testament) is a fundamental basis for their religion, but not the only one; for both religious communities, postbiblical traditions are of essential importance.

3. In both traditions, methods of interpreting the Hebrew (or Greek) Bible have developed that are peculiar to that particular community, and therefore cannot claim acceptance by the other.

4. Theological interpretation of the Hebrew Bible is not dependent on the theological system of the religious tradition to which the particular interpreter belongs: the Hebrew Bible is a theological book in its own right, which can be, and must be, interpreted theologically from the inside.

5. In doing so, the interpreter's theological approach will unavoidably be influenced by his or her own religious tradition; interpreters should be conscious of this influence and should reflect on its hermeneutical consequences.

6. Taking this into consideration, Jewish and Christian biblical scholars can work together toward a theological interpretation of the Hebrew Bible.

Let me try to unfold some of these postulates. One of the key points is the notion that the Hebrew Bible is itself a theological book. That means

16. See Levenson, "Why Jews Are Not Interested," 286.

that the Bible does not only become theological through interpretation by a later-elaborated theology, be it rabbinic or Christian; rather, it is possible and necessary to find the theological ideas and messages of the biblical texts themselves. At the same time, this implies that the authors of the biblical texts should be deemed to be in a certain sense theologians, who had theological ideas and purposes in mind when they spoke or wrote their texts, and even when they assembled the texts into larger units or books. This seems to be a truism. But if it is true, there would be no reason why Jewish and Christian scholars could not work together to explore the theological content of biblical texts.

Several objections might be raised against such a concept: What is theology? Does it not have to be defined by each particular religious and theological tradition? This is an interesting question because the answer turns out to be circular. Certainly, each religious community developed its own system of theological questions and answers. But they did so—and still do—on the basis of the traditions passed down to them, including first of all the Hebrew Bible. So it would be an important experiment to put certain present-day theological questions to the Hebrew Bible, and to see whether they prove to be appropriate.

This could be one of the great advantages of a common theological reading of the Hebrew Bible by Jewish and Christian scholars. In some cases, it would emerge that discussions among biblical scholars imply questions that also touch differences in the exegetical traditions of the two communities. Let me take one example. The identity of the Servant of the Lord, the עבד יהוה, in Isaiah 40–55 is disputed among Christian biblical scholars. Those who assume an individual understanding of the servant could be open in principle for a christological interpretation; those who make no such assumption will be unable to take the traditional Christian interpretation as being in accordance with the meaning of the text itself. On the other hand, those who are inclined to a collective or corporate understanding could be open for the dominant Jewish interpretation of the servant as representing Israel. In most cases the exegetical decision will be made, at least on the conscious level, independently of the Christian liturgical and dogmatic tradition. But it will have far-reaching consequences for the hermeneutical relations between the scholar's own exegetical-theological insights and the Christian tradition of interpretation. It would therefore be of great interest and value to discuss these different views with Jewish scholars committed to their own religious tradition.

Another example might be the traditional Christian notion that to speak theologically about creation can only mean creation through Jesus Christ.

One of the proof texts for such a dogmatic position is Col. 1:15-17, where it is said that Jesus Christ is "the firstborn of all creation," and that "in him all things were created, in heaven and on earth, visible and invisible." Another text is of course John 1:1-13: "In the beginning was the Word [ὁ λόγος], and the Word was with God, and the Word was God. He was in the beginning with God; all things were made through him, and without him was not anything made that was made."

It is obvious and well known that this text reflects certain Hellenistic Jewish speculations about the חכמה in Prov. 8:22-31, whose Greek equivalent is σοφία, which was then equated with λόγος. A dogmatic notion built on those extrabiblical speculations can scarcely serve as a hermeneutical key to a biblical text. Outside Protestant Old Testament scholarship, this dogmatic position is still widely held. But it is interesting to see that in von Rad's commentary on Genesis there is no hint of this Christian tradition. Westermann speaks in more general terms about God's history with humanity, which begins with creation and finally has its center in what happened in Jesus Christ; but he too does not mention the notion of creation through Jesus Christ.

Yet both commentators, and others as well (for example Walther Zimmerli), mention the aspect of the seventh day of creation and point to its relevance for the biblical Sabbath, as well as to certain eschatological elements involved. But they do not mention the importance of the Sabbath in postbiblical and contemporary Judaism. Possibly they would argue that this would go beyond the scope of their task as commentators on a biblical text. But it would in any case be interesting and useful to discuss these things with Jewish biblical scholars. Then Christian scholars would have to ask themselves what consequences the shift from Sabbath to Sunday as the weekly Christian holy day must have for the Christian interpretation of Gen. 1:1—2:3, and whether it is possible at all to interpret the creation story without taking the Jewish tradition of the Sabbath into account.

At this point I should like to add a remark about the question: Why do Christian biblical scholars usually ignore or negate postbiblical Judaism? The answer seems to me to be simple: nobody told them that they should be interested in that tradition. There is no scholarly custom for dealing with Judaism; even now there is little literature by Jewish biblical scholars that would demonstrate the use of the postbiblical tradition; there is scant relevant scholarly literature that could introduce Christian scholars to the problems of dealing with Jewish exegetical tradition; we lack translations of great parts of rabbinic literature, and so on. I fully understand the critical attitude of some Jewish scholars with regard to this deficiency among their Christian colleagues, and I do not want to defend it: but I feel that it is necessary to analyze the historical reasons carefully before blaming individual scholars.

THE FUTURE OF A COMMON BIBLICAL THEOLOGY

The two arbitrarily chosen examples just cited show that Christian biblical scholars are in many cases not eager to see their exegetical results in relation to a particular Christian tradition. Indeed the contrary is often the case. I believe that in the main Levenson is correct when he says:

Most Christians involved in the historical criticism of the Hebrew Bible today seem to have ceased to want their work to be considered distinctively Christian. They do the essential philological, historical, and archeological work without concern for the larger constructive issues or for the theological implications of their labors. They are Christians everywhere except in the classroom and at the writing table, where they are simply honest historians striving for an unbiased view of the past.[17]

That is one side of the coin. The other side (castigated by Levenson very sharply as being inconsistent, if not insincere) is the attempt nevertheless to interpret the Old Testament as part of Christian theology. I have tried to explain some of the reasons for this attitude, and I have tried to formulate my own view of how to change this situation. I agree with Levenson that the crucial point is the theological acceptance or, first of all, even the awareness, of the existence of contemporary Judaism as a living religion which uses the Hebrew Bible as its Holy Scripture. Christian theologians, Old Testament scholars included, have never been taught to realize that. I myself during more than ten years of teaching Old Testament was never aware of this problem. It was only through several visits to Israel and through personal acquaintance with Jewish biblical scholars in Israel and the United States that I gradually began to understand the whole problem, and I still feel that I am only beginning to discern the consequences of these insights. As far as I can see, there are still very few Christian biblical scholars who are aware of all this.

One of the main obstacles to progress in this field is the fact that there is almost no exchange between Jewish and Christian biblical scholars on theological questions involved in the biblical texts. At the same time, there is an increasing debate about the so-called hermeneutical questions of how to understand the Old Testament within the framework

17. Levenson, "Hebrew Bible, the Old Testament, and Historical Criticism," 49.

of Christian theology, and whether and how to write a biblical theology embracing both parts of the Christian Bible. Levenson quoted from several books on Old Testament theology to demonstrate these obvious inconsistencies. The most remarkable fact is that this kind of Christianizing interpretation is mainly, if not almost exclusively, to be found in the genre of books that try to embrace the Old Testament as a whole,[18] or in articles dealing with this problem, whereas in the commentaries on specific biblical books this kind of question is rarely raised at all.

What has to be done? In my view, the main point would be for Jewish and Christian scholars who feel challenged by the current situation to make efforts to bring to the awareness of Christian biblical scholars the crucial relevance of contemporary Judaism for any theological interpretation of the Hebrew Bible. This needs to be presented, of course, not with an attitude of imposing an absolute alternative, as if Christian scholars had to give up their present exegetical methods and take over Jewish exegesis. What would be necessary is to overcome the dichotomy that even now is used by Christians only one-way. There are *two* traditions of reading and interpreting the Hebrew Bible. Neither has a monopoly; neither is to be neglected, let alone excluded.

In my view, the only promising way forward would be to work together on biblical texts or certain biblical topics or themes, instead of discussing general hermeneutical questions about how to relate Jewish and Christian views of the Hebrew Bible to each other. One day in the future it may be useful, and I hope possible, to do that as well, but in my view it would be a fundamental mistake to begin there. Working on texts means asking about their theological meaning and relevance; the same is true in dealing with certain topics or themes. In his characterization (quoted above) of the general attitude of Christian biblical scholars, Levenson says: "They do the essential philological, historical, and archeological work without concern for the larger constructive issues or for the theological implications of their labors." Let us try to add to the essentials of their work the word *theological,* because a biblical text is never adequately interpreted unless attention is paid to its theological relevance, including the theological context of the text itself, of the chapter or book, and finally of the Hebrew Bible as a whole (here the discussion about canon and canonization becomes relevant).

---

18. Perhaps Levenson is right to characterize this kind of book as Midrash (see "Hebrew Bible, the Old Testament, and Historical Criticism," 48).

Let me conclude with a quotation from the New Testament that seems fitting for our situation:

> When he saw the crowds, he had compassion for them, because they were harassed and helpless, like sheep without a shepherd. Then he said to his disciples, "The harvest is plentiful, but the laborers are few; pray therefore the Lord of the harvest to send laborers into his harvest." (Matt. 9:36-38)

CHAPTER 5

The Importance of the Canon

for a Theology

of the Old Testament

In a postscript to the third edition of his history of form-critical research into the Old Testament (*Geschichte der historisch-kritischen Erforschung des Alten Testaments*), Hans-Joachim Kraus drew attention to recent developments in Anglo-Saxon theology, and advised continental European scholars to enter into more intensive dialogue with their English-speaking colleagues.[1] This advice is all too justified, for in the field of Old Testament theology particularly, highly important developments are taking place in the English-speaking world which have hitherto hardly been noticeably reflected at all in the German discussion.

This may even be said of Brevard S. Childs's book *Biblical Theology in Crisis* (1970), although this was a work of fundamental importance.[2] Initially, the book has to do with a purely American phenomenon, the "biblical theology" movement. This grew up during the Second World War and was an attempt to bridge the gap between fundamentalism and historical-critical scholarship through a rediscovery of the theological dimension of the Bible. Walther Eichrodt's *Theology of the Old Testament* (1933ff.) played an important part here (although it was not translated into English until 1961),[3] and the same may be said of Oscar Cullmann

1. H.-J. Kraus, *Geschichte der historisch-kritischen Erforschung des Alten Testaments,* 3d ed. (Neukirchen-Vluyn, 1982), 557, 559.

2. B. S. Childs, *Biblical Theology in Crisis* (Philadelphia: Westminster Press, 1970).

3. W. Eichrodt, *Theologie des Alten Testaments* (1933ff.); Eng. trans., *Theology of the Old Testament,* trans. J. A. Baker (London: SCM Press; Philadelphia: Westminster Press, 1961).

for the New Testament. But there were hardly any links with German exegetical work. This changed radically with the names of Gerhard von Rad and Rudolf Bultmann. Childs describes very impressively the crisis of the biblical theology movement, its gradual inward dissolution and its final collapse ("The Cracking of the Walls").

But the picture which Childs draws offers no reason for proclaiming the superiority of German exegetical theology. For the crisis sparked off by the new hermeneutic ("hermeneutic" instead of hermeneutics!)[4] drew that theology into the very same collapse. "One of the persistently weak points of the Biblical Theology Movement was its failure to take the Biblical text seriously in its canonical form. It accepted uncritically the liberal hermeneutical presupposition that one came to the Biblical text from a vantage point outside the text." Consequently "it was vulnerable to every shifting wind that blew, from Cullmann's 'salvation-history' to Bultmann's 'self-understanding' to Ebeling-Fuchs's 'linguisticality of being.' "[5]

Childs himself pleads for a new, different approach, propounding the thesis that "the canon of the Christian church is the most appropriate context from which to do Biblical Theology."[6] By saying this he set on foot a discussion which has meanwhile almost turned into a new "movement" in English-speaking theology. This is signalized by a whole series of book titles: *Torah and Canon* (J. A. Sanders, 1972, 2d ed. 1974), *Prophecy and Canon* (J. Blenkinsopp, 1977), *Canon and Authority* (ed. G. W. Coats and B. O. Long, 1977), and finally Childs's own *Introduction to the Old Testament as Scripture* (1979). There has also been a throng of essays on fundamental questions and individual aspects of the problem,[7] as well as discussions about method such as we find, for example, in the *Journal for the Study of the Old Testament*, no. 16 (1980) and in *Horizons in Biblical Theology*, vol 2 (1980).

At the same time, although I have just used the word "movement," this description must be expressly qualified. As far as I can see, it is never

---

4. Characterizing the influence in America of Bultmann's pupils E. Fuchs and G. Ebeling, Childs writes: "The term 'hermeneutic' was introduced in distinction from hermeneutics to designate 'the process of interpretation' which imposed upon man historical and ontological concerns" (Childs, *Biblical Theology*, 80).

5. Ibid., 102.

6. Ibid., 99.

7. J. A. Sanders, *Torah and Canon* (Philadelphia: Fortress Press, 1972, 2d ed. 1974); J. Blenkinsopp, *Prophecy and Canon: A Contribution to the Study of Jewish Origins* (Notre Dame, Ind.: Univ. of Notre Dame Press, 1977); G. W. Coats and B. O. Long, eds., *Canon and Authority* (Philadelphia: Fortress Press, 1977); B. S. Childs, *Introduction to the Old Testament as Scripture* (Philadelphia: Fortress Press; London: SCM Press, 1979).

used by the authors involved in this discussion; and in fact the discussion itself proves on closer examination to be much more differentiated than might appear at first sight. However, it is the common factors which must be stressed first of all, especially since the theme "canon" in the sense meant here has hitherto never been used in the German-speaking debate about the problems of an Old Testament theology.[8] All the authors involved are concerned with the question about the hermeneutical and theological importance of the final canonical form of the biblical texts—both the individual books and the canon as a whole. It is significant here that, although this new approach always develops in critical dispute with the methodological presuppositions and results of previous historical-critical exegesis, the scholars concerned still maintain and explicitly stress the continuity of the exegetical tradition.

If we go into the matter in more detail, we can discover three groups of questions. These are centered on: (1) the final form of the biblical books (or larger text complexes), and its relation to previous stages in the transmission history; (2) the development of the Old Testament canon in the context of the Jewish history of the time; and (3) the relationship between the Jewish and the Christian canon. These three groups of questions are in many ways intertwined, but in each of them we can find characteristic differences between the individual authors.

I

Up to now, it is the first point which has been most hotly debated— that is to say, the final form of the individual biblical books (or larger text complexes), and its relation to previous stages in the transmission history. Childs's *Introduction* contains a wealth of material on this question, together with a position which he puts forward with vigor and point; but even before this book was published, and independently of it, many individual studies had appeared. Here we can first of all again pick up what we have already said: many authors believe that it is an important and long-neglected task for exegesis to take the final form of the text seriously, in its existing and now canonical form, instead of viewing that as a mere fortuitous product, or the outcome of the work of editors and augmenters, which has grown up more or less uncontrolled. There is a new awareness of "the historical and theological dynamics of canonical

8. C. Westermann calls the "threefold division" of the canon the fundamental starting point for an Old Testament theology, but he is not relating this to the final form of the texts (*Theologie des Alten Testaments in Grundzügen* [Göttingen, 1978], 6; Eng. trans., *Elements of Old Testament Theology*, trans. D. W. Stott [Atlanta: John Knox Press, 1982]).

process—the collection, selection, interpretative sifting and application of traditions, a process which finally produced the body of writings now designated as canonical."[9]

This phraseology does not initially seem to offer any surprises to exegetical scholars belonging to the German-speaking tradition. It could be viewed as practically an exposition of what Martin Noth declared the task of transmission history to be: "to trace the long process, which was influenced by such manifold interests and tendencies, . . . from the beginnings to the end."[10] But if we look again, we immediately see the difference—indeed the contrast—in the general thrust of interest and the questions asked. Noth goes on: "Nevertheless, as things stand, this history will have as its major interest not so much the later processes of Pentateuchal development, which increasingly were purely literary, as rather the origins and first stages of growth which were decisive for the development as a whole." A comparison between the two quotations from Noth and from Coats and Long brings out very clearly the continuity and the discontinuity of method. There is continuity, because no new methods really have to be developed, since the question about the transmission history has provided the tools with which the development process of the text can be investigated and presented, right down to its final canonical form.[11] But these tools were not hitherto employed for this purpose, because "the major interest" tended in the opposite direction. So there is discontinuity, because eyes are now deliberately turned in a different direction—indeed in the diametrically opposite one.

But this does not simply mean that one partial and hitherto neglected aspect of the transmission history question is now given increased emphasis. The change is greater than that. For of course the direction of the viewpoint is not arbitrary. It is guided by exegetical interest. If interest is directed primarily toward "the beginnings," and the "first stages of growth which were decisive for the development of the whole," this means that an a priori decision has already been made. The later stages cannot attract the same interest, and the final "canonical" form generally

---

9. Coats and Long, eds., *Canon and Authority*, xi.

10. M. Noth, *A History of Pentateuchal Traditions*, trans. B. W. Anderson (Englewood Cliffs, N.J.: Prentice-Hall, 1972), 1 (translation slightly altered).

11. This link with the question about the transmission is less clearly expressed among American scholars, however. For example in Coats and Long, eds., *Canon and Authority*, xi, n. 2, we read: "Among American form critics especially, a newly awakened interest in directing traditional form critical questions in a new way to *whole* texts has cropped up."

does not enter the picture at all.[12] The change of direction in the line of sight therefore obviously has as its presupposition a changed exegetical interest.

This change seems to be most marked in the treatment of the prophetic books. Here the question about the final canonical form stands in particularly obvious tension to the question about the "original" words of the individual prophet as a historical figure; for it will probably be true to say that hardly a single prophetic book in its present form contains exclusively "genuine" prophetic sayings. So to take the final canonical form of a prophetic book seriously, means conceding theological relevance to a text which has deliberately altered the words spoken by one of the prophets. This is true, for example, in particularly marked form for Amos, where Childs too believes that the close, with its vista of salvation at the end of days (Amos 9:11-15), belongs to a later phase of interpretation. Yet it is precisely this which is the "canonical" form in which the book of Amos must now be read, or rather: in which its message must be heard.[13] The same is true of the book of Isaiah, which should now be read as a whole—as "God's word" to the postexilic community.[14] Here a fundamental concept emerges which applies, with the appropriate modifications, to all the prophetic books: they proclaim judgment and salvation, in a relationship of mutual tension.[15]

We shall have to discuss the reason and justification for this change of outlook at a later point (see section 2 below). But before that we have to ask how fundamentally the change is meant, and how far interest in the final stage of a text can still be linked with observations about the early phases of its development and history. Here wide differences emerge. Coats and Long initially say very cautiously that the new approach leads us to take the final stage of the Old Testament writings seriously, "simply because the *textus receptus* represents an important stage in the history of the book." And later they urge us "to treat the canonical form of the

12. R. Smend stresses that in his book *Die Entstehung des Alten Testaments* (Stuttgart and Berlin, 1978) he also began with the final canonical form of the text (see his "Questions about the Importance of the Canon in the Old Testament Introduction," *JSOT* 16 [1980]: 45–51, esp. 45). But the fundamental difference is precisely the fact that he does not return to this final form and does not consider it in its own intention.

13. Childs, *Introduction,* 505ff.

14. Ibid., 325ff.; cf. R. Rendtorff, *Das Alte Testament: Eine Einführung* (Neukirchen-Vluyn, 1983; 3d ed., 1988), 210ff.; Eng. trans., *The Old Testament: An Introduction* (Philadelphia: Fortress Press; London: SCM Press, 1986); also chapter 13 below.

15. Cf. R. E. Clements, "Patterns in the Prophetic Canon," in Coats and Long, eds., *Canon and Authority,* 42–55; J. Blenkinsopp, "A New Kind of Introduction," *JSOT* 16 (1980): 24–27; R. Rendtorff, *Das Alte Testament,* 255f.

Old Testament as something with integrity and meaning, which is worth fresh investigations, whether the motivation is religious or not."[16] Here Childs clearly takes up a different position. As long ago as 1970 he wrote: "Even though there is an obvious history of development that lies behind the formation of the canon, and even though there are a variety of modes of consciousness involved at various levels and periods, the confession of a canon holds *this* context to be normative for the Christian faith."[17] In his Exodus commentary he says: "It is the final text, the composite narrative, in its present shape which the church, following the lead of the synagogue, accepted as canonical and thus the vehicle of revelation and instruction. . . . The study of the prehistory has its proper function within exegesis only in illuminating the final text."[18] Consequently the canonical approach evokes the most vigorous contradiction from scholars committed to the tradition-history method, "for which the heart of the exegetical task is the recovery of the depth dimension."[19] "The depth dimension aids in understanding the interpreted text, and does not function independently of it."[20]

As far as I can see, with this postulate Childs has found few followers. Most scholars think that the earlier stages of the text are also worth independent interpretation.[21] But the difference of viewpoint is to be found not so much in the exegetical sector as in the field of dogmatics—in the question about the normative character of a particular stage in the history of a text. And here that means the final stage.[22] We shall come back to this question later. Before that we should note that, apart from this fundamental question, a growing number of scholars are viewing the final, existing stage of the text as something that has an integrity of its own and is based on an intention of its own. As a result, the aim of exegetical work to an increasing degree is to come to grips with this final stage.[23] In

---

16. Coats and Long, eds., *Canon and Authority,* xi.

17. Childs, *Biblical Theology,* 102 (my italics).

18. B. S. Childs, *Exodus,* OTL (London: SCM Press, 1974), xv.

19. Childs, *Introduction,* 75.

20. Ibid., 76.

21. This applies to most of the contributions in *JSOT* 16 (1980) and in *HBT* 2 (1980).

22. Childs himself is not quite so strict in his exegetical work. For example, in his fine essay "Psalm Titles and Midrashic Exegesis," *JSS* 16 (1971), 137–50, he views the psalm titles which are related to stages in the life of David explicitly as "exegesis" of the existing text.

23. I would include here the work A. H. J. Gunneweg has done on the books of Ezra and Nehemiah ("Zur Interpretation der Bücher Esra-Nehemia: Zugleich ein Beitrag zur Methode der Exegese," VTSup 32 [1981]: 146–61; "Die aramäische und die hebräische

the process, attention is often directed to particular "larger units" within the present complex, which are seen as having an independent purpose. As examples I may mention Peter Ackroyd's treatment of Isaiah 1–12,[24] and Bernhard W. Anderson's investigation of the primeval history (especially the story of the flood).[25] But other studies could also be cited. This shows that the change of direction in the line of sight does not prove fruitful only in connection with the final forms of the individual books. And from this angle too the position put forward by Childs would seem to be open to question.

Incidentally it is worth pointing out that even in earlier exegesis a particular stage in the textual history was frequently invested with outstanding, quasi-canonical dignity. This is true particularly in the sphere of the Pentateuch, where the question about the "kerygma" or the "theology" of the individual pentateuchal sources made one particular stage the preferred object of theological interpretation—and this stage neither the earliest nor the latest. This approach was to a great extent dependent on changing views about the separation of the source documents, and their relation to one another. Compared with this, to start from the final stage of the text offers a firmer point of departure.

II

To concern ourselves with the final form of the biblical text has a second very important aspect too, for it brings more clearly into view the community among whom, and for whose use, the texts were given their final form: that is to say, postexilic Judaism. This is always stressed in work on the canonical problem.[26] Here too we find an essential shift of emphasis in the way the exegetical question is formulated. This shows itself in a number of different ways. In the first place, it means that the postexilic period is not viewed as a late stage which could be neglected in the context of a holistic understanding of the Old Testament, or could even be seen as an aberration. On the contrary, this period is understood as being the formative epoch to which the Old Testament owes its

---

Erzählung über die nachexilische Restauration—ein Vergleich," *ZAW* 94 [1982]: 299–302).

24. P. R. Ackroyd, "Isaiah I–XII: Presentation of a Prophet," VTSup 29 (1978): 16–48; cf. also his "Isaiah 36–39: Structure and Function," in *Von Kanaan bis Kerala: Festschrift für J. P. M. van der Ploeg* (Neukirchen-Vluyn, 1982), 3–21.

25. B. W. Anderson, "From Analysis to Synthesis: The Interpretation of Genesis 1–11," *JBL* 97 (1978): 23–29.

26. Already by J. A. Sanders in *Torah and Canon.*

present configuration, not merely formally but in its theological shaping too. So here too the question is turned upside down, so to speak. The function of exegesis has changed. It is no longer supposed to free earlier, more primary layers of Old Testament tradition from later excretions. The transmission process is now looked at from the vantage point of its end—that is, from the Old Testament text in its existing form.

Here, in looking at the final stage of this process, the initial question is not about individual "authors," to whom we owe the final form of the text. Interest is now directed rather to the community whose self-definition is expressed in the final form of the Old Testament canon. We have to think of a mutual relationship: through its handling of the texts passed down to it, the community builds up the way it sees itself; while in the process it often gives these texts a new interpretation, which is ultimately reflected in the final form of the text and the canon as a whole.[27]

In order to clarify these questions further, we must intensify our efforts to throw light on the history of postexilic Israel. This period is generally considered to be wrapped in obscurity, since the sources provide us with hardly any direct information. In my view, however, lack of knowledge about this period is largely due to the lack of interest which it has hitherto evoked among scholars. Generally speaking, only very few have tried to delve into it more deeply.[28] Their work has been respectfully received, but it has hardly led to any more intensive study of the period.[29] In recent years Joseph Blenkinsopp has tried afresh to throw light on the groups and disputes in the Judaism of the time, and I believe that this attempt shows that if the sources are painstakingly interpreted, they yield much more than would at first appear.[30] If research into this era were to be pursued with the same intensity once devoted—and devoted still—to Israel's early period, I am sure that we could expect results which would

27. Cf. Blenkinsopp, *Prophecy and Canon*, 2: "What needs to be done ... is to take the formation of the canon as an important chapter in the history of nascent Judaism."

28. Deserving of special mention here are K. Galling, *Studien zur Geschichte Israels im persischen Zeitalter* (Tübingen, 1964) and H. G. Kippenberg, *Religion und Klassenbildung im antiken Judäa* (Göttingen, 1978, 2d ed. 1982).

29. However, here a number of writings dealing with the religious developments of the postexilic period must be mentioned, e.g., O. Plöger, *Theocracy and Eschatology*, trans. S. Rudman (Oxford: Blackwell, 1968) (German ed. 1959); O. H. Steck, "Das Problem theologischer Strömungen in nachexilischer Zeit," *EvT* 28 (1968): 445–58; P. D. Hanson, *The Dawn of Apocalyptic* (Philadelphia: Fortress Press, 1975, 2d ed. 1979). Cf. also Rendtorff, *Das Alte Testament.*

30. J. Blenkinsopp, "Interpretation and the Tendency to Sectarianism: An Aspect of Second Temple History," in E. P. Sanders, ed., *Jewish and Christian Self-Definition*, vol. 2: *Two Aspects of Judaism in the Greco-Roman Period* (London: SCM Press; Philadelphia: Fortress Press, 1981), 1–26.

provide a firmer basis for a reconstruction of the historical, social, and religious warp and weft of the time.[31]

As far as an Old Testament theology is concerned, this will then present us with a question: How are we to describe and weigh up the development which can be detected in the Israelite religion during Old Testament times? Here we shall have to take up once more another question which we already touched on in section 1—the question about what is "normative." The greater value attached to the preexilic period in earlier discussion would then seem to stand in irreconcilable antithesis to the normative validity of the final form of the canon which Childs stresses. But in this question too an intensive and differentiated discussion is still lacking. Here the question about the significance of prophecy undoubtedly plays an important role. Again, Blenkinsopp's approach seems promising, for he tries to show that the present form of the canon emerged from the tension between "Torah" and "prophecy," and that to overcome this tension means defining afresh the importance of prophecy for a "postprophetic" age.[32] This question is linked in a close mutual relationship with what was said above (in section 1) about the formation of the prophetic books in their final form.

III

Finally, in the light of this changed approach, the question about the importance of the Old Testament canon for Christian theology presents itself with new urgency. At this point views today diverge particularly widely. Christian Old Testament scholars have hitherto proceeded according to the method which Klaus Koch once called "the theory of the prophetic connection."[33] The New Testament (and with it Christian theology) links up more or less directly with the prophets and leaves the intervening era on one side, as something purely Jewish, and a phase which does not lead on to fulfillment in the New Testament. This is often the tacitly accepted procedure today: the postexilic portions of the

31. Cf. also F. Crüsemann, "Israel in der Perserzeit," and S. Talmon, "Jüdische Sektenbildung in der Frühzeit der Periode des Zweiten Tempels," both in W. Schluchter, ed., *Max Webers Sicht des antiken Christentums: Interpretation und Kritik* (Frankfurt, 1985), 205–32 and 233–80.

32. Blenkinsopp, *Prophecy and Canon*. Also R. E. Clements, *Old Testament Theology: A Fresh Approach* (London: Marshall, Morgan & Scott, 1978; Atlanta: John Knox Press, 1979), 120ff.

33. K. Koch, *The Rediscovery of Apocalyptic,* trans. Margaret Kohl (London: SCM Press, 1972), 36ff.

Old Testament and the religious developments of postexilic Judaism are simply ignored.[34] Other scholars explicitly claim that "a Christian theology . . . [may] never sanction the masoretic canon" because in that "continuity to the New Testament . . . is severed to a significant degree."[35] Whichever of these approaches is preferred, in neither of them is the Old Testament canon in its final form drawn into the deliberations about a Christian theology of the Old Testament.[36]

On the other hand, to take the Old Testament canon seriously raises a whole series of questions which we can only briefly touch on here. First, it becomes necessary to see the whole of the Old Testament in the light of its final canonical form as an expression of the self-understanding of postexilic Judaism. It makes no essential difference here if we stress that it was not the Hebrew canon of rabbinic tradition that was adopted as component of the Christian Bible, but the Hellenistic canon of the Septuagint; for in the Septuagint too the Holy Scriptures are summed up as "the Torah and the Prophets," as New Testament citations show (Matt. 5:17; 7:12, and frequently). In the framework of the canonical Old Testament, it is impossible to detach the Prophets from their relation to the Torah.

This brings us up against a second question, which was discussed in section 1: whether and how far the earlier stages of tradition can be an independent subject of interpretation, in the context of the canon as a whole. Here again, the heart of the matter is the question whether the final canonical form is accepted as having its own stature and dignity, or whether it is pushed aside as an improper alteration of what was originally intended. If this second procedure is adopted, insights into the history of the canon would require the proponents of that course to find a new way of explaining how there could be a theological reception of prophetic traditions which passes over and discounts the new definition of prophecy in its relation to the Torah arrived at by the postexilic Jewish community.

And finally: What did it really mean when the canon of the Jewish

34. Cf. here R. Rendtorff, "Die jüdische Bibel und ihre antijüdische Auslegung," in R. Rendtorff and E. Stegemann, eds., *Auschwitz—Krise der christlichen Theologie* (Munich, 1980), 99–116, esp. 113ff.

35. H. Gese, "Erwägungen zur Einheit der biblischen Theologie," *ZTK* 67 (1970): 417–36 (= *Vom Sinai zum Zion* [Munich 1974], 11–30), quotation from pp. 422f. (16f.).

36. I am unable to develop this problem more fully here; see here now J. Blenkinsopp, "Tanakh and the New Testament: A Christian Perspective," in L. Boadt et al., eds., *Biblical Studies: Meeting Ground of Jews and Christians* (New York: Paulist Press, 1980), 96–119.

Bible—first in its Greek form and since the Reformation in its Hebrew form too—became a component part of the Christian Bible? This initially raises a whole sheaf of historical questions about the time and nature of the canonization of the Old and the New Testaments, and about the mutual influence, and mutual demarcation, of rabbinic Judaism and the patristic church in this connection. But the most important question, it seems to me, is the question whether, in the view of Christian theology, the theological substance of the Old Testament itself is thereby changed, because it can—and may—now only be read as scripture tending toward the New Testament. As I see it, this viewpoint is possible only if the self-understanding of the Old Testament in its canonical form is surrendered. And it also means incidentally that, consciously or unconsciously, the Jews are being denied the right to carry on their own tradition in continuity with the Old Testament.

The better way—and, as I believe, the only appropriate way—would be the contrary one: to take the self-understanding of the Old Testament in its canonical form quite seriously, and at the same time to recognize, theologically as well, the historical fact that its influence has two separate strands, one Jewish and one Christian. To accept this would free Christian theology from the attempt to declare that its own exegetical history is canonical; and it would also make it possible for Jews and Christians to engage in dialogue about their common foundations in the Hebrew Bible, and to discuss together the relevance of those foundations today, in the light of our different interpretative histories and the different influence which the Hebrew Bible has exerted on our traditions.

CHAPTER 6

The Place of Prophecy
in a Theology
of the Old Testament

I

At the very time when Julius Wellhausen became aware of Karl Heinrich Graf's thesis, according to which the "Mosaic law" had emerged
later than the prophets, Bernhard Duhm published his foundational book
on the theology of the prophets. He too started from Graf's insights about
the later date of the priestly laws, but the conclusion he drew was much
more radical. For him now, the prophetic religion was not merely the
most important part of Israel's religion; it was the basis of its whole
development. The two-part title of his book is of great significance:
"The Theology of the Prophets as Foundation for the Inner Historical
Development of Israelite Religion" (*Die Theologie der Propheten als
Grundlage für die innere Entwicklungsgeschichte der israelitischen Religion* [1875]).[1] He felt that it was impossible to write a "theology of
the Old Testament," because of the diversity of developments within the
history of Israel's religion. But in the religion of the prophets he found
the basis from which all these developments started, and by which they
had been fundamentally shaped. The prophets "were understood as the
real creators of the authentic religion of Israel."[2]

Paper read at the SBL International Meeting in Vienna, 1990, hitherto unpublished in
English.
1. The English translation of the title is taken from J. Blenkinsopp, *A History of Prophecy
in Israel* (Philadelphia: Westminster Press; London: SPCK, 1983), 28.
2. J. H. Hayes and F. C. Prussner, *Old Testament Theology: Its History and Development*
(Atlanta: John Knox Press; London: SCM Press, 1985), 139.

Today, a hundred years later, things have changed. It is unnecessary in the framework of this paper to recapitulate the developments and changes that have taken place in Old Testament theology during this period. One of the main characteristics of the new type of Old Testament theology which began with Eichrodt was the turn from the history of Israel's religion to a systematic concept of its theology. The key words were taken from the vocabulary of Christian systematic theology. Eichrodt himself chose the idea of "covenant" as the first all-embracing concept. Many other theologies opened with a first chapter or paragraph on "God," followed by others on revelation, creation, covenant, sin and redemption, and the like. From these arrangements of theological topics one can in many cases learn much more about the theology of the author in question than about the theology of the Old Testament.

For our present topic, it is important to note that this kind of systematic arrangement does not offer any particular place for the prophets. In most cases they appear in the context of other leading religious figures such as judges, kings, priests, sages, and so forth, who are dealt with in a chapter on religious institutions, or as agents of God's rule, or the like. In this framework the history of prophecy is generally briefly outlined. Several authors feel the need to mention the prophets again under headings such as divine judgment, redemption, and promise. Sometimes the thinking and preaching of the prophets is given a more significant place in those frameworks, but generally speaking only in a later part of the exposition of Old Testament theology. Nowhere could the prophets win back the fundamental place they had at the end of the nineteenth century.[3]

II

On the contrary, Gerhard von Rad, whom I have not so far mentioned, wrote in the second volume of his *Old Testament Theology* (1960) that scholarship was still occupied with demolishing this nineteenth-century conception. He added that scholars had become increasingly uncertain how to define what was new in the message of the prophets.[4] Here things

---

3. Incidentally the prophets seem meanwhile to have disappeared altogether from theological discussion. In the new *Jahrbuch für Biblische Theologie (JBTh)*, whose fourth volume has meanwhile appeared, not a single article has hitherto dealt with the prophets.

4. G. von Rad, *Theologie des Alten Testaments,* vol. 2 (Munich, 1960, 4th ed. 1965), 18f. (4th ed., 14f.); Eng. trans., *Old Testament Theology,* trans. D. M. G. Stalker, vol. 2 (Edinburgh: Oliver & Boyd; New York: Harper, 1965), 4f.; the reprints of 1972 and 1975 by the SCM Press, London, are reissues, without the changes made in the 4th German edition.

have apparently made an about-turn. The prophets are no longer taken as the basis, in relation to which everything else is later; the question is now raised: What was new about the prophets themselves? But new related to what? What was before them? Von Rad himself gave the answer: one of the fundamental new insights in the Old Testament scholarship of that period—in Germany in particular—was recognition of the prophets' exceedingly strong bonds with the traditions ("[die] überaus starke übelieferungsgebundenheit der prophetischen Botschaften"), in contrast to the former focus on the prophets' immediate experience with God.

This was the crucial question: the relation of the prophets to tradition. What was the nature of that relation? Von Rad himself gave two answers which seem to be almost incompatible. In the first volume of his *Theology* (1957) he wrote that the prophets tried to convince their contemporaries that for them God's former gifts of salvation had lost their value, and that Israel, in order to be saved, had to venture out in faith toward new, future divine acts. This conviction put the prophets "basically outside the saving history" as it had been experienced by Israel up to that time. That is why they had to be dealt with in a separate (second) volume.[5]

Eight years later, in the revised edition of the second volume (1965), he added a paragraph that reads like a sort of retraction: "Of course it was not that with the prophets something totally new appeared, which was simply in contrast to everything that had gone before. On the contrary, it will be one of the main tasks of this volume to show how deeply the prophets were rooted in Israel's old, and even oldest, traditions."[6] And then follows, a little later, the sentence about these prophetic roots which I quoted above.

It would be interesting to reflect on what had happened between these two statements. If we look around in the literature of those years, we find among other things an article by Rudolf Smend from 1963 entitled "Das Nein des Amos" (The no of Amos).[7] His thesis is that the consequence of Amos's preaching is "the No to Israel's existence altogether, the announcement of her destruction" (p. 405 = 85). "Amos utters God's No, not God's Yes, he announces the wrath, not the grace" (p. 423 = 103). The later redaction of the book of Amos which, in view of the survival of the Israelite religion, tried to build a bridge where Amos saw only the

---

5. G. von Rad, *Theologie des Alten Testaments*, vol. 1 (Munich, 1957), 133f. (4th ed., 142) (Eng. trans., vol. 1 [1962], 128).

6. Ibid., vol. 2, 4th Germ. ed., 13 (no Eng. trans. of this passage).

7. R. Smend, "Das Nein des Amos," *EvT* 23 (1963): 404–23 (=his *Die Mitte des Alten Testament* [1986], 85–103).

gap, "paid the price of a betrayal of Amos," who never thought of such a survival. Interestingly enough, Smend continues: "But after God undertook to build a bridge which was not a betrayal of Amos, and through the cross of Jesus Christ turned his sharpest No into his greatest and ultimate Yes, Amos's threat became invalid." This manifests a characteristic and widespread canonical inconsistency among Christian theologians, who take the cross of Christ as God's Yes, while ignoring Israel's return from exile, which Israel herself had obviously understood as God's Yes, and which had inaugurated a great deal of canonical reworking of biblical books. (I will come back to this later.)

Perhaps it was this kind of radicalism, as expressed by Smend and others, that caused von Rad to reformulate the problem of the relation between prophecy and tradition, and to emphasize the prophets' dependence on the traditions. Nonetheless, he never revoked his former statements that the substance of the prophets' message was entirely new compared with the older traditions. But at the same time he insisted that it would be impossible to understand the prophets without scrutinizing these traditions and their relations to them. He called the message of the prophets "a dialogue with the traditions" ("Gespräch mit der Überlieferung"), and he defined this dialogue as "actualized" (that is, as making the traditions topical, relevant for the present situation),[8] but also as "critical."[9]

It was this critical element which von Rad finally declared to be the reason for reserving a special volume for the prophets. In so doing he broke with the canonical approach that had characterized the first volume of his *Theology,* or at least the first part of that volume. There he had first given an exposition of the "canonical saving history" as presented by the "Hexateuch." He had then followed God's history with Israel from the giving of the land down to the Babylonian exile. This was in fact the canonical story of the Torah and the Former Prophets, and von Rad explicitly declared that his conception was meant to be a canonical one. He wrote "that we have to yield ourselves to the sequence of events as Israel's faith saw them." So "retelling [*Nacherzählung*] remains the most legitimate form of theological discourse on the New Testament."[10]

But then von Rad continued in the second part of the first volume[11] (pt. 2 D) with a chapter on "Israel before YHWH," subtitled "Israel's

8. Von Rad, *Theologie,* 2:167 (4th ed., 183); Eng. trans., 2:160.
9. Ibid., 2:148 (4th ed., 144).
10. Ibid., 1:126 (134); cf. also 352 (4th ed., 366); Eng. trans., 1:121.
11. Ibid., 1:133 (142); Eng. trans., 1:355.

Answer." This part deals with elements taken from the Writings, mainly the Psalms and wisdom literature. So one might assume that he was following the canonical order of the German translation, which (like the English one) is mainly identical with that of the Septuagint, putting the Writings before the Prophets. But he never mentions this. So in fact the canonical approach already stopped with the end of the books of Kings. The order in which he treats the rest of the biblical books is determined by their content in relation to the Pentateuch and the historical books: first Israel's answer, reflecting God's mighty deeds, and then the prophets' critical dialogue with tradition about these deeds.

So one might say that von Rad's conception is semicanonical, with a strong canonical beginning which, however, comprised only the "historical" parts according to the division of the canon in the Septuagint and its followers, that is, the Torah and the Former Prophets. The other parts of the canon are seen only in their relation to this first canonical part. It is obvious that this has to do with von Rad's specific understanding of "traditions," which he saw first of all as creeds and similar texts which shaped Israel's understanding of her own history. (I do not think I need to explain that to this audience.)

III

From a canonical point of view, the relation of the prophets to the first part of the canon should be formulated as "Torah and Prophecy"— or "Prophecy and Torah." Von Rad never called the Pentateuch "Torah" (he did not even talk about the "Pentateuch," but spoke about the "Hexateuch"), and the same may be said of most other Christian scholars as well. Yet in some recent publications we find a new awareness of this problem. In Ronald E. Clements's book *Old Testament Theology: A Fresh Approach* (1978),[12] we find a paragraph on "*torah* and the prophets" (pp. 120ff.), and a corresponding chapter on "The Promise in the Law and the Writings" (pp. 149ff.). Here Clements absorbed into his viewpoint the canonical problem, which had been raised at the same time and with much greater determination by Joseph Blenkinsopp in his book *Prophecy and Canon: A Contribution to the Study of Jewish Origins* (1977).[13] Blenkinsopp's study is intentionally canonical. He tries

12. R. E. Clements, *Old Testament Theology: A Fresh Approach* (London: Marshall, Morgan & Scott, 1978).
13. J. Blenkinsopp, *Prophecy and Canon: A Contribution to the Study of Jewish Origins* (Notre Dame, Ind.: Univ. of Notre Dame Press, 1977).

to understand the relations between the individual parts of the canon, and in particular the canonical conception that stands behind the juxtaposition of the two main parts, "law" and "prophecy." One of his most illuminating observations is the interrelation between the last paragraph of the Torah and the last paragraph of the Prophets. The Torah ends with a definite word about law and prophecy:

> There has never since arisen in Israel a prophet like Moses whom the Lord knew face to face. (Deut. 34:10)

The prophetic part of the canon, in its turn, relates prophecy back to Moses' Torah, and at the same time points forward to the coming of a future prophet:

> Remember the law of my servant Moses, the statutes and ordinances that I commanded him at Horeb for all Israel. Behold I will send you Elijah the prophet before the great and terrible day of the Lord comes. And he will turn the hearts of fathers to their children and the hearts of children to their fathers, lest I come and smite the land with a curse. (Mal. 3:22-24)

It is obvious that in both cases there is a deliberate allusion to the other part of the canon. In Deuteronomy, the final paragraph refers back to the central chapter, chap. 18, where God says that he will send a prophet like Moses into whose mouth he will put his words, so that the prophet may pass on God's commandments to the Israelites (18:18). What we learn from that is first that God's Torah is given by prophets, and second that Moses was the first and authoritative prophet to deliver the Torah. Blenkinsopp summarizes: "The death of Moses is . . . the great divide between the paradigmatic prophetic age represented by Moses himself and the age following his death which belongs to all those who carry on his work and ministry" (p. 44).

According to Blenkinsopp, this represents the final stage of a canonical development that brought to an end the discussion—or even struggle— about claims to religious authority and legitimation. On the one hand "prophetic influence on the official version of the founding events and laws (that is, the Pentateuch) is unmistakable, profound and pervasive"; on the other hand "the emergence of a written Torah-canon contributed, paradoxically, to the eclipse of prophecy" (pp. 93f.). The statement about the death of Moses "puts the entire history of prophecy on a decisively lower level than the Mosaic epoch" (p. 86). But "the fact that the prophetic corpus came to be officially accepted alongside Torah sanctioned the view of prophecy as commentary on Torah" (p. 120).

In this understanding of "canonical" prophecy, still one other element is of great significance. In Deut. 18:15ff. Moses recalls the scene at Horeb when the people desired not to hear the voice of the Lord directly but requested a mediator (Exod. 20:18f.), and God accepted this, saying to Moses: "They have rightly said all that they have spoken," and then continues with the announcement of a prophet like Moses. "The implication seems quite clear. Prophecy is God's answer to Israel's request for mediation, and it is in this respect that the prophet is like Moses. Hence the prophet's essential function, whatever else he does, is to mediate the covenant between the Lord and his people and 'speak' the laws which guarantee its survival" (p. 45).

The "mediation and interpretation of the shared tradition in the light of contemporary reality" (p. 93, cf. 124) remains the main function of the prophets, even in their canonical subordination to the Torah. Of course "the tensions (between Torah and prophets) continued to exist but in a different form, and the difference was due to the fact that the words of the prophets were now available in writing" (pp. 124f.). From that point on, another chapter in dealing with the prophets begins.

IV

Blenkinsopp's methodological approach is quite different from that of Gerhard von Rad. But nevertheless, looking back we can discern that he has taken up a good number of von Rad's insights and questions. First of all, Blenkinsopp was the first since von Rad—and as far as I can see is still the only one—to take the prophets or prophecy as a whole to be a specific part of Old Testament theology. Like von Rad, he has realized the fundamental tensions between the Pentateuch and the prophets.[14] And, again like von Rad, he has seen that in spite of the tensions there are many interrelations between the two.

Yet by realizing that this is first of all a canonical problem, Blenkinsopp has opened up a new path for the theological interpretation of the whole problem. Let me add a few remarks from that point of view. None of the prophetic books has come down to us in a form which it received during the lifetime of the prophet in question. And none of them has come down to us in a form given to it in preexilic times. So the reader of the Hebrew

14. Recently Werner H. Schmidt wrote an article entitled "Pentateuch und Prophetie: Eine Skizze zu Verschiedenartigkeit und Einheit alttestamentlicher Theologie," in *Prophet und Prophetenbuch: Festschrift für O. Kaiser,* BZAW 185 (1989), 181–95. He begins by quoting von Rad's remarks in the first volume of his *Theology,* quoted above (without mentioning the qualification in the revised version of the second volume). But he does not mention Blenkinsopp's book at all, although this is precisely on his topic. In my view this is a typical example of the lack of communication between European (particularly German) and American scholarship.

Bible (or Old Testament) is confronted, not with the "historical" prophets, but with the "presentation" of the prophets (to use a term introduced by Peter Ackroyd),[15] and finally with the "canonical" prophets—that is, with the presentation of the prophets as the canonical editors of the Bible wanted to give it to the readers of later generations. This is by no means a simple image without tensions and contradictions; and in certain cases it might be possible to reconstruct some precanonical sayings of one or the other prophet. This might be useful, if one wishes to reconstruct the history of Israelite religion, or the like. But when doing Old Testament theology it is the canonical prophets we are dealing with. The "no" of the canonical Amos is followed by God's opening of a future for Israel:

> Behold, the eyes of the Lord God are upon the sinful kingdom, and I will destroy it from the surface of the ground; except that I will not utterly destroy the house of Jacob, says the Lord. (Amos 9:8)

There is no canonical Amos, and no other canonical prophet either, who speaks a radical "no" over Israel. And we as readers of the Hebrew Bible do not have any prophets at our disposal other than the canonical ones. For generations, biblical scholars tried to reconstruct the "original" sayings of the prophets, but they were only able to build prophets in their own image whose "originality" (or authenticity) stands or falls with acceptance of that particular exegetical method. In recent decades there has been a lot of discussion about the redaction history of prophetic sayings and books, sometimes with interesting and useful results. But in most cases the attempt to reconstruct this history stops before it has reached the canonical level.[16]

V

The canon-consciousness[17] which appears in the last paragraphs of the Torah and the Prophets shows the strong canonical link between the two. A canon-conscious Old Testament theology will have to follow this

15. P. R. Ackroyd, "Isaiah 1–12: Presentation of a Prophet," VTSup 29 (1978) (=his *Studies in the Religious Tradition of the Old Testament* [London: SCM Press, 1987], 79–104).

16. One of the most recent examples is the article by R. E. Clements, "The Prophet and His Editors," in D. J. A. Clines et al., eds., *The Bible in Three Dimensions: Essays in Celebration of Forty Years of Biblical Studies in the University of Sheffield,* JSOTSup 87 (1990): 203–20, where he does not mention the canonical aspect of the problem at all.

17. G. Sheppard, *Wisdom as Hermeneutical Construct,* BZAW 151 (Berlin, 1980), 109, used this term as a translation of I. L. Seeligmann's expression *Kanonbewusstsein* (in *Voraussetzungen der Midraschexegese,* VTSup 1 [1953]: 152).

line. The two parts will have to be presented as complementing each other. In the light of our discussion of the approaches of von Rad and Blenkinsopp, we shall have to consider two fundamental elements: the tensions between Torah and Prophets, and the final canonical relations binding them together as integral parts of the one canon.

Compared with von Rad's concept, there will be one fundamental shift. Von Rad related the prophets to the "traditions" which he found in the Pentateuch. We find similar concepts in other theologies. But we have now learned that there are much more profound interrelations. The main and central point is of course the description of Moses as a prophet, and even as the prophet of prophets—the prophet *kat' exochēn*. If we take prophecy as a canonical phenomenon, we cannot disregard this specific element, which appears in emphatic form in different contexts within the Pentateuch. This has one double consequence, among others. On the one hand the Torah is a fundamental prophetic phenomenon, given by the first prophet, who is the great example of a prophetic mediator. On the other hand the prophetic announcement of God's destructive judgment of Israel is prefigured by Moses at Sinai. At the same time, we encounter in this context the prophet's intercession for his people Israel, an intercession made even more forceful than in most of the prophetic books by Moses' self-sacrifice. The relations between Moses and, for instance, Jeremiah are quite obvious and fundamental.

These are only some preliminary reflections which will have to be given concrete form in the course of a detailed elaboration of Old Testament theology. For me it has once more been of great importance to work out a specific aspect of von Rad's concept in the light of more recent insights, in particular in the context of a new canon-conscious theology.

CHAPTER 7

The Image of Postexilic Israel in German Old Testament Scholarship from Wellhausen to von Rad

Several years ago Shemaryahu Talmon directed some "critical inquiries" to European Christianity. His point of departure was the different approaches toward the Hebrew Bible that are to be found in Judaism and Christianity. His summary was that in many crucial points "in Christian theological thinking Judaism represents the negative pole, while Christian faith claimed the positive one for itself."[1]

One of the most characteristic fields of this kind of Christian behavior is the depiction of postexilic Judaism in modern German Old Testament scholarship, where we find a certain well-known set of stereotypes. The intention of this paper is, first, to look for the origins of those stereotypes; second, to follow their development through certain significant stages; and, third, to ask how we might deal with these traditions in our present theological situation.

DE WETTE: FROM HEBRAISM TO JUDAISM

It was Wilhelm Martin Leberecht de Wette who in the earliest period of modern biblical scholarship established the distinction between preexilic

Paper read in English at the Annual Meeting of the American Academy of Religion, Chicago, November 1988, in the History of Judaism section. The paper has undergone some stylistic revision.

1. S. Talmon, "Kritische Anfragen der jüdischen Theologie an das europäische Christentum," in W. Licharz and M. Stöhr, eds., *Einladung ins Lehrhaus: Beiträge zum jüdischen Selbstverständnis* (Frankfurt, 1981), 65.

and postexilic Israel. In 1813 he divided the Old Testament part of his *Biblical Dogmatics* into two parts, which he called Hebraism (*Hebraismus*) and Judaism (*Judentum*).[2] In his view, during the Babylonian exile the Hebrew nation was changed so deeply by foreign religious influences that it actually became a different nation with a different way of thinking and a different religion (§76). The most characteristic element of this new religion was *faithfulness to the letter*. The Hebrews understood their disastrous fate as divine punishment for their violation of the law, and therefore now tried to fulfill the law as strictly as possible (§77). But by this faithfulness to the letter of the Mosaic law, they became estranged from Moses' spirit. This occurred under the influence of the Chaldean or Persian religion (§78). The first sentence of de Wette's chapter on the "doctrine of Judaism" reads: "Judaism is the unsuccessful restoration of Hebraism and a mixture of its positive components with foreign mythological-metaphysical doctrines . . . : a chaos which is longing for a new creation" (§142). Here already almost all the stereotypes are present.

A more detailed study of de Wette's conception, however, reveals a remarkable inconsistency. He takes a considerable part of postexilic literature to be a continuation of the spirit of Hebraism (cf. §74), and therefore develops his description of Judaism mainly from the postcanonical literature (§149ff.). In the New Testament part of the book, Jesus' teaching is depicted as a "spiritually reborn and developed prophetism" (§211), whereas Pharisaism is the "cutting contrast" to his teaching. Here it becomes obvious that the main interest in the negative characterization of postexilic Judaism is to build up a dark background for the New Testament, and at the same time to save the "better" parts of the Old Testament as a precursor of Jesus and the New Testament.[3]

WELLHAUSEN: THE LAW CAME IN BETWEEN

Let me now turn to Julius Wellhausen, with whom begins the era of Old Testament scholarship in which we are still living. In his work the antithesis between preexilic Israel and postexilic Judaism is omnipresent. In 1879 he wrote in a letter that for ten years he had been "exclusively

2. W. M. L. de Wette, *Biblische Dogmatik Alten und Neuen Testaments, oder kritische Darstellung der Religionslehre des Hebraismus, des Judenthums und Urchristenthums* (Berlin, 1813, 2d ed. 1818).
3. The relation of Jesus' teaching to Mosaism is like that of "the full light to a glimmer, the perfect idea to the unperfect picture": he is in harmony with the "original [Mosaic] spirit full of presentiment" (§211).

taken up" by the historical study of "Judaism and ancient Israel in all its contrast."[4] The results of these studies shaped his later publications.

Wellhausen's basic characterization of the contrast between the two epochs of Israelite and Jewish history is closely related to that given by de Wette. It is above all the *law* that achieves a predominant role in postexilic Judaism. Wellhausen makes it quite clear upon what he bases his evaluation of the law when he quotes from Paul's Letter to the Romans (5:20): "The Law came in between."[5] Paul's understanding of the law, in its Lutheran (or Augustinian) interpretation, explicitly serves as a criterion for Wellhausen's own assessment of the law.[6]

In Wellhausen's view, as in that of de Wette, the function of the law had undergone a fundamental change since the Babylonian exile. Two aspects seem to me to be of particular relevance. The first one is the *individualization* of religion and thereby of the law also. Earlier, religion had been "a common possession of the people." "Now, the Jew by birth still had to make himself a Jew through his own deliberate labor" because the core of the ideal of justice was "individual morality."[7] Here the main point is the separation of the law from the nation, which contravenes the naturally given connection between the two. This aspect later played a crucial role in Martin Noth's concept.

The second point is the relation of law and *cult.* According to Wellhausen, the cult had become part of the law and had thereby changed its real nature: "Religious worship was a natural thing in Hebrew antiquity; it was the blossom of life.... The law ... severed this connection"—in

4. Cf. R. Smend, "Wellhausen und das Judentum," *ZTK* 79 (1982): 252.

5. Wellhausen uses this verse as motto for the section on "Israel and Judaism" (pt. 3) in *Prolegomena zur Geschichte Israels* (Berlin, 1883). Quotations are from the English translation by J. S. Black and A. Menzies (Edinburgh: A. & C. Black, 1885, with preface by W. Robertson Smith; reprint, New York: Meridian Books, 1957), but the wording has in some cases been slightly altered. Wellhausen has taken this quotation from Wilhelm Vatke, as he explicitly indicates (p. 363). The German reads: "Das Gesetz ist zwischenein getreten." Ever since Luther's translation, "Das Gesetz aber ist neben ein kommen," German translations usually stress the double preposition of the Greek παρεισῆλθεν, which is not expressed in the RSV version: "Law came in." Lou Silberman, with references to Sanday and Headlam, proposes the translation "to sidle in"; see "Wellhausen and Judaism," *Semeia* 25 (1983): 75–82. According to Liddell and Scott's Greek Lexicon, the word means "come or go in beside."

6. Silberman ("Wellhausen and Judaism," 76) refers to the first edition of the *Prolegomena* where (in a passage omitted later) Wellhausen makes it clear that he "has admittedly pushed Paul beyond what Paul said, that legalism sidled in."

7. J. Wellhausen, "Israelitisch-jüdische Religion," in P. Hinneberg, ed., *Die Kultur der Gegenwart* (Berlin and Leipzig, 1905), 1/4:1–38; reprinted in Wellhausen, *Grundrisse zum Alten Testament,* ed. R. Smend, TBü 27 (Munich, 1965), 65–109, quotation from 102–3.

particular through the centralization of the cult. "The warm pulse of life no longer throbbed in it to animate it; . . . [the cult] had its own meaning all by itself. . . . The soul had fled; the shell remained. . . . Technique was the main thing, and strict fidelity to rubric." Wellhausen concludes by saying: "The connection of all this with the Judaising tendency to remove God to a distance from man, it may be added, is clear." And: "The cult, after nature had been killed in it, became the shield of supernaturalist monotheism."[8]

In sum, in Wellhausen's romanticizing view[9] the main aspect of the decline from preexilic Israel to Judaism is the separation of law and cult from the original, natural religion.[10] Yet there is a remarkable inconsistency since on the one hand individualization is highly praised—for example, in the case of Jeremiah—but on the other hand is viewed as an indication of denaturing.[11]

NOTH: ONLY THE LAW REMAINED

Compared with Wellhausen's picture, Martin Noth's view of postexilic Israel shows some similar features, but also some characteristic differences. First of all, Noth felt it to be a problem where to draw the line between "Israel" and "Judaism." In his earlier writings he followed the approach which was traditional from de Wette to Wellhausen by taking the Babylonian exile as a dividing line. He made a distinction between "an *earlier* period up to the end of the independent states of Israel and Judah, and so to the factitive end of the Israelite nation, . . . and a *later* period, in which . . . there was no more than a small community in and about Jerusalem, with a widely scattered diaspora."[12] His interest is clearly

---

8. Quotations in this paragraph from Wellhausen, *Prolegomena*, English trans. 77, 78, 79 and 425 (but see n. 5 above).

9. For the influence of romanticism on Wellhausen see also J. Blenkinsopp, *Prophecy and Canon: A Contribution to the Story of Jewish Origins* (Notre Dame and London: Univ. of Notre Dame Press, 1977), 17ff.: "Wellhausen and the Origins of Judaism."

10. Smend ("Wellhausen und das Judentum") tries to defend Wellhausen against the accusation of anti-Semitism. In so doing he is responding to my own article, "Die jüdische Bibel und ihre antijüdische Auslegung," in R. Rendtorff and E. Stegemann, eds., *Auschwitz—Krise der christlichen Theologie* (Munich, 1980), 99–116. Yet I should like to emphasize that I never claimed that Wellhausen was an anti-Semite. I am fully aware of the fact that there were, and still are, many Christian theologians who in their theological thinking and writing express themselves in a strictly anti-Jewish manner, while in the political and social field fighting anti-Semitic discrimination.

11. For Noth's evaluation of individualism, see n. 16 below.

12. M. Noth, *Die Gesetze im Pentateuch: Ihre Voraussetzungen und ihr Sinn* (Halle, 1940) (= his *Gesammelte Studien zum Alten Testament,* 2d ed. [Munich, 1960], 1:9–141).

focused on the political, and in particular on the institutional aspect. "Israel" existed only as long as its institutional form existed, in the shape of one or two states. But despite this clear distinction, Noth speaks only about the preexilic and postexilic periods, avoiding the term "Judaism" for the latter.

Later he changed his opinion. In his *History of Israel* (1950) he writes that the disappearance of the institution of the Davidic kingdom "did not mean the end of Israel, just as its emergence had not represented the beginning of the history of Israel."[13] Instead he speaks explicitly about "Israel's end" in connection with the Jewish war against the Romans and the destruction of the Second Temple in 70 C.E. Now he prefers to use the term "Judaism" for the new phenomenon which arose out of Israel's downfall (*Untergang*).[14]

There is nevertheless in this concept also a fundamental difference between preexilic and postexilic Israel. While the former had been constituted in varying forms of political structures, the latter existed only as a *cultic* community. Noth calls it "the cultic congregation of Jerusalem" (*die Jerusalemer Kultgemeinde*). In this respect he had not changed his view, since earlier he had already characterized postexilic Israel in this way. But now he made his view more explicit so that the consequences are clearer: if Israel in postexilic times existed only as a cultic congregation which gathered around the Temple in Jerusalem, then it is evident that after the destruction of the Temple this congregation ceased to exist. From that time on there is no Israel any more, but only diaspora.

Moreover, another basic element of Noth's approach makes itself felt here. His hypothesis of an ancient Israelite tribal league, the "amphictyony," has the consequence that actually an Israelite *people* had never existed. Even during the period of the monarchy the tribal system acted as a substructure. But how then could Israel continue to exist after the end of an independent political organization?

Here the *law* comes in. According to Noth, originally and essentially the Israelite laws had their *Sitz im Leben* only within the tribal league. This league was built upon the idea of a covenant between YHWH and "Israel," the latter being the name of the league. Only because of the

Quotations are from the English trans. by D. R. Ap-Thomas, *The Laws in the Pentateuch and Other Studies* (Edinburgh: Oliver & Boyd, 1966; Philadelphia: Fortress Press, 1967), 12.
13. M. Noth, *Geschichte Israels* (Göttingen, 1950). Quotations are from the English trans. by S. Godman, revised by P. R. Ackroyd, *The History of Israel*, 2d ed. (London: A. & C. Black; New York: Harper, 1960), 290.
14. Noth, *History of Israel*, 7.

continuing existence of the tribal substructure could the laws serve as a legal basis for monarchically organized Israel as well. But what happened to the laws after the cessation of this structure?

According to Noth, not only had the tribal structure come to an end, and with it the political structure in general; the covenant between YHWH and Israel was also terminated and dissolved, as the prophets had announced. So in every respect the basis for the validity of the laws was lost. Only the expectation and hope for a "new covenant" according to Jeremiah 31, for a restoration of the previous order of things, enabled the Jerusalem community to survive. One of the means for this survival was the continuing observance of the laws, notwithstanding the fact that they had actually lost their raison d'être. This development had fundamental consequences:

> Actually the primary relationship of affairs and regulations became more and more reversed. Whereas it was originally the relationship of God and man depicted as a "covenant" which had constituted the ancient sacral confederacy of the tribes, and whereas it had been the presence of this institution which had provided the necessary prerequisite for the validation of the old laws, it was now the acknowledgement and observance of the law by the individuals which constituted the community—for whoever undertook to keep the law joined the community.[15]

There is a slight but very revealing shift of language in the above quotation. In the first part of this long sentence dealing with the original order, Noth speaks of "laws," but in the second part dealing with the individual acceptance and observance, he shifts to "law." And later he writes "the law" (*das Gesetz*) in quotation marks. In Noth's concept of postexilic Israel, this is the decisive turning point. He explains its consequences again and again: "The reason for this was the transfer of the decisive emphasis from *divine* activity to the behaviour of individual *mortals*—which is a decline from the original basis of the faith."[16] Finally "the law" became an "*absolute entity*," which was

> no longer tied to anything. . . . The law became a power in its own right. . . . It was the law, as the unprecedented primary entity, which fashioned this com-

---

15. Noth, *Laws in the Pentateuch*, 80.
16. Ibid. Immediately before this sentence there is an interesting remark on the function of individualism: "It is customary to speak of the 'individualism' which arose during exilic and post-exilic times in place of an earlier 'collectivism,' and often we tend to see an element of progress in this change." The following sentence explains that in Noth's view the opposite is true. For a similar ambivalence in Wellhausen's evaluation of individualism see p. 69 above.

munity, which was nothing but the union of those people who submitted to the law on all points. . . . So when the edifice of the old establishment collapsed, the law which had formed a single pillar in the framework of the whole was the only part which finally remained erect. It then became the centre column and stay of a new edifice erected on the ruins of the old.[17]

One special feature of Noth's conception should at least be mentioned, if only briefly. Noth argues that in postexilic times the terms "law" and "covenant" were separated from each other. I cannot discuss this point in the present framework, but wish to say only that in my opinion there is no exegetical evidence for this thesis.

In sum, Israel did not exist any longer; only a group of individuals remained whose sole relation to each other was submission to the law. As long as this group gathered around the Temple in Jerusalem it deserved the name of "the cultic congregation of Jerusalem"; "but as the centre of worship had been abolished and there was no homeland and therefore no chance of united historical action it was in fact something substantially new," namely "Judaism."[18]

At first glance, there is an obvious continuity between Wellhausen and Noth in their view of postexilic Israel. For both of them the law is of crucial relevance. But while for Wellhausen the loss of naturalness is the decisive negative point, for Noth it is the loss of the institutional structure of the community. For Wellhausen, Judaism ossifies in legalism; for Noth, Israel ceases to exist and turns into an assembly of individuals who keep the law.

VON RAD: A NEW APPRECIATION OF THE LAW

In his *Theology of the Old Testament,* Gerhard von Rad depicts postexilic Israel more or less along the same lines. In particular, speaking about the law he quotes Noth: "The law becomes an absolute entity, unconditionally valid irrespective of time or historical situation." But while he admits that "it is now beginning to become the 'law' in the theological sense of the word," he explicitly denies that there is as yet "any

17. Ibid., 86–87.
18. Noth, *History of Israel,* 7. Noth adds that the modern state of Israel "is separated from the Israel of old not only by the long period of almost 2000 years but also by a long history full of vicissitudes and it has come into being in the midst of entirely different historical conditions. It would therefore be improper to extend our historical enquiry from the end of the 'Israel' of old to the 'Israel' of the present day."

legal casuistry proper."[19] His own depiction of the Priestly Code is full of sympathetic empathy.

But for him the crucial point is the problem of *history*. Since in Israel's understanding the law had become absolute and timeless, von Rad sees as consequence that Israel had to step out of its history with YHWH, out of salvation history (*Heilsgeschichte*). It was only with such a timeless and ahistoric concept of the Torah as a "law" that Judaism finally came into being.

In a certain sense one could say that what the law was for Noth, history was for von Rad. Nevertheless, it was his conception of the law that elicited harsh criticism from a dogmatic point of view. One year after the first volume of von Rad's *Theology* had appeared, Gerhard Ebeling published an article on the doctrine of law. In that article he criticized von Rad, not because of his view of the postexilic understanding of law but, on the contrary, because of his opinion that the earlier concept of law, in particular that of Deuteronomy, was less legalistic than the usual Christian interpretation assumes. Ebeling comments on von Rad's position: "That of course would lead perforce to the further conclusion that the way to overcome the late Judaistic [!] view of the law is to return to the deuteronomic concept of the Torah"—an idea which from his own dogmatic standpoint appears to be simply absurd. In contrast to von Rad's evaluation of Deuteronomy, he argued that the Old Testament in general had not yet realized the very nature of the law, and that Paul was the first to recognize the existence of two lines in the Old Testament, the one coming from Abraham and the other coming from Moses, the line of promise (ἐπαγγελία) and faith (πίστις) as over against the line of law (νόμος) and deeds (ἔργα). So according to Ebeling, Paul does not argue against the "late Judaistic" understanding of the law but "has in view the Mosaic Law as a whole, and precisely as it is embedded in the totality of the Old Testament revelation of the divine will."[20]

Von Rad took up the challenge. In the revised fourth German edition of the first volume of his *Theology of the Old Testament* (1962), he writes

19. G. von Rad, *Theologie des Alten Testaments,* 2 vols. (Munich, 1957–60). Quotations are from the English translation by D. M. G. Stalker, *Old Testament Theology* (Edinburgh: Oliver & Boyd; New York: Harper, 1962–65; reissued London: SCM Press, 1972 and 1975), 1:91. In the revised 4th German edition (Munich, 1962), as a consequence of G. Ebeling's criticism (see below), he changed the expression in the second quotation from "theological sense of the word" to "dogmatic sense of the word." (Changes made in the 4th edition do not appear in the English translation.)

20. G. Ebeling, "Erwägungen zur Lehre vom Gesetz," *ZTK* 55 (1958): 270–306, (=his *Wort und Glaube* [Tübingen, 1960]). Quotations are from the Eng. trans. by J. W. Leitch, *Word and Faith* (London: SCM Press; Philadelphia: Fortress Press, 1963), 264–66.

the following: "Our task is clear enough: To understand theologically, as precisely as possible, YHWH's will for Israel, and to take care that this emerging knowledge is not obscured by a traditional yet no longer appropriate terminology."[21] With this, he virtually denies the applicability of preformulated dogmatic conceptions and terminologies to theological problems of the Old Testament.

From this discussion von Rad drew a remarkable conclusion. In the second volume of his *Theology* we find a final chapter on "the law" where he summarizes the whole discussion about the theological understanding of the law. There he writes that it would be a complete misunderstanding of the prophets to believe "that they made the renewal of the broken covenant relationship dependent upon a more meticulous fulfillment of the commandments." And he adds: "It is not easy to give an answer to the question of when it was precisely that Israel began to seek her salvation along the road of the meticulous fulfillment of divine commandments." He is convinced that this did not happen in Old Testament times at least, and that "there is no basis in the Old Testament for the well-known idea which early Lutheranism exalted to almost canonical status, that Israel was compelled by God's law to an ever greater zeal for the Law."[22]

This debate made it evident how Protestant theologians tried to judge the Old Testament by their own theological criteria, even by those that are explicitly not applicable.[23] Von Rad, though having grown up in the same tradition, intensively and successfully tried to develop a new theological understanding and appreciation of the theological thoughts and intentions of the Hebrew Scriptures from within, avoiding, as far as possible, the application of prejudices and theological systems alien to them. When Ebeling attacked him, he clearly decided in favor of an independent theological evaluation of the Hebrew Bible on its own terms.

By doing so he opened the eyes of many readers of his *Theology,* including myself, to the dangerous and illegitimate dependence of Old Testament theology upon theological values and systems drawn from outside. He insisted, in other contexts as well, that Protestant theology in particular—with its claim to be based on "Scripture"—has to work in the opposite direction, not imposing its own theological ideas on the

---

21. Von Rad, *Theologie,* 4th ed., 1:214.

22. Von Rad, *Old Testament Theology,* 2:404f.

23. G. Ebeling writes: "Admittedly, his [i.e., Paul's] own concept of law is then not identical with that of the Old Testament, and cannot be identical with it" (*Word and Faith,* 266). This goes even beyond Wellhausen, who himself "has admittedly pushed Paul beyond what Paul said, that legalism sidled in" (see n. 6 above).

Scriptures, but taking the Scriptures themselves as a starting point, and first of all developing their intrinsic theological thoughts and insights.

It would go beyond the scope of this paper to discuss the influence of von Rad's approach in the years since. I personally feel it to be significant, but still in a stage of development. I hope that one fruit of this new approach might be better mutual understanding, and even cooperation between Jewish and Christian biblical scholars.

CHAPTER 8

Christological Interpretation
as a Way of "Salvaging"
the Old Testament?
Wilhelm Vischer and
Gerhard von Rad

Looking back, Gerhard von Rad said: "But when National Socialism came, with its repellent and gross 'no' to the Old Testament, . . . the situation became critical, for this challenge found Old Testament scholarship almost completely unprepared. With an almost religious earnestness, it had trained people to the ethic of an incorruptible historical discernment; but it had not trained them to acknowledge the Old Testament publicly, indeed in the political sector, in a crucial situation—what theologians call *in statu confessionis.*"[1]

With these sentences von Rad puts his finger on a problem which even in retrospect has seldom been recognized, or at least openly defined. In the nineteenth century, Old Testament scholarship had increasingly ceased to see itself as a *theological* discipline; and in this respect nothing very fundamental had changed right down to the 1920s or 1930s. It was first and foremost a historical science, with all the aspects and facets which had developed over the years—in historical studies, the history of religion, literary and form criticism, philology, and archaeology. Its link with theology was in many cases no more than fragmentary, or was even specifically denied, at least where theology as a discipline linked with, and bound to, the church was concerned. When, in 1882, Julius

Lecture delivered at the Kirchliche Hochschule, Bethel, on January 24, 1989. I am dedicating this text to Claus Westermann on his eightieth birthday, in grateful awareness of our common ground in the concern discussed here.

1. G. von Rad, "Gerhard von Rad über Gerhard von Rad" (1966), in H. W. Wolff, ed., *Probleme biblischer Theologie: G. von Rad zum 70. Geburtstag* (Munich, 1971), 660.

Wellhausen applied to be moved out of the theological faculty into the faculty of philosophy, he put the matter as follows: "I became a theologian because the scientific treatment of the Bible interested me. It was only gradually that I came to realize that a professor of theology also has the practical function of preparing students for service in the Protestant church, and that this practical function was one I could not fulfill. Indeed, in spite of all restraint on my part, I was rather making my students incapable of carrying out their ministry."[2]

What distinguished Wellhausen from other representatives of his field was primarily, no doubt, the honesty with which he recognized this dilemma, and took the consequences. For how little the theological importance of the Old Testament was at the forefront or center of the work of most Old Testament scholars emerged years later when, for example, not a single Old Testament scholar, as far as I know, made any public declaration in response to Adolf von Harnack's unequivocal rejection of the Old Testament in his book about Marcion, published in 1921. In that book von Harnack declared: "To have gone on since the 19th century conserving [the Old Testament] in Protestantism as a canonical document is the result of religious and ecclesiastical paralysis."[3] "To wipe the slate clean here . . . is the mighty feat required—almost too late—of Protestantism today."[4] So it also comes as no surprise to find that a good ten years after the appearance of Harnack's book, most German Old Testament scholars remained silent in the face of the multifarious disparagements and contemptuous appraisals of the Old Testament by the "German Christians," which went as far as the demand made at the notorious assembly at the Berlin Palace of Sport in November 1933 "that our regional church, as a German folk church, should liberate itself from everything that is un-German in its worship and creed, especially from the Old Testament, with its Jewish 'recompense' morality."[5] There were certainly a few Old Testament scholars who responded to these questions in congregational lectures, some of which have been printed. But these very publications bring out the truth

2. Cf. A. Jepsen, "Wellhausen in Greifswald: Ein Beitrag zur Biographie Julius Wellhausens," appendix 5, in *Festschrift zur 500-Jahr-Feier der Universität Greifswald* (1956), 2:47–56 (= A. Jepsen, *Der Herr ist Gott* [Berlin, 1978], 254–70).

3. A. Von Harnack, *Marcion: Das Evangelium vom fremden Gott* (Leipzig, 1921), 248f. (2d ed. 1924, 217).

4. Ibid., 245 (222).

5. J. Beckmann, ed., *Kirchliches Jahrbuch für die Evangelische Kirche in Deutschland 1933–1944* (Gütersloh, 1948, 2d ed. 1976), 38.

of what Gerhard von Rad said in the sentences quoted at the beginning: that this challenge found Old Testament scholarship almost completely unprepared.[6]

So when the first volume of Wilhelm Vischer's book *The Witness of the Old Testament to Christ* was published in 1934[7] it came out into what was almost a complete vacuum. An essay of Heinrich Vogel's entitled "How Do We Preach about the Old Testament?," published in 1935 in the new periodical *Evangelische Theologie,* shows how important this new book was felt to be; for he writes that "where the Holy Scripture of the Old Testament is concerned [Vischer's book] means for us today a breakthrough battle of theological or, to put it more incisively, christological perception."[8] A few years later Rudolf Abramowski wrote: "Vischer's book has become *the* Old Testament book of our day, because it is necessary and right. It is *necessary* because the theological and political situation required a Christian testimony in the light of the Old Testament, not merely an opinion about the Old Testament. . . . It is *right* . . . because the New Testament and the Reformation proclaim to us with a single voice that the Old Testament witnesses to Christ."[9]

This was undoubtedly the essential reason for the book's rapid and sweeping success: that here the Old Testament was consistently interpreted as a "Christian" book. Vischer says this quite unequivocally right at the beginning: "The two main words of the Christian confession 'Jesus is the Christ' . . . correspond to the two parts of the Holy Scriptures: the New and the Old Testament. The Old Testament tells us *what* the Christ is; the New *who* He is."[10] And from this he draws a completely unambiguous conclusion: "The distinctive doctrine of apostolic preaching is that Jesus is the Christ of the Old Testament. If that is true, if Jesus really

---

6. W. Zimmerli (*TRE* [1980], 6:438) put together the few attempts made in the 1920s and 1930s to outline a "theology of the Old Testament." With regard to the matters discussed here, there is no detectable influence, as far as I can see, of Walther Eichrodt's *Theologie des Alten Testaments,* which appeared in 1933 (Eng. trans. only 1961) and has since often been regarded as the beginning of a new epoch in this discipline.

7. W. Vischer, *Das Christuszeugnis des Alten Testaments,* vol. 1: *Das Gesetz* (Munich, 1934; 6th ed. 1943); vol. 2: *Die Propheten,* pt. 1, *Die früheren Propheten* (1942; 2d ed. Zurich: Zollikon, 1946; no further vols. published); Eng. trans., *The Witness of the Old Testament to Christ,* trans. from 3d ed. by A. B. Crabtree (London: Lutterworth Press, 1949).

8. H. Vogel, "Wie predigen wir über das Alte Testament?" *EvT* 2 (1935): 339–60, quotation from 346 n. 1.

9. R. Abramowski, "Vom Streit um das Alte Testament," *TRu* 9 (1937): 65–93, quotation from 91.

10. Vischer, *Christuszeugnis,* 1:7 (*Witness,* 1:7).

is the Messiah, the Old Testament belongs to those who believe in Him, i.e., the Church."[11] Here, therefore, was a clear counterposition to the contempt poured on the Old Testament as "Jewish." Because it was now claimed as "Christian," the dispute shifted to totally different ground. We could even say that here an attempt was being made to "salvage" the Old Testament from the attacks and persecutions of its opponents. (What this meant for the relationship to the Jews is something we shall have to ask later.)

A further reason for the success of Vischer's book was doubtless the fact that it offered a continuous, essentially narrative and paraphrastic interpretation of biblical texts such as was very rare at the time. Where practical dealings with the Old Testament in the church were concerned, it gave hardly any help that could be called theological.

The introduction to the first volume then offers one of the first detailed, modern theological reflections about the relationship between the Old and New Testaments. But it does not merely deal with the question about the use of the Old Testament by Christians. It also takes into its viewpoint the attitude to the Jews in the light of this kind of Christian interpretation of the Old Testament. In this way the book was also able to offer a contribution to the discussion in the church about the "Arian" paragraphs,[12] as well as to theological questions about the relations between Christians and Jews generally.

And finally, Vischer's interpretation offered some very pronounced, one might almost say spectacular, christological interpretations of key Old Testament texts, interpretations which we may presume were soon the subject of widespread discussion at the time. It was probably this last aspect particularly which helped to make the book so popular, and we shall no doubt not go far wrong if we suspect that many readers picked out these passages especially.

The differentiation between these different aspects makes the problem clear: How, from our contemporary standpoint, can we talk about Vischer's book in an appropriate way? Here the most important thing must be to distinguish carefully between what Vischer meant, or could have meant, at the time, and what we have to say today "in the light of our necessary—theologically necessary —new sensitivity *after Auschwitz* to the

---

11. Ibid., 1:32 (*Witness*, 1:27).

12. In 1933 a law was passed in which it was stated that "no one of non-Arian descent or who is married to a person of non-Arian descent may be appointed to the ranks of the clergy or as official in the general administration of the church."

problem, to the church's tradition, and above all to the men and women concerned."[13]

I

Let me begin with some characteristic examples of Vischer's christological interpretations. On the first day of creation, we are told in Gen. 1:4, God said, "Let there be light!":

> The light which the Creator here sends forth is, far above the brightness of the heavenly bodies called forth on the fourth day for particular purposes, the epitomy of the miracle whereby God allows His invisible Being to be seen. This light is—the expression can no longer be avoided if we are to expound our text faithfully and guard it against every kind of speculative misinterpretation—"the glory of God in the face of Jesus Christ" (2 Cor. 4:6). Heaven and earth are the scene of this radiant "brightness of His glory" (Heb. 1:3), and "wherever the eye looks, there is no part of the world where the radiance of at least some sparks of His glory are not discernible" [Note: Calvin, *Inst.* 1.5.1]. Yet always in such a way that the light by which He reveals Himself is at the same time a garment in which He hides Himself (Ps. 104:2), and His strong tower into which none may enter (1 Tim. 6:16). Only "by faith", and that means in New Testament language "by faith in Jesus Christ", can we know that the world is completed by the Word of God (Heb. 11:3), and only by faith in Jesus Christ can "His invisible nature, His everlasting power and divine being, be perceptible in what He has made" (Rom. 1:20, Moffat).[14]

This quotation makes Vischer's expository method plain. He interprets a central concept in the Old Testament text by way of a New Testament quotation in which the same word appears, related to Christ; and he then expands the christological aspect, a detailed quotation playing a central role (in this case Calvin, but more frequently Luther or Hamann). So here, on the basis of the keyword "light" in Gen. 1:4, he develops in essentials the beginnings of a christological theology of creation. He sums up Genesis 1 in a similar way:

> For everything in this chapter proclaims the Christ. . . . Anyone who believes in a Jesus who either has nothing to do with this chapter or only in so far as He is a member—perhaps even the noblest member—of the created world, does not really believe at all in Jesus the *Christ*. For the Christ is more than the ripest fruit of creation; He is its root, its meaning, its truth. He is the Word

---

13. F. Crüsemann, *Bethel* 30 (Bielefeld, 1985): 4.
14. Vischer, *Christuszeugnis,* 1:55f. (*Witness,* 1:44).

that was in the beginning, which was with God and partook of the nature of God.

And then the appropriate quotation from John 1:1-5 follows, with an extensive quotation from Luther, and other New Testament references. And finally he reiterates:

> In Him and alone in Him, is the truth of what is written in the first chapter of the Bible.[15]

This passage is hermeneutically interesting because Vischer does not merely interpret the Old Testament text christologically, anchoring its truth and validity in the New Testament; he also conversely binds faith in Christ retroactively to creation: "Anyone who believes in a Jesus who ... has nothing to do with this chapter ... does not really believe at all in Jesus the *Christ.*" As many passages show, he wishes to make clear the irrelinquishable dependence of the New Testament—and with that the dependence of the Christian faith generally—on the Old Testament.

Let me give a few other examples. When he interprets the curse on the serpent in Gen. 3:15 as "proto-gospel," Vischer is following church tradition. One of the "spectacular" interpretations is then his explanation of the mark of Cain in Genesis 4. It is not only, he says, the first sign of the covenant in the Bible. According to Ezek. 9:3 it must be interpreted as the Hebrew taw, and since in Old Hebrew this letter was written in the form of a (recumbent) cross, Vischer comes to the following conclusion:

> The Christian amulet in the form of a cross thus probably had its origin not in the cross of Christ but in the sign which Yahweh set upon Cain, though it remains true that it was filled with new meaning by the crucifixion of Christ, or rather renewed in its inmost meaning. In both cases the sign symbolizes the same most holy paradox—that he who as a murderer falls under the judgment of God is nevertheless upheld by the grace of God.... The Christian sign of the cross, like the sign of Cain, imprints on its bearer the *character indelebilis* of a servant of God. "Servant of Christ Jesus" or "servant of God" the apostle calls himself, and grounds his inviolability which becomes him as a servant of Christ upon the fact that he bears in his body the marks of Christ (Gal. 6:17).[16]

The boldness of Vischer's constructions and his design often compels admiration. But at the same time, the exegetical scholar is frequently faced with the question whether he is not led by mere associations, which

15. Ibid., 1:64f. (*Witness,* 1:51f.).
16. Ibid., 1:93f. (*Witness,* 1:75).

are not merely unsupported by the exegesis of the text but are also incapable of contributing anything to the theological understanding of it. Here again, let me give a few examples. He says about Genesis 14: "In Melchizedek's bringing of bread and wine we have a clear allusion to the sacrament of the New Covenant which Jesus instituted for the completion and dissolution of the old."[17] No connection is discernible here exegetically or theologically. "The undeclared name of the man" with whom Jacob wrestles at the Brook Jabbok is Jesus Christ, according to Vischer's interpretation: "We are able with Luther to say [this] without the slightest contradiction." But this is then expanded to such a degree that there is no longer any connection with the text at all: "Where Christ is, there is Israel, there begins God's fight. His gospel summons all who hear it to wrestle for the blessing of Abraham, for the mercy of God upon all races of the earth."[18] The blood of the red heifer (Numbers 19) is equated with the blood of Jesus Christ: "That is the gospel which is proclaimed in the passage concerning the red heifer and confirmed in the sacraments of baptism and communion."[19] Finally we may cite a highly imaginative example from the second volume on "the early prophets," where Vischer tells us that the capture of Jericho after a seven-day-long procession, accompanied by the trumpets of the Year of Jubilee, is "unmistakably" the prophetic foreshadowing of the great Sabbath at the end of days, when at the sound of the last trump "the kingdoms of this world shall become the kingdoms of the LORD and of his Christ."[20]

II

In a detailed review in the *Theologische Blätter* of 1935, Gerhard von Rad subjected Vischer's book to a critical scrutiny.[21] His criticism goes right to the root of the matter. He begins by pointing out that "the link between the churches and Old Testament scholarship has been almost completely broken off for more than a generation." And he goes on: "It is self-evident that this situation has brought with it new obligations for Old Testament scholarship too. Here I can only say how the rift *cannot* be healed; and that seems to us to be a very serious subject in our present

---

17. Ibid., 1:164 (*Witness*, 1:132).
18. Ibid., 1:190 (*Witness*, 1:154).
19. Ibid., 1:277f. (*Witness*, 1:227).
20. Vischer, *Christuszeugnis*, 2:30.
21. G. von Rad, "Das Christuszeugnis des Alten Testaments: Eine Auseinandersetzung mit Wilhelm Vischers gleichnamigem Buch," *TBl* 14 (1935): 249–54.

situation." Von Rad therefore cannot find in Vischer's approach any contribution that could point the way toward a solution of the fundamental problems as he sees them.

Now, it is by no means the case that von Rad's criticism is primarily directed against the book's strained christological interpretations—"certain heightenings," as he calls them. On the contrary, he says explicitly that his objections are directed, not to what is too much but rather to what is too little; he objects, that is, "to this way of deducing the testimony to Christ from the Old Testament by reducing the Old Testament utterances in every case to the greatest possible generality, or common denominator, so that the true meaning of the texts is levelled out to the point of unrecognizability." And he adds: "This has to be resisted. . . . The choir of the voices that witness to God's judgment and salvation is infinitely more varied than Vischer describes it as being. God has spoken in the Old Testament in 'diverse manners,' not just in one."

Let us briefly call to mind the situation in Old Testament scholarship which formed the background to what von Rad said. In the 1920s, his teacher Albrecht Alt had begun to develop a new picture of Israel's history and religion, linking together the history of religion and form criticism, with the addition of certain aspects of territorial history (keywords were: the God of the patriarchs; the settlement of the Israelites in Palestine; the origins of Israelite law). His pupils, Martin Noth and Gerhard von Rad, had expanded this picture by a number of other aspects (keywords here being amphictyony and the doctrine of creation; Joachim Begrich's work belongs here too, he being a pupil of Gunkel's and at that time Alt's colleague in Leipzig). Von Rad himself was already developing the concept of his book *Das formgeschichtliche Problem des Hexateuchs,* which appeared in 1938 (Eng. trans., *The Problem of the Hexateuch,* 1965/1984). This is already clearly evident from his critical comments on Vischer. He describes the situation in the following way: "Vischer is as much aware of this situation as I am: through the research of the last hundred years into history, into the history of religion and into literary history, the Old Testament testimonies of faith have shown themselves to us in a positively confusing diversity and dynamic. Much has not yet been seriously grasped at all theologically, but what we do see at the moment eludes any kind of theological systematization— this parallelism, indeed interweaving, of traditions and movements and counter-movements, theological schools and prophetic and theological outsiders or 'lone wolves.' " In short, what is heralded here, and what von Rad is characterizing in his own inimitable way, is a concept of the Old Testament seen under the aspect of tradition history.

In von Rad's opinion, all this would have to be embodied and made fruitful in a theological interpretation of the Old Testament. Hence his complaint: "And what has happened to all this in Vischer's book? Where has it all disappeared to? The Pentateuch is read as if it is a unified and, it must be said, an ultimately somewhat monotonous book of prophecy pointing to Christ." That is the one reproach: all that the texts have to say has been leveled down and reduced to uniformity. Against this von Rad says: "One must listen to the Old Testament, even at the risk of hearing voices which cannot by any means be made immediately and deftly christologically comprehensible and of theological utility. In Vischer we sense nothing of this necessity, which is laid on the interpreter of the Old Testament." This is indeed, in my view, an important hermeneutical aspect: that the theological interpretation of the Old Testament must not exempt itself from a scholarly examination of the texts; it must be developed and justified in the light of that examination, difficult though this venture may often be.

Von Rad's second objection is this: "The great text complexes are forcibly broken down into innumerable little units, each of which, on the basis of an eclectic biblicism, is given its theological meaning in the light of the New Testament." This too is an important hermeneutical viewpoint: not to split up the texts into small units, but to ask about the wider contexts and to seek in these above all the essential theological utterances.[22]

Yet a third objection seems to me noteworthy: "What Vischer himself says is restricted to a few sentences. Much more space is given to extensive quotations from Luther and Hamann." And he goes on: "It would be a blessing—and here I am speaking frankly, at the risk of shocking a good many people—if interpreters of the Old Testament would for the time being be exceedingly restrained in their use of quotations from Luther or Calvin, however fine these may be. For one can be sure that the result for us will in most cases be to obscure the situation in which *we* inescapably stand with regard to the text, either in hermeneutical method or substantially, in the exegesis. . . . It is impossible to step out of our own situation

---

22. Von Rad himself, however, argues from a standpoint based on literary criticism, and this would today no longer be shared by some of his pupils or by other younger Old Testament scholars—or at least not without reservation. Thus he criticizes the fact that Vischer takes the Pentateuch on its own, without including the book of Joshua (the "Hexateuch"), and stresses the theological importance of the different profiles of the pentateuchal sources. But this does not diminish the correctness and importance of this hermeneutical principle.

and to turn back the clock of history four hundred years."[23] Here too we must in principle agree with von Rad. Of course light can occasionally be thrown on important aspects of a text by way of quotations from the Reformers, or from other theologians belonging to the past. But we cannot overlook the danger that this can also go hand in hand with an evasion of today's exegetical problems, and that the theological utterances can be lodged at a level that is detached from the rest of Old Testament research.

These last reflections particularly once again show clearly where the antithesis between Vischer and von Rad really lies. Von Rad thinks that it is necessary to develop theological statements about the Old Testament out of scholarly exegesis, even though he is aware that this is a long and laborious process. Vischer, on the other hand, has no such confidence in modern Old Testament scholarship: "But the question is whether the methods and results of this research do not awaken justifiable doubts. Is this modern research not under the spell of the tenets of modern scientific scholarship to a greater degree than is permissible in the interpretations of ancient texts? Does it not introduce alien points of view? Does it not make use of concepts and categories unknown to the ancient writers?"[24]

We can and must understand both positions in the light of Old Testament scholarship. Vischer had good reasons for his suspicion that nothing could be expected in the way of a theological interpretation of the Old Testament from Old Testament scholarship in the form it had hitherto taken. He therefore saw no alternative except to cut himself free from it, for the most part,[25] and to develop a theological interpretation of his own, in the context of Karl Barth's theology (by which he was molded), as well in recourse to the Reformation and post-Reformation Fathers. Von Rad, on the other hand, had already begun some years earlier to think further theologically the new approaches of the group around Al-

23. The varying use of the word "speculative" is interesting here. Von Rad writes: "For... when Vischer emancipates himself from this awareness of the unique character of the Old Testament testimonies (an awareness which for us today is simply obligatory), his interpretation is bound to take on dangerously *speculative* features" ("Christuszeugnis," 253; von Rad's italics). Vischer, on the other hand, writes that the light in Gen. 1:3 has to be understood as "the glory of God in the face of Jesus Christ if we wish to interpret the text correctly, and to secure it against every kind of speculative reinterpretation" (quotation from n. 13). Apparently the word is being used in both cases as a polemical term, designed to discredit a statement which does not accord with one's own approach.

24. Vischer, *Christuszeugnis,* 1:34.

25. We do, however, find here and there in Vischer too allusions or references to the findings of modern Old Testament research, for example when he says that the categories and concepts of Genesis 1 belong to the "stringent system of a priestly theology," a fact which he uses here as a warning against slipping into "natural philosophy or mysticism" (ibid., 1:55).

brecht Alt,[26] although this had hardly as yet been reflected in any of his published work.[27] But it is quite understandable that he should have considered Vischer's attempt to be an aberration which was bound to lead to further alienation between Old Testament scholarship and the church's theology.[28]

In retrospect, two things must be said about this controversy. First, Gerhard von Rad himself fulfilled what he had indirectly announced by way of his criticism of Vischer. He developed a theology of the Old Testament which grows out of a scrupulously scholarly exegesis. He provided the first, and up to now the most convincing, example of this approach, and the fact that in the last thirty years or more his *Theology* has been continually reprinted and made available to students in cheap editions, speaks for itself.[29]

But that is only one side of the matter. Where the other aspect is concerned, Rudolf Abramowski hit the nail on the head in 1936. He shared von Rad's criticism of Vischer for the most part,[30] but for all that he considered that Vischer's book was necessary and right at that particular point in time. *"Necessary* because the theological and political situa-

26. I am avoiding here the internationally usual (and objectively undoubtedly justifiable) description "the Alt school," because Alt's own pupils, especially Martin Noth, always rejected it. Von Rad occasionally talked about "the Alt clan."

27. Von Rad's contribution to the Congress of the International Organization for the Study of the Old Testament in Göttingen in 1935 on "Das theologische Problem des alttestamentlichen Schöpfungsglaubens" (The theological problem of the Old Testament doctrine of creation) may be viewed as his theological "breakthrough."

28. Incidentally, von Rad's criticism of Vischer was apparently unwelcome at that time in the theological circles to which both belonged or with which both were associated. This emerges from an "editorial note" appended to his essay in *Theologische Blätter* (see n. 21 above): "We feel obliged to give this essay space here. It was first offered to *Evangelische Theologie,* but for editorial reasons it would have been difficult to find a place for it there." If we inquire into these "editorial reasons," we quickly discover what they were. The same year, 1935, saw the publication in *Evangelische Theologie* of Heinrich Vogel's essay (see n. 8), with its hymn of praise over Vischer's book. Parallel to this, there was apparently no room for von Rad's criticism.

29. G. von Rad, *Theologie des Alten Testaments,* vol. 1: *Die Theologie der geschichtlichen Überlieferungen Israels* (Munich, 1957); vol. 2: *Die Theologie der prophetischen Überlieferungen Israels* (Munich, 1960); 6th ed. of both volumes, 1987; Eng. trans., *(Old Testament Theology,* trans. G. M. Stalker (Edinburgh: Oliver & Boyd; New York: Harper, 1962–65; reissued London: SCM Press, 1975).

30. "Of course Gerhard von Rad was right in all his misgivings.... And it is true that much, surprisingly much, of that which Vischer offers is exegetically rashly concluded and by no means satisfactory.... And von Rad is surely even more correct in fearing that less knowledgeable and talented people would, in Vischer's discipleship, also arrive at rash conclusions of a very different kind" (Abramowski, "Vom Streit um das Alte Testament," 91).

tion requires a Christian testimony in the light of the Old Testament, not merely an opinion *about* the Old Testament. It was impossible to wait for this testimony until Old Testament scholarship had come to terms with this fact, for von Rad also agrees that this could take a very considerable time."[31]

Here again we see the same dilemma emerging: the tension that exists between the inevitably long-term developments of scholarly theology, and the ad hoc necessities of taking up positions toward questions of the day. So I would agree with Abramowski that at that time Vischer's book had its function and its great importance, quite irrespective of its position in Old Testament scholarship. In those years it undoubtedly helped many theologians and lay Christians to hold on to the Old Testament as the church's book, and to withstand attacks on it. Insofar, in the situation of the *Kirchenkampf,* the church's struggle in Hitler's Germany, it made an important contribution toward "rescuing" the Old Testament for the Christian church. But it is noticeable that, although at first the book was enthusiastically received—the first volume went through six editions in Germany between 1934 and 1943—it was just as swiftly forgotten, and there was no new edition after the Second World War. The book had had its day.

I should like here to add a note relating to the history of theology. In the further course of the hermeneutical discussion there has been a strange development. The method of interpreting the Old Testament in the light of the New, without considering the exegetical findings of Old Testament research, came to be practiced especially by scholars at the opposite theological pole from Vischer. This was already true of Emanuel Hirsch,[32] and may also later be said of Rudolf Bultmann[33] and Friedrich Baumgärtel.[34] The same applies, finally, to A. H. J. Gunneweg, whose "hermeneutics" has recently appeared in a new but unrevised edition.[35] All these scholars

31. Ibid.

32. E. Hirsch, *Das Alte Testament und die Predigt des Evangeliums* (Tübingen, 1936); see von Rad's review, "Gesetz und Evangelium im Alten Testament," *TBl* 16 (1937): 41–47.

33. R. Bultmann, "Weissagung und Erfüllung," *ZTK* 47 (1950): 360–83 (= *Glauben und Verstehen,* 6th ed. [Tübingen, 1980], 2:162–86, = C. Westermann, ed., *Probleme alttestamentlicher Hermeneutik* [Munich, 1960], 28–53).

34. F. Baumgärtel, *Verheissung: Zur Frage des evangelischen Verständnisses des Alten Testaments* (Gütersloh, 1952).

35. A. H. J. Gunneweg, *Vom Verstehen des Alten Testaments: Eine Hermeneutik*

extract from the New Testament the theological criteria for the evaluation of the Old, without any recognizable attempt to make the findings of modern Old Testament research fruitful for a theological understanding of the Old Testament *on its own ground.* Conversely, among those who do make this attempt,[36] we find an intensive attempt to extract the Old Testament's theological utterances from the Old Testament texts themselves; and here there is considerable reservation about any endeavor to relate the Old Testament all too directly to the New. It is hardly more than an oblique indication when Zimmerli talks about "the openness of the Old Testament proclamation" (§23), restricting himself to quoting Heb. 1:1. Westermann differentiates, working out both the fundamental assertions shared by the two parts of the Christian Bible, and the contrast between them, and bringing out the different relationship to the New Testament of the prophecy of judgment and the prophecy of salvation.[37] Vischer has therefore found no theological successors among Old Testament scholars, and his hermeneutical methods have been pursued by people who are theologically his opponents.

III

One important aspect of Vischer's book still has to be mentioned: the position of the Jews in his theological concept of the Old Testament. It must first of all be said here that Vischer was one of the very few who asked this question at all—and he has remained so down to the present day. As a general rule the question about Christian use of the Old Testament is discussed without mentioning the Jews at all. (This may be said even of Gerhard von Rad.) But Vischer does ask the question. Let me quote the decisive passage:

(Göttingen, 1977, 2d ed. 1988); Eng. trans., *Understanding the Old Testament,* trans. J. Bowden (London: SCM Press; Philadelphia: Westminster Press, 1978).

36. Particularly deserving of mention here are two outlines which appeared after von Rad's *Theology:* W. Zimmerli, *Grundriss der alttestamentlichen Theologie* (Stuttgart 1972, 5th ed. 1985); Eng. trans., *Old Testament Theology in Outline,* trans. D. W. Green (Edinburgh: T. & T. Clark; Atlanta: John Knox Press, 1978); and C. Westermann, *Theologie des Alten Testaments in Grundzügen* (Göttingen, 1978, 2d ed. 1985); Eng. trans., *Elements of Old Testament Theology,* trans. D. W. Stott (Atlanta: John Knox Press, 1982).

37. Westermann, *Theologie,* pt. 4: "The Old Testament and Jesus Christ." In especially striking contrast to Vischer's methods are the statements about "The Relations of the Prophecy of Salvation to Christ" (German ed. 198f.). Here Westermann largely rejects any direct relationships: "The center of gravity in the relation between the prophecy of salvation and Christ is to be found in the history of the promises as a whole, not in individual sayings which may or may not point to Christ."

Consequently the patristic church took over Israel's Holy Scriptures complete, saying: we who believe that Jesus is the Son of God, we who believe his promise that we are his brothers, we and not the synagogue, which rejected his messianic claim, are the legitimate heirs of the divine Testament. By adopting it in this way the church did not wish to take the Old Testament away from the Jews. On the contrary, the apostles continually expressly assert that the Israelites still have first claim, "to whom pertaineth the adoption, and the glory, and the covenants, and the giving of the law, and the service of God, and the promises; whose are the fathers, and of whom as concerning the flesh Christ came" [Rom. 9:4f.]. They must only acknowledge this one thing: that God has made the Jesus whom they rejected Lord and Christ. This metanoia, this change of heart, is the sole condition. Then they too, and they first of all, can draw upon the riches of the divine Testament.

With the assertion: "By adopting it in this way the church did not wish to take the Old Testament away from the Jews," Vischer puts his finger on a problem which, as I have said, is as a general rule neither perceived nor discussed. In his case this belongs in a wider context. In 1933, at Friedrich von Bodelschwingh's request, he had already written a section on "The Church and the Jews" for the preliminary draft of the "Bethel Confession." But in this form it found no place in the confession itself.[38] Today, in retrospect, one is surprised at the differentiated way in which Vischer treated this problem, for hardly any other voices of this kind are known to us from those years.

At the same time, even against this positive background, we still have to ask the critical question whether Vischer's remarks do not permit the very thing to happen which he says is not the intention: that the Jews *as Jews* have taken from them their Bible, to which we give the name Old Testament. (N. B.: We know today that this is in any case an inappropriate way of speaking, since as Christians it is not our business to decide about the use the Jews make of their Bible. The whole question at issue is the internal Christian debate as to how we wish to define theologically our relation to the Jews and our common Bible.) Vischer says: No, we do not wish to take it away from them. "They must only [*sic*] acknowledge this one thing: that God has made the Jesus whom they rejected Lord and Christ." But this really means: they must become Christians and thus cease to be Jews. Once they take this step, they will even become a kind of specially privileged Christians: "This metanoia, this change of heart, is the sole condition. Then they too, and they first of all, can draw upon the riches of the divine Testament."

38. The text is printed in Vischer, "Zeugnis eines Zeitgenossen," *Bethel* 30 (Bielefeld, 1985): 79–85. Cf. also his essay "Zur Judenfrage," in ibid., 62–69.

Here we see emerging the limits of what could evidently be thought and said by Christians at that time about "the Jewish question." Dietrich Bonhoeffer, together with Vischer, continually tried to awaken awareness in the Confessing Church for the importance of this subject. But even in Bonhoeffer we find statements to which we could not possibly still assent today.[39] And we must be permitted—indeed we are enjoined—to term these statements insufficient *today*, and to go beyond them. I am saying that here especially, because a few years ago Wilhelm Vischer, to my great regret, reacted vehemently to some remarks I made along these lines with reference to his book.[40]

I am convinced that in the theological question about the relations between Christianity and Judaism we are today standing on a threshold. Theologically too, we must unreservedly acknowledge the independence and dignity of postbiblical and contemporary Judaism. Where the Old Testament is concerned, this means that we must affirm that Testament's double later history, and must do so theologically too, without casting doubts on the legitimacy of the history of Jewish exegesis, and later Jewish history. It is clear that this attitude includes—or rather presupposes—a renunciation of the assertion that we are the sole possessors of the truth, and particularly so where the biblical history of revelation is concerned.

All this has far-reaching theological implications and consequences, and we have not nearly arrived at a perception of them all in their full scope. Here the discussion about the theological significance of the Old

39. See above all D. Bonhoeffer, "Die Kirche vor der Judenfrage" (1933) (= *Gesammelte Schriften*, vol. 2 [Munich, 1959], 44–53; also in W. Huber and I. Tödt, *Ethik im Ernstfall: Dietrich Bonhoeffers Stellung zu den Juden* [Munich, 1982], 245–50).

40. These remarks were made in an essay of mine on the Jewish Bible and its anti-Jewish interpretation, which appeared in French in the periodical *Foie et vie* (January 1982): 52–72. The editors asked Vischer to comment ("A propos de la conference de R. Rendtorff," ibid., 73–80). In this essay among other things I quoted Abramowski's remarks about the importance of Vischer's book at that time. I should perhaps have made it even clearer that today we approach, and must approach, these questions in a different way from what was possible then. But (in a contribution more than four times as long as the relevant passage in my essay) Vischer insists that everything he had said is to be found in exactly the same way in the New Testament, and that he himself had tried to read the Old Testament in the same manner as the New Testament writers and the Reformers. The difference between us becomes particularly clear in Vischer's criticism of my requirement that as Christians we have to respect the Jewish way of understanding the Old Testament: he describes this as "laissez-faire" (p. 79). The true solidarity of Christians and Jews, he says, is rather "the preparedness to be challenged by the other at whatever cost." But his book never talks about a *mutual* challenge, nor would this have been possible at that time. I am only sorry that he now brings up against me Jewish authors such as Geza Vermes and Emil Fackenheim, as witnesses that what is at issue is something completely different from the "useful dialogue" which I maintained was necessary.

Testament as this was pursued in the 1930s proves to be one of the most important points of departure for a further theological development and differentiation of the problems. Wilhelm Vischer and Gerhard von Rad were among the pioneers in this theological work; they helped to blaze the trail. We can still gratefully learn from them today, even at points where we go beyond what they were able to say at their own time.

"Where Were You When I Laid the Foundation of the Earth?" Creation and Salvation History

"In the beginning God created the heavens and the earth." These are the first words of the Hebrew Bible, which we are accustomed to call the Old Testament. So we might expect, quite as a matter of course, that summary accounts of "the theology of the Old Testament" would begin with creation too. But that is not the case. The last survey of this kind to treat creation first of all was the volume containing Gustav Friedrich Oehler's posthumously published lectures; and Oehler died in 1872.[1] Here the first section is entitled "The History of Revelation from Creation to the Settlement of the People of the Covenant in the Holy Land." Oehler's intention is "to give an account of the Old Testament's whole economy of revelation."[2] He criticizes the concept of revelation held in earlier Protestant theology as too static, claiming that it failed particularly to appreciate *"the stages of development* which revelation undergoes in Scripture itself." The point here is not primarily the development of human perception of revelation; in Oehler's view, biblical theology must rather be "a theology of divine accomplished *facts.*"[3] Here he is explicitly coming forward as disciple of the great Erlangen theolo-

---

Lecture given in Heidelberg in the winter semester of 1985/86 on the occasion of the university's six hundredth anniversary.

1. G. F. Oehler, *Theologie des Alten Testaments,* ed. H. Oehler (Tübingen, 1873), 3d ed., ed. T. Oehler (1891); Eng. trans., *Theology of the Old Testament,* trans. E. D. Smith and S. Taylor (Edinburgh: T. & T. Clark, 1874-93).

2. Oehler, *Theologie,* 8.

3. Ibid., 26 n. 1.

gian Johann Christian Konrad von Hofmann (1810–77), whose theology was centered on the concept of salvation history.

The other great standard Old Testament theology published during the second half of the nineteenth century came out at almost the same time as Oehler's lectures, and was written by Hermann Schultz.[4] He takes a completely different, consistently historical approach and describes *the development of Israel's religion,* beginning with what he supposes were its origins in a "simple religion of the Semites" (which he sees reflected in the Genesis accounts),[5] by way of Moses and the prophets down to the postexilic period. It is only in the final section that he treats "The Religious View of the World," and here, under the heading "God and the World," we also find the subject "Creation and Providence."[6] In this exposition Schultz certainly takes the view that the idea that God created the world was a component of Israelite religion from the very beginning and that, in a limited sense, this idea doubtless already belonged to "the Semitic religion" too.[7]

Under the influence of increasing knowledge about the religious history of the ancient East, however, this view soon changed. In his *Biblische Theologie des Alten Testaments* (1905), Bernhard Stade treated creation in a section called "The Age of Syncretism,"[8] by which he means the period of Manasseh and his successors, in the seventh century B.C.E. According to Stade, it was the influence of Assyrian and Babylonian religion which first allowed the idea of the creation of the world to enter Israelite awareness at all. Talking about the previous period, he writes: "A people whose gaze hardly reached beyond the frontiers of Canaan had naturally enough never concerned itself with cosmological problems."[9]

The effects of this radically new approach can still be felt even today. The question whether there were ideas about creation at all in early Israel is often left cautiously open; but the most commonly accepted view is that it was only in a later phase of Israel's history—round about the period

---

4. H. Schultz, *Alttestamentliche Theologie: Die Offenbarungsreligion auf ihrer vorchristlichen Entwicklungsstufe* (Frankfurt, 1869), 3d ed. 1885; 4th rev. ed. 1889; 5th completely rev. ed. 1896; Eng. trans., *Old Testament Theology,* trans. J. A. Paterson (Edinburgh: T. & T. Clark, 1892).

5. Schultz, *Alttestamentliche Theologie,* 74 (Eng. trans., 1:108).

6. Ibid., 446–70 (Eng. trans., 2:100ff.).

7. Ibid., 446 (Eng. trans., 2:180f.).

8. B. Stade, *Biblische Theologie des Alten Testaments,* vol. 1: *Die Religion Israels und die Entstehung des Judentums* (Freiburg and Leipzig, 1905), 235–46.

9. Ibid., 239.

of the monarchy—that Israelite thinking took over and reshaped ancient oriental traditions about creation.

Since Stade's time, however, theological interest in this question has undergone a radical transformation. The change in the question asked found most clear-cut expression in the lecture which Gerhard von Rad, then a young professor in Jena, delivered in Göttingen on September 7, 1935, at the Congress of the International Organization for the Study of the Old Testament. His lecture was entitled "The Theological Problem of the Old Testament Doctrine of Creation."[10]

The lecture begins: "The Yahwistic faith of the Old Testament is a faith based on the notion of election and therefore primarily concerned with redemption. This statement, which requires no justification here, poses simply and precisely the problem with which we are here concerned. How are we to define theologically the relationship between the predominating belief in election and redemption, and that belief in Yahweh as Creator which is also attested by the Old Testament? How far is the idea of Yahweh as Creator a relevant and immediate conception, over against his redemptive function?"

We can sense that the purpose of these statements is not merely to pass on historical insights about particular developments in Israelite religion, but that von Rad's remarks are determined by a direct involvement. He makes this clear beyond the shadow of a doubt by quoting in his first sentences Wilhelm Lütgert's book *Schöpfung und Offenbarung* (Creation and revelation [1934]), and rejecting his approach as "not a tenable view."[11] By saying this he is indicating that what is at issue here is really the dispute over the question of "natural theology"—a theology, that is, which tried to see the nation too as one of the orders of creation; and he is also making it plain that in this question he himself was unequivocally on the side of Karl Barth. Here, however, he had first to raise an objection

---

10. G. von Rad, "Das theologische Problem des alttestamentlichen Schöpfungsglaubens," in *Werden und Wesen des Alten Testaments,* BZAW 66 (Berlin, 1936), 138–47 (=his *Gesammelte Studien zum Alten Testament,* TBü 8 [Munich, 1958, 4th ed. 1971], 136–47); Eng. trans., "The Theological Problem of the Old Testament Doctrine of Creation," in *The Problem of the Hexateuch and Other Essays,* trans. E. W. Trueman Dicken (Edinburgh and London: Oliver & Boyd, 1966; reissued London: SCM Press, 1984).

It was not originally my intention to give a lecture on Gerhard von Rad. But it soon emerged that to enter into this subject almost inevitably leads to that. It was von Rad who fifty years ago again made the theme of creation a subject for Old Testament theology; it was he who shaped the question under which the subject was treated for very many years; and, finally, it was he too who again gave the theme a new direction. Consequently this lecture has inevitably turned into a kind of "homage to Gerhard von Rad," nor is this something I shall try to avoid.

11. Von Rad, "Das theologische Problem," 136 (Eng. trans., 2).

to the Old Testament itself in its existing form when he said: "We shall certainly have to correct radically the suspiciously simple picture of this matter which is drawn for us in many theological studies of the Old Testament, and which is particularly widespread in the non-theological world as a result of the circumstance that Genesis 1 stands at the beginning of the Bible."[12]

The apologetic intention is unmistakable. Von Rad's purpose is to preserve, or to attain for the first time, a particular theological understanding of the Old Testament which will make possible an interpretation in the context of Karl Barth's theology. In the same year, 1935, in the second volume of his *Old Testament Theology* (which was conceived entirely in the light of Barth's theology), Walther Eichrodt wrote that in the Old Testament "creation [was understood] as the work of the covenant God."[13] Exactly the same concern finds expression in the final sentence of von Rad's lecture, when he says: "The doctrine of redemption had first to be fully safeguarded, in order that the doctrine that nature, too, is a means of divine self-revelation might not encroach upon or distort the doctrine of redemption, but rather broaden and enrich it."[14] The same concern lest what von Rad calls "the doctrine of redemption" (*Heilsglaube*) should be distorted can be found more than thirty-five years later in Walther Zimmerli's *Old Testament Theology,* where he writes: "Thus the question arises whether in its wisdom lore and approach to the world Israel comes upon a second source of revelation, independent of the first."[15] But Zimmerli himself had already given the answer in advance by stressing, entirely along Barth's lines, that even in the Christian creed, the first article, which talks about God the "maker of heaven and earth," certainly precedes everything else, but that it is only in the light of the second article that it can actually be understood.[16]

In 1935, however, this subject was dynamite, politically speaking. In the final section of his Heidelberg dissertation entitled "The Creation of the World and the Creation of Man" (1972), Rainer Albertz writes: "Against the attempts of the time to link theology and the church with

12. Ibid., 137 (Eng. trans., 2 [slightly altered]).

13. W. Eichrodt, *Theologie des Alten Testaments,* vol. 2: *Gott und Welt* (Leipzig, 1935), 2/3, 6th ed. (Göttingen, 1974), 60; Eng. trans., *Theology of the Old Testament,* trans. J. A. Baker (London: SCM Press; Philadelphia: Westminster Press, 1961), 98.

14. Von Rad, "Das theologische Problem," 147 (Eng. trans., 143).

15. W. Zimmerli, *Grundriss der alttestamentlichen Theologie* (Stuttgart, 1972, 5th ed. 1985), 138; Eng. trans., *Old Testament Theology in Outline,* trans. D. E. Green (Edinburgh: T. & T. Clark; Atlanta: John Knox Press, 1978), 158.

16. Zimmerli, *Grundriss der alttestamentlichen Theologie,* 25.

National Socialist ideology by way of 'creation,' von Rad denied 'the Old Testament doctrine of creation' any independent status at all, consistently subordinating it to 'the doctrine of election.' This was justifiable then, for the purpose was to secure the center of the faith and to establish that neither for Israel nor for the church was this center creation."[17]

By stressing the theological concern that prompted von Rad and others, I am by no means intending to declare that this position was without foundation. My intention is rather to make us aware of a hermeneutical problem: the fact that a particular initial question—a particular concern or thrust behind the investigation—brings to light exegetical correlations which would otherwise not emerge. In the context of the leading question he put, von Rad's position was undoubtedly both sustainable and well sustained, and to this he himself essentially contributed.

Considerations based on the history of religion have already been mentioned. There is widespread agreement nowadays among Old Testament scholars that the doctrine of creation in the form in which we have it in the Old Testament today was shaped in the process of grappling with the creation traditions of other ancient oriental religions, and that it only took on its present form during the period of the monarchy—if not later still (in recent years there would seem to be a certain inclination toward a later date). A second argumentation complex is based on examinations of the Old Testament texts in the light of form criticism and tradition history. In his book *Das formgeschichtliche Problem des Hexateuchs* (1938),[18] von Rad himself developed a new model by which to understand the genetic history of the Pentateuch (or Hexateuch). In our present context the essential aspect here is the observation that each of the larger individual tradition complexes within the Pentateuch had initially its own history, before these complexes were all welded together. This means that the traditions about creation were first formulated and worked out independently of the traditions about the patriarchs, the exodus from Egypt, the giving of the law on Sinai, and so forth, all of which now follow the creation accounts in the Pentateuch. A few years ago, in the Festschrift for Hans Walter Wolff, Frank Crüsemann also convincingly worked out "the independence of the primeval history."[19]

Here we can see a many-faceted interplay between ideas drawn from

---

17. R. Albertz, *Weltschöpfung und Menschenschöpfung: Untersucht bei Deuterojesaja, Hiob und in den Psalmen* (Stuttgart, 1974), 174.

18. G. von Rad, *Das formgeschichtliche Problem des Hexateuch*, BWANT 78 (Leipzig, 1938) (= his *Gesammelte Studien zum Alten Testament*, 9–86); Eng. trans. in *The Problem of the Hexateuch*.

19. F. Crüsemann, "Die Eigenständigkeit der Urgeschichte: Ein Beitrag zur Diskus-

the history of religion, from tradition history, and from theology. The really interesting thing here is the theological interpretation of the data arrived at by historical and exegetical methods. In 1935 von Rad's main thesis was that the Old Testament belief in YHWH's creation of the world was never something on its own but was "always . . . related to—indeed subordinated to—the interests and content of the doctrine of redemption." Indeed "the doctrine of creation is at times altogether swallowed up in the doctrine of redemption." He therefore talks about a "soteriological interpretation of the work of creation" which he believes to be "the primary expression of Yahwistic belief concerning Yahweh as Creator of the world,"[20] and which he thinks did not radically change even later. So where the two beliefs come together as parallel or intertwining threads, he puts the stresses accordingly.

Here the term "doctrine of redemption" (which can occasionally alternate with the term "doctrine of election") stands as a kind of shorthand for belief in God's acts in Israel's history, acts which found their special, exemplary expression in Israel's deliverance from Egyptian slavery, that fundamental saving act which, as it were, establishes Israel's history. In almost all modern surveys of Old Testament theology, this aspect stands at the forefront or the center. For example, the first main section of Claus Westermann's *Old Testament Theology*, which appeared in 1978, is headed "The Saving God and History";[21] as introductory argument for this he cites Martin Noth and Gerhard von Rad, and he might also have added Walther Zimmerli and others.

How long this consensus had already existed may be shown by a quotation taken from the year 1954: "The question about the position of the doctrine of creation in the whole complex of Old Testament statements of faith requires no further discussion today. Gerhard von Rad has clearly shown that in the Old Testament the doctrine of creation is intimately linked with the doctrine of redemption, and ministers to that." These were the opening sentences of my inaugural lecture as university teacher in Göttingen, published in 1954.[22] That today this question

---

sion um den 'Jahwisten,' " in *Die Botschaft und die Boten: Festschrift für H. W. Wolff* (Neukirchen-Vluyn, 1981), 11–29.

20. Von Rad, "Das theologische Problem," 142 (Eng. trans., 138 [altered]).

21. C. Westermann, *Theologie des Alten Testaments in Grundzügen*, GAT 6 (Göttingen, 1978, 2d ed. 1985), 28–71, quotation from p. 29; Eng. trans., *Elements of Old Testament Theology*, trans. D. W. Stott (Atlanta: John Knox Press, 1982).

22. R. Rendtorff, "Die theologische Stellung des Schöpfungsglaubens bei Deuterojesaja," *ZTK* 51 (1954): 3–13 (= his *Gesammelte Studien zum Alten Testament*, TBü 57 [Munich, 1975], 209–19.

does in fact again require discussion is something I should like to show here.

Let us first return to von Rad's 1935 lecture. The really new thing about his approach was that he did not take the creation accounts in Genesis as starting point; he took the Psalms and above all Deutero-Isaiah—that anonymous prophet of the Babylonian exile whose sayings have been passed down to us in the book of Isaiah, chaps. 40–55. He demonstrates that, often in the Psalms and always in Deutero-Isaiah, utterances about God the Creator are closely linked with utterances about his acts in history on Israel's behalf. This is so, for example, in Psalm 136, the famous litany with its congregational response, repeated after every verse, which the 1611 Bible translates as: "For his goodness endureth for ever." Here the psalm talks first about God's acts as Creator of the world, using phraseology which is very close to the language of Genesis 1:

> Who alone does great wonders,
> who in wisdom made the heavens,
> who founded the earth upon the waters,
> who made the great lights:
> the sun to rule by day,
> the moon and the stars to rule by night . . .

And then comes a sudden turn, a turn so abrupt as to be almost painful:

> . . . who smote the first-born of Egypt,
> and brought Israel out from among them,
> with a strong hand and an outstretched arm.

A leap from Genesis 1 to Exodus 11 and 12, without preparation and without transition! Von Rad writes here: "The hymn presses on beyond [belief in creation] to the saving acts of God, and we shall surely not be mistaken if we regard this second part as the climax of the psalm."[23] We find something similar in other psalms too, and then repeatedly and pre-eminently in Deutero-Isaiah. The transition in Isa. 51:9ff. is particularly subtle:

> Awake, awake!
> Put on strength, O arm of the Lord;
> Awake, as in days of old, in the generations of long ago!
> Was it not thou that didst cut Rahab in pieces,
> that didst pierce the dragon?
> Was it not thou that didst dry up the sea,
> the waters of the great deep;

---

23. Von Rad, "Das theologische Problem," 138 (Eng. trans., 133).

that didst make the depths of the sea a way
for the redeemed to pass over?
The ransomed of the Lord shall return,
and come to Zion with singing;
everlasting joy shall be upon their heads.…

Here we are first told in the language of mythical tradition about the struggle of the Creator God against Rahab and Tannin, the great sea serpent. Then we find the word תהום, the mythical primordial flood which Gen. 1:2 talks about too ("the deep" as our Bible calls it). God has "dried it up." This still echoes Genesis 1, where we are told that on the third day of creation the water was assigned a particular place, so that "the dry land" appeared. We might also think of Psalm 104, where we read that the waters of chaos fled in terror at the thunder of God's voice, so that hills and valleys could be seen.

But another theme has all of a sudden crept in. The depths of the water became a path so that the redeemed could pass through. Here the water of the chaotic primordial seas has all of a sudden become the water of the Reed Sea; the scene has shifted from the creation to the exodus, without our being able to say exactly where the transition takes place. We find the same ambivalence, incidentally, in the great song in Exodus 15, which we know as "the song of the Reed Sea," in which God's saving act for Israel is extolled. Here too the water of the Reed Sea, in which the Egyptian pursuers sink, is several times called תהום, the primordial flood.

Von Rad impressively describes the fusing of these two constellations of ideas and utterances in Deutero-Isaiah. In "what at first sight appears to be an incredible transposition from one category to another … [the prophet] maintains with passionate conviction his belief that what appear theologically to be two distinct acts are in fact one and the same act of the universal redemptive purpose of God … [so that] the doctrine of creation and the doctrine of redemption are both included in the one picture of the battle with the primeval dragon."[24] But the decisive thing is the theological stress which von Rad now puts here. In the extract from his lecture which I have just quoted I have left out two phrases. At the beginning of the passage he writes: "The prophet takes his stand here on his faith in salvation with such passionate exclusiveness … "; and a little later: "Here the incorporation of the doctrine of creation in soteriological ideas is complete.… "* The coincidence, or conspectus,

---

24. Ibid., 140f. (Eng. trans. 136).
*These last two sentences translated directly from the German text.—TRANS.

of the two traditions of belief is therefore interpreted by von Rad with resolute one-sidedness in favor of faith in redemption.

He traces this approach consistently through to the end by now seeing the creation account at the beginning of Genesis as included in this concept: "Genesis 1 is not an independent theological essay, but one component of a great dogmatic treatise which moves in ever-narrowing concentric circles. The writer naturally takes his own theological stand in the innermost circle, representing the redemptive relationship between Yahweh and Israel. . . . Thus here, too, the creation of the world by Yahweh is not being considered for its own sake, nor as of value in itself. On the contrary, P's presentation of it, even in Genesis 1, is wholly motivated by considerations of the divine purpose of redemption."[25] Later he put it by saying that creation is part of "Israel's aetiology,"[26] indeed even that the primeval history as a whole is itself Israel's "aetiology of aetiologies."[27] Thus everything is entirely related to God's acts for and with Israel and belongs to the sphere which von Rad, in unembarrassed acceptance and remolding of an important but disputed theological term, called "salvation history."

The approaches which von Rad developed here initially remained essentially unchanged. They can be seen in his Genesis commentary of 1949,[28] and in his *Old Testament Theology* of 1957 as well.[29] But parallel to these, we begin to hear some new notes. We find these, for example, in his treatment of one of the Old Testament's particularly interesting creation texts, Psalm 19. The psalm begins with the words: "The heavens are telling the glory of God, and the firmament proclaims his handiwork. . . ." In 1935 von Rad's comment here was as follows: "[In Psalm 19] we find a quite new phenomenon in the thought that the cosmos itself bears witness to God. It certainly cannot be said that this notion finds any very wide support in the Old Testament. On the contrary, it occurs nowhere else with the same clarity." He then also draws attention to the fact that here there is no mention of a revelation of Elohim, let alone a revelation of YHWH, but that the phrase here is "the כבוד of El" ("the word 'El' being

---

25. Von Rad, "Das theologische Problem," 143 (Eng. trans., 139).

26. G. von Rad, *Theologie des Alten Testaments* vol. 1: *Die Theologie der geschichtlichen Überlieferungen Israels* (Munich, 1957, 8th ed. 1982), 152; Eng. trans., *Old Testament Theology*, vol. 1, trans. G. M. Stalker (Edinburgh: Oliver & Boyd; New York: Harper, 1962).

27. Von Rad, *Das formgeschichtliche Problem*, 73.

28. G. von Rad, *Das erste Buch Mose: Genesis*, ATD 2–4 (1949, 11th ed. 1981); Eng. trans., *Genesis: A Commentary*, trans. J. H. Marks (London: SCM Press, 1961).

29. Von Rad, *Theologie*.

here the equivalent of 'divinity' "). And finally he goes on to stress that "Here we have a fragment of an ancient Canaanitish hymn subsequently adapted to Yahwistic beliefs."[30] He could hardly have marginalized this text more thoroughly.

In his *Old Testament Theology* the comment then sounds very different. There this text is certainly treated only quite marginally in the section on creation, but it is emphasized all the more under the heading "Israel's Praise." There he writes: "Besides the saving history, the other great theme in the hymns of the Old Testament is the action of Yahweh in nature."[31] "Praise still had something special to say about the world over and above this. Since it was so wonderfully created by Yahweh and is so wonderfully preserved, it has a splendour of its own, from which praise and witness issue." And now he quotes other psalms too, which say: "All thy works praise (confess) thee" (Ps. 145:10), or "The heavens praise (confess) thy wonders" (Ps. 89:5), as well as Deutero-Isaiah's saying that even the regions which are very far from Israel are to praise God—the ends of the earth, the sea, the islands, the deserts, the Arabian desert-dwellers (Isa. 42:10-12), and he adds: "What do these know of Yahweh and his people?" We might even put it by saying: What do they know of salvation history? Even the song of the seraphim in Isaiah 6 plays a part here: "Holy, Holy, Holy is the Lord Sabaoth; what fills the whole earth is his glory." Incidentally here we have the same word כבוד which is used in Psalm 19, but here it is used not of El but of YHWH Sabaoth! And finally we have Psalm 19 itself, which says: "Day to day pours forth speech and night to night declares knowledge." Von Rad says here: "[The psalm] even insists on the undoubted legitimacy of this witness: day and night are passing it on from creation down to today—an absolutely unbroken chain of tradition."[32]

Here, incidentally, our homage on this six hundredth anniversary [of Heidelberg university] finds an additional legitimation. Twenty-five years ago, when the university was celebrating its 575th anniversary, Gerhard von Rad delivered a lecture entitled "Faith and Knowledge of the World in Ancient Israel."[33] Here—as already in his *Old Testament Theology*—he discusses the problem of why this psalm about the praise of God

---

30. Von Rad, "Das theologische Problem," 143f. (Eng. trans., 140).

31. Von Rad, *Theologie,* 1:371 (Eng. trans., 1:360).

32. Ibid., 1:373 (Eng. trans., 1:362).

33. G. von Rad, "Glaube und Welterkenntnis im Alten Israel," in *Ruperto Carola XIII,* 39 (1961): 8490 (=his *Gesammelte Studien zum Alten Testament,* vol. 2, TBü 48 [Munich, 1973], 255–66); no Eng. trans. of this essay.

in creation should have had a second "psalm" added to it, a psalm dealing with the Torah, the divine precepts given to Israel (Ps. 19:7ff.). Von Rad calls this "a highly deliberate addition, theologically." For "is the witness that proceeds from the cosmos . . . heard by human beings? . . . At all events there is reason enough to talk also about the revelation which they can hear"[34]—that is to say, the Torah. And von Rad sums up his whole lecture as follows: "Thus according to Israel's ideas the situation of human beings in the world is a very curious one. They are living in a creation from which a never-ending song of praise proceeds (Psalm 19). But human ears are by no means full of it. Human beings have much more in common with the ever-reasoning Job, who is at odds with God, and who has first to be told that at the very beginning, when God began to make the world, the morning stars sang together and the heavenly beings shouted for joy (Job 38.7). Men and women have to be told as if they were blind and deaf that they are living in a world which desires to open itself to them, a world indeed in which—according to the wonderful conception of Proverbs 8—the self-revealing mystery of creation plays round them and caresses them."[35]

The road which Gerhard von Rad had traveled in these twenty-five years from 1935 to 1960 can hardly be estimated: from the almost curt isolation and marginalization of the utterances in Psalm 19 about the witness given by creation itself, to the ironic indictment that human beings are like the blind and the deaf, who fail to hear the sonorous testimony of creation which ought really to fill their ears. It is the road which reached its culminating point and its conclusion in his book *Wisdom in Israel* (1970).[36] And there, right at the end, he again expresses with almost staggering emphasis the decisive thing about this wisdom view: "The unshakeable certainty that to the person who gives himself up to it and trusts it, creation will itself demonstrate its truth, because it in fact unceasingly does so. This self-demonstration of the orders of creation . . . remained the final decisive word."[37]

Gerhard von Rad knew very well what he was requiring of his hearers and readers, if they wished to accompany him along this road. At the point in his wisdom book where he begins to develop this train of thought stands the sentence: "All this raises the questions which a bibli-

34. Von Rad, "Glaube und Welterkenntnis," in *Gesammelte Studien,* 260.
35. Ibid., 266.
36. G. von Rad, *Weisheit in Israel* (1970, 3d ed. 1985); Eng. trans., *Wisdom in Israel,* trans. J. D. Martin (London: SCM Press; Nashville: Abingdon, 1972).
37. Von Rad, *Weisheit,* 403.

cal theology surely still has to confront."[38] And again and again comes the question: How, then, is all this related to what could be summed up under the headings "Doctrine of Redemption," "Doctrine of Election," and so forth? And again and again his answer is: they are irreconcilable; "a deep cleft has been driven" between these different attempts to arrive at knowledge.[39] Thus, for example, the Deuteronomist's question about what is unique and what is recurrent in history "cannot possibly be linked with the attempts at knowledge of [Wisdom] teachers";[40] and from the "kerygma" of the Yahwist, as Hans Walter Wolff has expounded it, "there is ... quite simply no bridge to Wisdom." Indeed von Rad even warns us that "it is probably advisable to stress the differences more strongly than the points in common"[41]—and for us, his pupils and readers, that means: the differences between that which we learned from him first of all, and which became an accepted "school of thought," and that which he wrote in the last ten years of his life.

If I am not mistaken, this final phase—the phase of the book on wisdom—has been much less generally "received" up to now than the previous period, which culminated in the two volumes of his *Old Testament Theology*. But again: if I am not much mistaken, inherent in his questions, and even in his assertions about irreconcilability and indeed impossibility, is also a challenge to his readers *not* to resign themselves to this state of affairs. So we shall at least tentatively try to think his questions through a little further.

I should like to do this especially under two headings. The first is "Job and Deutero-Isaiah." The Job quotation in the lecture which von Rad delivered at the Heidelberg celebrations in 1960 was taken from the great divine address in chap. 38, in which God replies to Job's accusations:

> Then the Lord answered Job out of the whirlwind and said:
> "Who is this that darkens counsel by words without knowledge?
> Gird up your loins like a man!
> I will question you, and you shall teach me.
> Where were you when I laid the foundation of the earth?
> Tell me, if you know it!
> Who determined its measurements—surely you know!
> Or who stretched the line upon it?
> On what were its pillars sunk,

38. Ibid., 211.
39. Ibid., 367.
40. Ibid., 369.
41. Ibid., 374 n. 9.

or who laid its cornerstone,
when the morning stars sang together,
and all the sons of God shouted for joy?
Or who shut the sea with doors,
when it burst forth from the womb?...
Have you ever commanded the morning since your days began,
and caused the dawn to know its place...?
Have you entered into the springs of the sea,
or walked in the recesses of the deep?
Have the gates of death been revealed to you,
or have you seen the gates of deep darkness?
Have you comprehended the expanse of the earth?
Declare, if you know all this!
Where is the way to the dwelling of light,
and where is the place of darkness...?
Have you entered the storehouses of the snow,
or have you seen the storehouses of the hail...?
Can you bind the chains of the Pleiades,
or loose the cords of Orion?
Can you lead forth the stars of the zodiac in their season,
or can you guide the Bear with its children?
Do you know the ordinances of the heavens?
Can you establish their rule on earth?..."

A positively endless series of rhetorical questions! They unfold a pan-
orama of what was known about nature in ancient times, knowledge for
which the author of this text has drawn on the treasury of experience of
Israel's older neighbors, especially the Egyptians. But the question about
the origin of this material is not so important, for here at least it has become an integral part of a completely independent Old Testament text.
What is its intention?

One can read this text in very different ways. Detached from its context
in the book of Job, it is a great didactic poem about the mighty interlock-
ing structures of nature which awaken our wonder. The way the author
describes the parts of nature which are quite remote from human beings
is deeply impressive, and similar to what we have already encountered in
Psalm 19, in the doxology of the heavens. Here the human being is an apparently far-off observer of the great marvels of creation. We could react
to this with the cry of Psalm 104: "O Lord, how manifold are thy works!
In wisdom hast thou made them all; the earth is full of thy riches!" But in
the context of the book of Job, the function is a very different one: God is
answering Job's charge. He is replying to Job's great and ever more im-
passioned impeachment, with its continual new beginnings, a speech full

of provocations. Job stresses that justice is on his side; he accuses God of withdrawing his rights from him; he reproaches him with destroying the guilty and the innocent; and he challenges him to stand trial.

God presents himself to respond to the charge. He answers. But is this an answer? Is it not in fact shocking that this divine address does not touch on Job's difficulties at all, but simply confronts his accusations with God's supremacy, doing so, moreover, in an ironical way which cannot fail to be hurtful? But this is evidently not the way the author of the book of Job saw the matter, and he undoubtedly assumed that his readers too would see things differently. We must again call to mind what we said before about the witness of creation itself. For it was precisely Job whom Gerhard von Rad described as "the ever-reasoning human being at odds with God," who first has to be told everything. It is told him to counteract his doubts. And it is told him in the form of rhetorical questions—as in Deutero-Isaiah (Isa. 40:12ff.):

> Who measures the waters in the hollow of his hand
> and marks off the heavens with a span?
> Who encloses the dust of the earth in a measure
> and weighs the mountains in the scales
> and the hills in a balance?

Here too rhetorical questions which have to do with creation. And here too the ironical criticism:

> Who has directed the Spirit of the Lord,
> or as his counselor has instructed him?
> Whom did he consult for his enlightenment,
> and who taught him the path of justice?

And here again we see that in this rhetorical disputation about creation another theme is involved as well. There is talk about "the path of justice." A few verses later this is quite explicitly made the theme:

> Why do you then say, O Jacob,
> and speak, O Israel,
> "My way is hid from the Lord,
> and my right is disregarded by my God"?

Is this not Job's question?

> Oh, that I knew where I might find him,
> then I would lay my case before him. (Job 23:3f.)

And in Job's sharper tones:

> I cry out, "Violence!" but I am not answered;
> I call for help, but there is no justice. (19:7)

"No justice," we read in Job; "my right is disregarded by my God," says Deutero-Isaiah. And the answer is: "Have you not known? Have you not heard? God from everlasting is the Lord, the Creator of the ends of the earth" (Isa. 40:28).

The complaint that justice has been withheld is answered by a reminder of what the plaintiff has long known: that God is the Creator. But *why* this should be an answer here is immediately explained:

> He does not faint or grow weary,
> his understanding is unsearchable.
> He gives power to the faint,
> and to him who has no might he increases strength.
> Even youths shall faint and be weary,
> and warriors shall stumble and fall;
> but they who wait for the Lord shall renew their strength,
> so that they mount up with wings like eagles,
> run and are not weary,
> walk and do not faint.

Both Job and the Israelites in exile to whom Deutero-Isaiah is speaking are complaining because justice is withheld from them. But neither Job nor the exiles are concerned about justice as such—as an abstract legal position. They are quite specifically aggrieved because things are going badly for them. Job in his sufferings and the Judean deportees in their miserable situation—both accuse God of withholding justice from them. It is the right to "a good life" which is at issue here—in Job in the form of the individual life of the person who, with good reason, sees himself as "just" or "righteous"; in the case of the Judean deportees, the good life as a matter of justice for Israel which, with good reason, interprets itself as the nation under God's guidance. Both see themselves as having right on their side—and in neither case is this right denied. But both are reproached with apparently having forgotten what they had once known: that before God their righteousness and their redemptive history do not represent isolated legal positions, but are embedded in the world which God has created, and in his dealings with that world. "Have you not known? Have you not heard?" we read in Deutero-Isaiah, and the psalmodic phrases that follow show that the Israelites are being reminded of their own worship, in which they have so fervently sung the hymns about God's power as Creator. Job needs no explicit reminder, for the reader of the Job dialogue knows what Job himself had said earlier:

> How can a man be just before God?
> If one wished to contend with him,
> one could not answer him once in a thousand times . . .

> he who removes mountains, and they know it not . . .
> who shakes the earth out of its place,
> so that its pillars tremble . . .
> who alone stretched out the heavens,
> and strides upon the waves of the sea,
> who made the Bear and Orion,
> the Pleiades and the chambers of the south;
> who does great things beyond understanding,
> and marvelous things without number. (Job 9:2ff.)

Job himself had said all this, before he had worked himself up to his despairing protest. So it is not that he is silenced through a demonstration of God's power as Creator: he is simply reminded of the premises from which he himself started, and which he had forgotten—like the deported Judeans in Babylon. Both are once again initiated into the connection between their faith and thinking, into the great total cohesion which the Hebrew Bible depicts for us. For that is precisely the framework whose restoration is at issue here: "In the beginning God created the heavens and the earth"—and then he created human beings and assigned them their place in this creation, right at the end—"at the very apex" one might say, if one wished to see the marvelous design of Genesis 1 as a pyramid; "at the center" one could say, looking at the other pattern in Genesis 2, where the garden of the world, with its trees and animals, is built up round about the human being. But in both cases the design includes a charge which gives the human being a piece of responsibility for creation: "to till and keep" the garden, says Genesis 2; "to have dominion" over the earth, says Genesis 1—not like a despot but like a ruler with a sense of responsibility, whose charge is the well-being of the creation entrusted to him.

It is only in this framework that there can be any talk about the "rights" of the individual and the "rights" of Israel. This solves neither Job's immediate problems nor those of the deported Judeans. But in the framework of our subject it makes something else clear: that the questions which concern Job and Deutero-Isaiah only differ superficially. And this brings us back to our starting point, to the question which Gerhard von Rad raised in 1935 about the relation between the doctrine of creation and the doctrine of redemption. If we draw upon his own later insights about the significance of creation in Job and in the rest of wisdom literature, the result is a correction to his earlier thesis that the doctrine of creation always remained dependent on the doctrine of redemption—a correction which emerges almost of its own accord. We can now put it differently: faith in God the Creator was perceived and experienced as the all-embracing framework, as the fundamental, all-underlying premise for any talk about God, the world, Israel, and the individual. As so often, the fundamental insight takes on its most distinct form and formulation in periods of crisis: the crisis of personal "religion," which attempts to deduce "rights" from a formalized thinking in categories of human action and resulting destiny, and the crisis of the nation, which deduces from its "salvation history" a "right" to permanent national prosperity. Only the restored incorporation of personal and national destiny in the all-embracing cohesion of creation puts the standards right. Of course the price is loss of calculability and the capacity to see ahead; God is removed from apparent disposability, personal and national prosperity are withdrawn from the sphere of what can be claimed as a right. But this does not mean surrendering to the arbitrary disposal of a *deus semper absconditus*—a permanently hidden God.

This brings us to the second heading under which I should like to pursue this train of thought. I am calling it "Creation and Covenant." Let us begin once more with the quotation from von Rad's book about wisdom, where he writes that "to the person who gives himself up to it and trusts it, creation will itself demonstrate its truth," and where he talks about the "self-demonstration of the orders of creation."[42] But why is it possible to have this trust in creation and its orders? For what reason? At the close of the creation account in Genesis 1 we read: "And God saw everything that he had made, and behold it was very good" (Gen. 1:31). But a few chapters later we read: "And God saw the earth, and behold, it was corrupt" (6:12). The two sentences are built up in a completely parallel way. The earth was no longer "very good," and God resolved to destroy all living things, because it was from them, from "all flesh," that the corruption of the earth proceeded. But God makes an exception. Noah is saved, only Noah and his family, and just one pair of each species of animal. With these God makes a new beginning. The earth has lost its innocence; it is no longer "very good." Its existence is endangered. And what support is there for the assumption that after this new beginning everything will not repeat itself, that the corruption will not grow rampant, and that God will not again surrender the earth to annihilation, this time perhaps finally and without any exceptions?

The answer of the primeval history is unequivocal: nothing at all suggests that this will not repeat itself. On the contrary, the declaration that "the imagination of man's heart is evil from his youth" is explicitly repeated (8:21; cf. 6:5). But remarkably enough: before the flood this observation is followed by the sentence, "And the Lord was sorry that

---

42. Cf. p. 102 above.

he had made man on the earth"; whereas after the flood the sequel is quite different: "I will never again destroy every living creature as I have done." And then follows the solemn obligation to which God commits himself:

> While the earth remains,
> seedtime and harvest, cold and heat,
> summer and winter, day and night
> shall not cease.

The reason for the danger therefore still exists; the earth is no longer "very good" and can never again become so. And yet God lets it go on existing. He pledges himself to do so. And he does not only guarantee this through his word; he institutionalizes his promise through a "covenant," a בְּרִית, a self-imposed obligation in solemn form that there will never be another flood (9:8ff.). He makes this covenant with Noah and his sons, but at the same time with all other living things too (v. 12)—indeed simply with the earth (v. 13). So according to the idea behind the Bible's primeval history, the reason that human beings can trust the orders of creation is not to be discovered simply in creation itself. On the contrary, creation's existence is profoundly endangered by all the things that constantly happen in it, which are anything but good. The fact that it still goes on existing in spite of this is due to God's self-imposed obligation, his covenant with Noah. And that is the reason why human beings can have confidence in creation; that is why they can hear and see its witness; that is why they can learn wisdom from it; and that is why they can ultimately say: "O Lord, how manifold are thy works! In wisdom hast thou made them all" (Ps. 104:24).

It is curious how little importance is attached to God's covenant with Noah in surveys of Old Testament theology. In the theologies of Zimmerli and Westermann it is not referred to at all. Even in von Rad it is mentioned almost by the way. But I found it consoling to discover in his book at least one or two sentences about it—sentences which also take us a step further: "Yahweh even guaranteed the preservation of the continued physical existence of the universe by the making of a covenant (Gen. ix.8ff.). It is within the stability thus established by the grace of Yahweh that the saving history is in due time to operate."[43]

It is in a world stabilized through God's grace that everything else takes its course. It is again Deutero-Isaiah who shows most clearly an aware-

---

43. Von Rad, *Theologie* 1:170 (Eng. trans., 1:157).

ness of the connections between these things. In a saying to Jerusalem
we can read:

> For a brief moment I forsook you,
> but with great compassion I will gather you. . . .
> For this is like the days of Noah to me:
> as I swore that the waters of Noah should no more go over the earth.
> So I have sworn that I will not be angry with you and will not rebuke you.
> For the mountains may depart and the hills be removed,
> but my steadfast love shall not depart from you,
> and the covenant of my peace shall not be removed,
> says the Lord, who has compassion on you. (Isa. 54.:7ff.)

That is the one thread: the covenant with Noah is a warranty that creation
will endure, and at the same time it is a model and pattern for God's acts
with and for Israel—after the catastrophe. Here the Babylonian exile
becomes the flood, as it were, but here too, as after the flood, the covenant
follows, the covenant of peace, the ברית שלום.

But the covenant with Noah throws open another dimension too. We
hear about the covenant of peace in very different connections—for
example in the prophet Ezekiel's vision of the future:

> I will make with them a covenant of peace
> and banish wild beasts from the land,
> so that they may dwell securely in the wilderness
> and sleep in the woods. . . .
> And I will send down the showers in their season;
> and they shall be showers of blessing.
> And the trees of the field shall yield their fruit,
> and the earth shall yield its increase;
> and they shall be secure in their land,
> and they shall know that I am the Lord,
> when I break the bars of their yoke, and deliver them
> from the hand of those who enslaved them. (Ezek. 34:25ff.)

Here too the prophet is talking about the liberation from exile. But
in the promised peace in the people's own land, nature is also included.
The wild beasts which multiplied and spread in the country once it was
emptied of people, and which threaten to make living there impossible, will yield it up again so that it can be lived in. The rain will fall
at the proper time, and the earth will give its fruits. Seedtime and harvest will take place once more, as God had already promised in Noah's
time. So the promise that Israel will again dwell securely in its land has
two dimensions: the political one—the ending of foreign domination—

and the other, in which nature is included. God's covenant with Israel simultaneously endorses the covenant with Noah.

We already hear something similar in Hosea (2:18), long before Ezekiel and in a different political situation. And if we follow this thread in the Old Testament we find still other clues pointing in the same direction. Helga Weippert has investigated the theology of creation in the book of Jeremiah[44] and in this context has also drawn attention to the link between creation and covenant. Thus in Jer. 5:22-25 we can read:

> Me you will not fear, says the Lord,
> nor tremble before me,
> I who placed the sand as the bound for the sea,
> a perpetual barrier which it cannot pass. . . .
> This people has a stubborn and rebellious heart;
> they have turned aside and gone away
> and do not say to themselves:
> "Let us fear the Lord our God,
> who gives the rain in its season,
> the autumn rain and the spring rain,
> and keeps for us the weeks appointed for the harvest."
> Your iniquities have brought this into confusion,
> your sins keep the good from you.

Here we find echoes of the creation in which God set bounds for the sea, and of the covenant with Noah in which he promised the alternation of the seasons, seedtime and harvest. The whole has been disrupted because Israel has turned to other gods. In Jeremiah 14 the term "covenant" is expressly used here:

> We acknowledge our wickedness, O Lord,
> and the iniquity of our fathers, for we have sinned against thee.
> Do not spurn us, for thy name's sake,
> do not dishonor thy glorious throne [i.e., Zion]!
> Remember and do not break thy covenant with us!
> Are there any among the false gods of the nations that can bring rain?
> Or can the heavens give showers of themselves?
> Is it not thee, O Lord our God?
> Should we not set our hope on thee,
> because thou doest all these things? (Jer. 14:20-22)

The direct link between remembrance of the covenant and the reference to the rain which only God himself can give shows here again

---

44. H. Weippert, *Schöpfer des Himmels und der Erde: Ein Beitrag zur Theologie des Jesajabuches,* SBS 102 (Stuttgart, 1981).

how the covenant with Noah belongs to the foundations of the relationship between God and Israel. In Jeremiah 5 we now find the astonishing statement that this order has been destroyed by Israel's sins. It is no great intellectual leap to statements about the destruction of the ecological balance through the arbitrary intervention of human beings, although now these human beings have not put other gods in God's place; they have put themselves, or their self-made surrogate gods of economic expansion and the adaptation of nature to the wishes and alleged needs of human beings.

The echoes of the covenant with Noah in the book of Jeremiah therefore bring out a further important aspect: God's assurance as it is formulated in Genesis 8 and 9 is not a carte blanche which now permits human beings to do whatever they like at will. It certainly breaks through the inevitability with which human acts would again be bound to lead to catastrophe. It designates the order to whose fundamental sustaining God has committed himself. We human beings cannot destroy it "as long as the earth remains." But we can enduringly disrupt it to the point of interrupting the alternation of day and night, summer and winter, through the permanent night and permanent winter which we have acquired the ability to produce, and from which we distance ourselves in polite paraphrase through the word "nuclear." We can destroy the countryside, exterminate species, make life impossible in rivers and lakes, allow forests to die, and much more. We are doing everything, for our part, to thwart the promise of the covenant with Noah. And we can no doubt even manage to remove the foundation from the covenant with Noah altogether, for that foundation is: "as long as the earth remains." With our so-called satellites we have already created something like an Archimedean point outside the earth. It is true that this is not yet sufficient for us from that point to move the earth; but it could well be enough for us from that point to destroy it.

The human sins which destroy the orders of the covenant with Noah have changed since the time of Jeremiah. The most important difference is that they are now turned directly against creation—a notion which the authors of the biblical era would have found inconceivable. Today there is a widespread notion afloat that Christians are mainly responsible for the exploitation and destruction of nature, because they have followed the instruction of their Bible: "Subdue the earth!" According to this it would really be the Bible itself that is responsible. As I have said this is no more than a false report; for it was never this biblical saying that was the cause or occasion for the exploitation of nature. It was at most subsequently brought in as a legitimation, often by people who were not much concerned about the Bible and Christianity otherwise. Moreover only people who do not know the Bible can view this as the Bible's central assertion on the subject of "human beings and nature." Both the creation accounts at the beginning of the Bible show in their different ways how human beings are included in the cohesion of creation's order, and that they have their place and their task within that.

But above all, the Bible knows a great deal about the endangering of creation—its endangering through human beings especially. The covenant with Noah stands in the way of this imperilment, as what the prophets called a "covenant of peace." In the Old Testament the concept of the covenant is strangely asymmetrical: God establishes it, he commits himself to keeping it—but for all that, the enduring nature of the covenant is not wholly independent of human behavior. Men and women can keep it or break it. Whether they can shatter it entirely— whether they can make God's self-commitment null and void through their behavior—ultimately remains an open question in the Bible. As yet, God still considers himself bound by it. But the prophets know and tell us that it is endangered by our sins. Perhaps it is not so very much wide of the mark when we talk about "sins against the environment," for here it really is a matter of sins against creation and against the covenant of peace which God has established for the preservation of creation.

What the Bible has to say about creation is by no means merely idyllic. And above all it is not remote from the realities in which we live. The more seriously we take the Bible and the more seriously we take the realities of the present threat to creation, the clearer it becomes how much the two have to do with one another. God set the rainbow in the heavens as sign of the covenant with Noah. Human beings can look at it, and can see from it that God is standing by his covenant; and God looks at it in order to remember his covenant and to preserve the orders of creation. Let us see to it that the rainbow remains visible, that it does not become faded through the destruction of the water cycle between heaven and earth, that it is not darkened by the smog caused by the emissions of our civilization, or it does not finally become totally invisible in the nuclear night. For up to now it still holds good that

> while the earth remains,
> seedtime and harvest, cold and heat,
> summer and winter, day and night,
> shall not cease.

CHAPTER 10

Revelation and History:
Particularism and Universalism
in Israel's View of
Revelation

I

When I am asked today to talk about "history and revelation," it would seem obvious to begin with a few thoughts about the program "revelation as history," which was first presented publicly at the beginning of the 1960s.[1]

This program grew up out of the attempt of a small group of young theologians to subject fundamental positions in the theological situation of the time to a critical examination. Theologians belonging to the various theological disciplines cooperated in this attempt. One of our shared points of departure was the theology of Rudolf Bultmann, in whose train we tried to interpret "history" in the sense of "historicity." But at the same time our theological development had been firmly molded to a greater or lesser degree by Gerhard von Rad; this was true for us all. And when we attempted to reconcile with Bultmann's approach the Old Testament understanding of history which von Rad had developed, the Old Testament proved resistant. This became irrefutably clear to us when the thesis "Christ, the end of history," came up for discussion. We saw ourselves faced with the alternative of surrendering either our approach via the Old Testament, or the approach via Bultmann's theology.

1. W. Pannenberg, ed., *Offenbarung als Geschichte* (Göttingen, 1961, 2d ed. 1963; 5th ed. 1982); Eng. trans., *Revelation as History*, trans. D. Granskou and E. Quinn (New York: Macmillan, 1968; London: Collier-Macmillan, 1969).

This of course was not a genuine alternative, for to start from the Old Testament was the self-evident and indispensable presupposition for our theological work. So this dilemma led us to try to find a new theological interpretation of history. And that inevitably brought us into opposition to dialectical theology.[2]

Our primary concern, then, was not the problem of revelation; it was the problem of history. But the concept of revelation seemed to us to be the horizon against which a new understanding of history could be most readily acquired and developed.

There was another fundamental aspect as well. In the discussion about the earliest Christian interpretation of Jesus' resurrection, Ulrich Wilckens had drawn our attention to the fact that in the End-time expectation of Jewish apocalyptic the resurrection of the dead is one of the signs of the dawning eschaton. From this he went on to develop the thesis that the resurrection of the *one* man Jesus was, as it were, the anticipation, in this one person, of the End. Wolfhart Pannenberg took up this idea and developed from it the thesis about the "anticipatory coming about" of the End in Jesus' cross and resurrection; for this he then used the term "prolepsis." This idea was further developed, in the direction of the notion that the full significance of all happening is unveiled only in the light of its end. Related to the interpretation of revelation, this meant that God's self-disclosure—that is his revelation—can be perceived only from the perspective of the End; indeed that revelation in the real sense only takes place at the end of history.

This understanding of revelation was developed in continual reference to the biblical texts, especially the Old Testament. The focus here was particularly on texts which suggested that historical events were interpreted in the light of their end—texts which already played an important part in von Rad's work; for example Gen. 50:20: "You meant to do me evil, but God thought of turning it to good, in order to bring about what is now taking place" (following von Rad's translation); or Exod. 14:31: "When Israel saw the strong hand with which Yahweh acted against the Egyptians, the people feared Yahweh, and they believed in Yahweh and in his servant Moses." The "cognition formula" worked out by Walther Zimmerli: "You shall know that I am Yahweh," also acquired great importance, since we meet it for the most part in connection with historical

---

2. See the postscript to the second edition of *Offenbarung als Geschichte,* 132ff.; also J. M. Robinson and J. B. Cobb, eds., *Theology as History* (New York: Harper & Row, 1967), esp. the part on "The Location of the New Position within the Theological Spectrum."

events. So in this way the Old Testament too could be understood under this aspect: the interpretation of Yahweh's acts in history is only possible in the light of the End.

Finally, the whole complex came to be considered under a holistic aspect, the aspect of universal history: the *one* revelation of the *one* God is a universal historical event which finds its realization only at its end— and for us that means in the anticipatory coming-about of the End in the resurrection of Jesus Christ.

My theological understanding at the time was such that I had no objection to this whole concept. To regain theologically the historical dimension of the Old Testament, and the possibility of understanding God's activity in historical events under the aspect of revelation, even if in a provisional sense, seemed to me an important step forward in the theological rehabilitation of the Old Testament. For in this way the Old Testament had become not merely an important presupposition for Christian theology, but one of its irrelinquishable components. For Pannenberg too, the Christ-event was the revelation of God only "inasmuch as it is part of God's history with Israel."[3]

I was not then conscious of the fact that the God who is being talked about here is only the God of Israel insofar as the Christian church has taken Israel's place. The program "revelation as history" has as its implicit basis a "substitution theory" of extremest consistency.

II

Between then and now there intervened what was for me a decisive event: my encounter with Judaism. The diverse aspects which made this encounter important for me biographically and theologically have their center, and also quintessence, in one thing: in the recognition that there is a living Judaism *today* which still exists, in unbroken continuity, in the traditions of the Jewish Bible, the "Old Testament," and which has developed these traditions in such a way that they could, and can, be at all times the foundation for Jewish life.

Where the Old Testament is concerned, this means one thing above all: that the Christian appropriation of the Old Testament is not self-evident, but that it needs grounds and justification—grounds, moreover, which state explicitly how the Christian appropriation of the Old Testament is to be understood—how it stands in relation to the Jewish interpretation

---

3. Thus the fifth of his "Dogmatic Theses on the Doctrine of Revelation" in *Offenbarung als Geschichte,* 107.

and application of that Testament. I am far from disputing the right and legitimacy of a Christian use of the Old Testament. But a clear distinction must be made between the *interpretation* of the Old Testament in its canonical framework—that is, under the presuppositions and conditions of its development up to the close of the canon—and its *appropriation* by the Christian church, especially since that church has become an exclusively Gentile one; so that the Old Testament has been introduced as canonical document into a religious society which came into being only after the close of this canon and on its foundation.

In the context of our present subject and the program "revelation as history," this means that the "universal history" aspect does not belong to the interpretation of the Old Testament at all; it belongs to the Christian appropriation of that Testament. Its legitimacy in the framework of Christian theology is not the object of our investigation here. But what must be disputed is its claim to be *the* interpretation of the Old Testament, and hence the understanding of revelation which accords with the Old Testament and is elicited from it. On the contrary, *this* aspect—the viewpoint of universal history—cannot be discerned from the Old Testament itself, or find any justification there. It would have to be developed under the explicit premise that Christian appropriation of the Old Testament has meant departing from, and going beyond, the Old Testament's own self-understanding; and that there is no methodological way of introducing the viewpoint of universal history into the Old Testament itself.

III

I should like to supplement these general hermeneutical reflections by a few individual observations based on exegesis and biblical theology.

The text I have already quoted, Exod. 14:31, says that Israel "saw" and believed. As we have seen, it was an already completed event in which the Israelites perceived God's activity and in that activity God himself: God had "revealed" himself to them in what he did. We find the same thing in Deuteronomy 4, where at the end of the first introductory speech in Deuteronomy we read, in recollection of Israel's deliverance from Egypt: "To you it was shown, that you might know that Yahweh is the God; there is no other besides him" (v. 35; similarly v. 39). Here too, a past, already completed act of Yahweh's is to bring about knowledge—though not a random act, but *the* fundamental event of salvation history, which laid the foundation for Israel's existence as God's people in his land (cf. also Deut. 7:8f.).

The verb יָדַע, "know," has a central function when texts talk about the revelation of God as a *self*-revelation or *self*-disclosure. It is often used in the perfect in the Old Testament, so that it points back to a self-revelation of God which has already taken place.[4] For example, in Ps. 76:1 we find: "In Judah God is known, his name is great in Israel." The rest of the psalm shows that this divine making-himself-known has come about in God's acts (cf. also Ps. 48:3 and the context). In Ps. 77:14ff. God's making-himself-known is related to the deliverance from Egypt.

Psalm 98, finally, is particularly interesting. Here again the psalm talks about God's making-himself-known, and here the verb יָדַע (hiph'il) is set over against the verb גָּלָה, which—in the wake of the Septuagint—is generally translated by "reveal" (v. 2). This "revealing" takes place "in the sight of the nations." Verse 3 then makes an explicit distinction between Israel and the nations: "He has remembered his steadfast love and faithfulness to the house of Israel; all the ends of the earth have seen the salvation of our God." So YHWH's act takes place for Israel's sake, because he "remembers" Israel. But it takes place before the eyes of the nations, and in this way all the ends of the earth can also "see" the salvation (or to be more exact: "the help") of God—the God whom the psalmist in this context especially calls "our God." So here the particularist and the universalist aspects are linked.

Before we go into this question any further, we must first look at the other side of the process in which knowledge comes about, namely human perception of God, that is, human reaction to the fact that God makes himself known. In a whole series of texts we are explicitly told that people came to "know" God. Let me mention three of them.

In Exod. 18:11, Jethro, Moses' father-in-law, after hearing Moses' account of the deliverance of the Israelites from Egypt, says: "Now I know that Yahweh is greater than all gods." In 2 Kings 5:15 another devout non-Israelite, Naaman the Syrian, says: "Behold, now I have come to know that there is no god in all the earth but in Israel." Finally, in 1 Kings 18:39, after Yahweh has sent down fire from heaven to consume the sacrifice on the altar dedicated to him, the whole people cries: "Yahweh, he is the God, Yahweh, he is the God!" We might almost talk about a climax of perception in these three texts: (1) Yahweh is greater than all other gods. (This presupposes the existence of other gods—at least in the way the acknowledgment is formulated). (2) There is no god in the whole of the earth except in Israel. (3) The "monotheistic" acknowledgment: "Yahweh (alone) is (the) God."

4. I neglected this aspect in my own contribution to *Offenbarung als Geschichte* (on "The Concept of Revelation in Ancient Israel"), 21–41, esp. 25ff.

This last observation is important. The utterances about the content of what is known change. In a question determined by the interests of systematic theology, there is a danger that the Old Testament will be looked at too much as if it were a single, level plane. The statement that God discloses himself in his revelation is so wholesale that it conceals the fact that a highly differentiated history of reflection can be found in the Old Testament—reflection as to who this God is who lets himself be known, reflection about the way men and women experience his self-disclosure, and the way in which they assimilate and express their experiences.

There are texts which say that God reveals his *power*—for example the passage I have already several times cited, Exod. 14:31, which talks about Yahweh's "strong hand." So to say that Yahweh is God means here that he is able to act and does act, and that those who believe in him can rely on him. Other texts (for example Exod. 18:11; Pss. 95:3; 96:4; and frequently) say that Yahweh is greater and more powerful than other gods. So here the point of reference is not so much personal experience of Yahweh's help; it is rather his position compared with other gods. In still other texts, the existence of these gods is explicitly denied, for example in the already cited passage 2 Kings 5:15.

This utterance is frequent and widely dispersed in the Old Testament. We find it in especially pregnant form in Hosea, for example: "I am the Lord your God from the land of Egypt; you know no God but me, and besides me there is no helper" (13:4). Here again we see the way the knowledge of God is historically anchored in the deliverance from Egypt: the exclusivity of Yahweh's divinity is expressly related to Israel; Israel has no other "helper." In Deut. 4:35, 39 too the "monotheistic" formula is related to the deliverance from Egypt. Because of that, Yahweh alone is acknowledged as the One who deserves the predicate "God."

In the examples from Hosea and Deuteronomy, closeness to the language of Deutero-Isaiah is quite evident, for example, Isa. 45:5: "I am Yahweh and there is no other, besides me there is no God." Here the universalist aspect now emerges once more: Yahweh has called Cyrus "so that they may know from the rising of the sun to its setting that there is none besides me. I am Yahweh and there is no other. I form light and create darkness, I make weal and create woe—I am Yahweh, who do all these things" (vv. 6f.). God's uniqueness is to be known "from the rising of the sun to its setting." And yet in Deutero-Isaiah there is no doubt about the fact that the prophet is talking about *Israel's* God. So this universalism does not in any way imply that the idea of a special relation between this God and Israel has been abandoned, and that the universal knowledge of God is therefore a step beyond the particularist narrows of the Israelite religion, as it were, in the direction of a more comprehensive, universalist understanding of God. Deutero-Isaiah himself makes it unmistakably clear that this is not his view. On the contrary: in 49:26, in words addressed to "Zion," we read: "Then all flesh shall know that I am Yahweh your savior and your redeemer, the Mighty One of Jacob." Here, therefore, the two aspects are bracketed together in a single sentence: "*all flesh*" knows that Yahweh is *Israel's* "savior" and redeemer.

The nations' knowledge of God therefore does not bypass Israel, nor is it achieved in such a way that the nations leave Israel's knowledge of God behind them in the process of their own knowing. On the contrary, by recognizing God as Israel's God they recognize him as the one and only God. To put it another way: God reveals himself to the nations as the *one* God who he is, by revealing himself to them as Israel's God.

IV

Let us turn back to our point of departure. What is the relation between the universalism of Deutero-Isaiah's utterances about revelation, and the viewpoint of universal history under which Pannenberg developed the program "revelation as history"? Pannenberg writes: "Only in the course of the history which is experienced in the light of Yahweh does this tribal God show himself to be the one true God. Strictly speaking and in the ultimate sense, this demonstration results only at the end of all history. But in the destiny of Jesus the end of all history has come about in advance, as anticipation."[5] From this he concludes: "In the history of Israel Yahweh has not yet shown himself to be the one God of all human beings. He has only shown himself to be Israel's God."[6]

How does he arrive at this assertion, which is patently false exegetically, and goes against numerous texts which Pannenberg himself cites? Here I must quote what I myself wrote: "Yahweh's self-demonstration which is still to come and future, increasingly draws to itself expectation and hope. What was earlier—above all what was foundational in the deliverance from Egypt—is not forgotten; but it can no longer be understood as Yahweh's sole and final self-disclosure. Something new and greater is expected; the full revelation of Yahweh becomes an eschatological dimension."[7] Here it becomes plain that at that time we interpreted the whole of the Old Testament eschatologically—one might even say

5. *Offenbarung als Geschichte*, 98.
6. Ibid., 103.
7. Ibid., 27.

apocalyptically. It is explicitly said several times that the catastrophe of the political end of the state of Judah and the destruction of Jerusalem by Nebuchadnezzar in 587/86 B.C.E. meant a profound caesura, and that through its historical experiences Israel arrived at the recognition "that Yahweh's last and ultimate revelation was still to come."[8]

The preconditions in theological history for this view are obvious enough. Behind it stands the separation (practiced ever since de Wette and Vatke at the beginning of the nineteenth century) between preexilic and postexilic Judaism, the latter being a degeneration, "a chaos which awaited a new creation."[9] For Vatke, Deutero-Isaiah represented the absolute peak of Israelite religion. This view has continued to prevail down to the present day. For Wellhausen, Noth, and von Rad (to mention only these great names) the exile is the great caesura—afterwards there was only decline.

But there was not decline alone. There was one thread, the eschatological, apocalyptic one, which makes it possible to establish a link between the Old Testament and the New. Klaus Koch once called this view "the theory of the prophetic connection."[10] It was a way of bridging the "ugly ditch" of postexilic Judaism, so that the New Testament can take up directly where Deutero-Isaiah leaves off, and document the fulfillment of his expectations and promises.

Of course Christian Old Testament scholars too have always seen that the Old Testament frequently establishes that promises are fulfilled; Josh. 23:14 is an example: "Know in your hearts and souls that not one thing has failed of all the good things which the Lord your God promised concerning you; all have come to pass for you; not one of them has failed." But a particular interpretation of the connection between promise and fulfillment had developed, which Zimmerli in particular formulated, saying that every time a promise is fulfilled, the fulfillment again gives rise to a new promise. Fulfillment is never something final. It points beyond itself to new fulfillments. And in this way the whole of the Old Testament ultimately points beyond itself—to the New, in which it is said that all promises are fulfilled in Jesus Christ.[11]

Pannenberg took up this viewpoint: "The historical self-demonstration

---

8. Ibid., 41.

9. Quoted in R. Smend, *Wilhelm Martin Leberecht de Wettes Arbeit am Alten und am Neuen Testament* (Basel, 1958), 103.

10. K. Koch, *The Rediscovery of Apocalyptic*, trans. M. Kohl (London: SCM Press; Naperville, Ill.: A. R. Allenson, 1972), 37.

11. W. Zimmerli, "Verheissung und Erfüllung," *EvT* 12 (1952/53): 34–59 (= C. Westermann, ed., *Probleme alttestamentlicher Hermeneutik* [1960, 3d ed. 1968], 69–101); Eng.

of Yahweh through his acts, although it was often seen as final, always still retained a provisional character in Israel. It was continually over-taken by new events, new historical acts, in which Yahweh showed himself in a new way. It is only the end of all happening which can...bring the final self-demonstration of Yahweh, the fulfillment of his revelation."[12] It is plain that here a dogmatic—or philosophi-cal—postulate is falsifying the exegetical facts. The statement that the self-demonstration of Yahweh through his acts has "a provisional char-acter" finds no support anywhere in the Old Testament. Above all, in my view there is an essential fallacy in Pannenberg's system here. It is of course true that in the texts belonging to the exilic and postexilic period the expectation of a great new divine act in history found expression in multifarious forms. This may be said of Deutero-Isaiah in a very special way. And yet it is precisely Deutero-Isaiah who stresses more than al-most anyone else that God *has already* shown himself as *the one* God, as himself, and that this is the very reason why there can be hope for his future acts. It is impossible to detect here any suggestion that Yah-weh's self-demonstration has a provisional character. On the contrary: the markedly hymnal and confessional language which Deutero-Isaiah employs actually stresses again and again the unequivocal and definitive self-unveiling of this God. The multifarious variations of the formula "I am Yahweh" in Deutero-Isaiah have precisely this intention.

Let me again make this clear by adding another quotation to the Deutero-Isaiah texts quoted above: "Thus says Yahweh, the King of Is-rael and its Redeemer, Yahweh Sabaoth: 'I am the first and I am the last; besides me there is no god' " (44:6). Nowhere is this unambiguity subsequently declared to be something provisional—except by Christian dogmatics. And anyone who has a feeling for tight-knit language will perhaps find Deutero-Isaiah's brief formulation even more unequivocal, where the text simply reads: "I am He" (אֲנִי הוּא), especially emphati-cally perhaps in 48:12: "I am He, I am the first and I am the last." This "I am He" is the most pregnant abbreviated form of the "monotheis-tic" acknowledgment as we find it in 1 Kings 18, Deuteronomy 4, and elsewhere.

God has manifested himself in Israel as himself—that is, he has done so for us, Jews, Christians, and Muslims: *only* in Israel. We know no God

---

trans., *Essays on Old Testament Interpretation,* trans. ed. J. L. Mays (London: SCM Press, 1963).

12. *Offenbarung als Geschichte,* 103.

other than the God of Israel, who has made himself known to us in Israel. But this "in Israel" has different aspects.

First of all it means: in Israel's history, in God's historical acts for Israel. That is what the Old Testament says. But it also says that this is not equally true of every random historical act. Thus the beginning of the Decalogue says: "I am Yahweh your God, who brought you out of the land of Egypt, out of the house of bondage." And in Hosea we read similarly: "I am Yahweh your God from the land of Egypt" (13:4). Bringing Israel out of Egypt is the foundational saving act. The others are based on that, and can be experienced as self-demonstrations of the God who is mighty in history inasmuch as they confirm him to be the God who brought Israel out of Egypt.

We therefore have to reverse Pannenberg's sentence: "The self-demonstration of Israel's God is to be found not only at the end, but at the beginning of Israel's history." The whole history of Israel's faith—*and* the faith of the religions that followed it—has its foundation in this. For we do not believe in a God of whom we do not know how he will show himself and manifest himself to us; we hope that the God who at the beginning demonstrated himself as himself in Israel will also demonstrate himself as himself in the future too, in the sense of the paraphrase of his name in Exod. 3:14: "I will be there as the one I will be there as," or: "I will manifest myself as the one I will manifest myself to be." He is "Yahweh, the God of your fathers, the God of Abraham, the God of Isaac, and the God of Jacob—this is my name for ever" (v. 15).

But it is not enough—theologically and philosophically—to talk in this way about God's revelation in Israel's history. For after all, historical events only become the revelation of God when they are *experienced* as such by the people affected, and when this experience is assimilated, thought about, formulated, and passed on. We cannot in all honesty simply say: God has revealed himself in the deliverance of Israel from Egypt. We can only say: Israel experienced this event as the fundamental salvific act in which God revealed himself as the One who he is. For Israel, this event belongs within a wider context: this God is the God of the patriarchs—Abraham, Isaac, and Jacob—and he is the God who gave Israel the land in which it is to live as his people, and in which it thinks about, formulates, and passes on to succeeding generations the experiences which it has had with this God—generations which in their turn will have to think about them afresh and formulate them as their experience with this God.

The history of these experiences and theological insights is part of what we mean when we say that God revealed himself "in Israel." The history of experience, the history of reflection, the history of reception all belong to this assertion. Not merely the bare facts—this was what was often thrown at us in the hermeneutical discussion of the early 1960s— but their appropriation and assimilation belong to the revelation of God in Israel. Insofar the Old Testament is not merely a witness to God's revelation, but itself has a share in the process of revelation.[13]

But to say "in Israel" now does not exclude the universalist aspect; it includes it. I have already tried to show this from biblical texts. Israel's God reveals himself to all human beings as Israel's God, that is to say as the One who has made himself known to Israel first and enduringly as himself. Let me once again set two texts over against one another: In Ps. 76:1 we read: "God has made himself known in Judah, his name is great in Israel." And in Mal. 1:11: "From the rising of the sun to its setting my name is great among the nations." It is the same *one* name of the same *one* God, who is revealed in Israel and among the nations. The opening to the nations is not merely a late stage. It is occasionally more strongly stressed in the late period, but this does not mean that what has been hitherto has now been overstepped; least of all does it mean that "particularism" has now been surmounted.

The tension between Israel's particularism and the universalism of its knowledge of God remains—for Israel, and for "the nations." For these nations the problem is turned upside down, so to speak: they cannot have the universalist "monotheist" understanding of God except through Israel's particularism. It is not their particularism—on the contrary, they are denied the right to any such particularism. But they have to endure the fact that Israel adheres to its own particularism, and must adhere to it, and that this means that an unsurmountable difference between Israel and the nations continues to exist; but that in spite of this they are still conjoined in their knowledge of the *one* God who has revealed himself in Israel for all nations.

---

13. Cf. here also, considerably earlier, R. Rendtorff, "Geschichte und Überlieferung," in R. Rendtorff and K. Koch, eds., *Studien zur Theologie der alttestamentlichen Überlieferung* (Neukirchen, 1961), 81–94 (= R. Rendtorff, *Gesammelte Studien zum Alten Testament* [Munich, 1975], 23–38).

CHAPTER 11

"Covenant" as a Structuring
Concept in Genesis and Exodus

Old Testament scholarship is on the move. This is, of course, a truism. But I feel it necessary to emphasize the experimental character of much of what we are doing at the moment. In German scholarship, which is my own background, the majority still hold to the traditional methods established since the end of the nineteenth century, such as *Literarkritik,* or since the beginning of this century, such as *Formgeschichte,* or developed in the 1940s and 1950s, such as *Überlieferungsgeschichte.* In other parts of the world, Old Testament scholarship meanwhile has undergone fundamental changes.[1] It is out of this complex context that I am attempting to break new ground.

As befits a student of Gerhard von Rad, my main interest is a theological one. What would be the most appropriate approach to a theological understanding of Old Testament texts? This question has been the subject of deep reflection by several Old Testament scholars during the last decade. In the limited framework of these introductory remarks, I want to quote only two of them.

In his book *Old Testament Theology: A Fresh Approach,* Ronald Clements thoroughly analyzes the problems, in particular the "inescapable tension in the very goal of writing an Old Testament theology." He writes:

Lecture delivered in English at the Annual Meeting of the Society of Biblical Literature in Chicago in 1988.
1. Cf. chapter 3 above.

The Old Testament is a literature, whereas a theology is concerned with the world of ideas and their systematic formulation. . . . It is possible for us to extract the ideas, so far as is attainable, and to pay little attention to their literary setting. Conversely we may concentrate our attention upon the literature and its complex history, giving only scant attention to the systematic ordering of the religious ideas which we find in it.[2]

I want to go beyond this alternative, not only by an "as well as" but also by assuming that the Old Testament texts in their present form are theological by nature, and that, therefore, the texts themselves contain the—or at least a—theological message.

My position is close to that of Brevard Childs in the introductory chapter of his *Old Testament Theology in a Canonical Context*. Childs puts the question differently by posing the problem of "the relationship between text and process":

The final canonical literature reflects a long history of development in which the received tradition was selected, transmitted and shaped by hundreds of decisions. . . . That the final form of the biblical text has preserved much from the earlier stages of Israel's reflection is fully evident. However, the various elements have been so fused as to resist easy diachronic reconstructions which fracture the witness of the whole.[3]

Indeed, "the witness of the whole," that is, the text as we have it before us, in my view, should be the first and main subject of our theological interpretation of the Hebrew Bible. I want to demonstrate this by focusing on a central aspect of the first two books of the Pentateuch.

I

Let me begin with the primeval history in Genesis 1–11. It is obvious that in these chapters different aspects of the beginnings and foundations of the world's and humanity's history are closely interwoven. The narrative begins with creation, but there follows immediately the endangering of the original intention of the Creator by human sin (Genesis 3–4). This development reaches its peak in Genesis 6, where God himself declares that he is going to destroy his own creation. The structure of the text makes the contrast between God's intention and the actual situation of

2. R. R. Clements, *Old Testament Theology: A Fresh Approach* (London: Marshall, Morgan & Scott; Atlanta: John Knox Press, 1978), 32.

3. B. S Childs, *Old Testament Theology in a Canonical Context* (Philadelphia: Fortress Press; London: SCM Press, 1985), 11. In the framework of this paper it is not my intention to discuss the structure of a "theology of the Old Testament," but I consider Childs's *Theology* to be much more "systematic" than "canonical."

the creation evident. In Gen. 1:31, after the completion of God's work it is stated:

וירא אלהים את־כל־אשר עשה והנה־טוב מאר

"And God saw everything that he had made, and behold, it was very good."

In contrast, Gen. 6:12 reads:

וירא אלהים את־הארץ והנה נשחתה

"And God saw the earth, and behold, it was corrupt."

The parallelism in the Hebrew text of these two passages is evident and obviously intentional.

The world is no longer "very good," and God decides to destroy it. But he makes one exception: "But Noah found favor in the eyes of the Lord" (6:8). God announces his decision to Noah by saying: "But I will establish my covenant with you" (v. 18). This is the first time that the word ברית appears in the Old Testament. It is spoken as a promise to Noah that God will spare Noah himself together with all living beings that enter the ark together with him (v. 19). This points to chap. 9, where the term *běrît* is developed in detail.

But before that, after the flood, God declares: "While the earth remains, seedtime and harvest, cold and heat, summer and winter, day and night, shall not cease" (8:22). The introduction to that promise is given by an almost word-for-word repetition of the statement God made as a reason for his decision to destroy the earth: "For the imagination of humanity's heart is evil from its youth" (8:21; cf. 6:5: "that every imagination of the thoughts of its heart was only evil continually"). This repetition is a well-known crux for the interpreter because the same assessment of human nature seems to serve two contradictory functions; the first time, as a reason for the coming of the flood; the second time, however, as a reason for the opposite. Yet the intention is clear: human beings have not changed after the flood. Their יצר־הרע, their evil inclination, still exists. Nevertheless, God promises not to do again what he has done and guarantees the continuation of the basic preconditions for life upon the earth.

Chapter 9, in particular vv. 8-11, serves as a solemn confirmation of that promise. What God has just declared will be the content of his *běrît:* not to bring a flood over the earth again and not to destroy living beings again. But before that confirmation, God makes it clear that this world is no longer "very good." God reconfirms his blessing of fertility (v. 1), but immediately he adds that peace no longer prevails between human beings and animals (v. 2), or among human beings themselves, so that a strict commandment is needed to prevent murder (vv. 5-6). This commandment is related to Genesis 1. Every human being is created in God's own image (9:6; cf. 1:26-27); therefore, according to rabbinic tradition, to kill one human being means to kill all humanity. Within the composition of the primeval history, this commandment is also related to chap. 4, Cain's murder of his brother Abel. This murder was the first deed committed after human beings were released into autonomy. It demonstrates what human beings are able to do. Therefore, the first commandment given to them after the flood with regard to interhuman relations is the prohibition of murder.

The importance of Genesis 9, in addition to its fundamental function in the structure of the primeval history (to which I shall return below), lies in the different elements related to the idea of bĕrît. I want to mention two of them: first, the term זכר, "to remember." God will "remember" his covenant (vv. 15-16), with the consequence that he will do (in this case: not do) what he has promised. The reader of chap. 9 recalls having met the word זכר before, namely, at the turning point of the flood story: "And God remembered Noah and all the beasts and all the cattle that were with him in the ark" (8:1), after which the flood subsided. Now the reader understands the relation between the bĕrît promised to Noah in 6:18 and God's remembering.

The second element is the "sign of the covenant" (אות־הברית, vv. 12-17). In addition to God's remembrance, the covenant is confirmed by a visible sign. It is the rainbow, which God himself will look at and then remember his covenant. But also human beings will be able to see it and then will be assured that, however terrible the thunderstorms might be, God will be faithful to his promise and will not bring the flood back upon the earth. (At this point, I couldn't help thinking what would happen if on "the day after" the rainbow were to become invisible in the "nuclear night," as the experts nicely call it. Will God's covenant be valid even after humanity has committed the final sin of self-destruction? But this question goes beyond the interpretation of Hebrew Scripture.)

Now let me come back to the composition of the primeval history. If my reading of these chapters is correct—or at least possible—the first result would be that Genesis 9 is an integral part of the primeval history, perhaps one could even say, the key to understanding the primeval history as a whole. Here all the lines meet, and only from here can the whole story be interpreted.

The message is, first of all, that humanity does not live in a creation that God has called "very good." This creation does not exist any longer. It has nearly been destroyed because of human sin, in spite of which it still exists because of the grace of God. The guarantee for its continued existence is the covenant God has established with humanity and with the whole creation. The addressees of this message are those who live in the real world as it is, that is, from the biblical point of view after the flood. Therefore, we should not read Genesis 1 apart from its continuation, the story of the fall as well as that of the flood, and finally that of the covenant after the flood.

From a diachronic point of view Genesis 1 and 9 form a frame surrounding the first main part of the primeval history. At the same time, these chapters, in particular chap. 9, are not comprehensible without the material enclosed by this frame. It seems highly unlikely, therefore, that these "Priestly" chapters ever existed apart from the present context; rather, they were formulated in order to be put where they are now.[4] Whether the rest of the material could be interpreted without the frame formed by chaps. 1 and 9 is another question. It may be possible and to a certain degree meaningful to interpret the individual stories independently, but in my view it would not make sense to try to "reconstruct" a "non-Priestly" primeval history.

II

Let me turn to another key text of the Pentateuch: the Sinai story. Usually Exodus 19–24 is treated as an independent unit. Taking this as a starting point, we may observe that this unit is framed by passages using the word *běrît*. In the first divine speech in 19:4-6, the word has a central function: "Now therefore, if you will obey my voice and keep my covenant..." (v. 5). Here the vocabulary related to ברית is enlarged by the word שמר, "to keep." Whereas in the primeval history the covenant was given by God without mentioning any human reaction or activity, here the human side is particularly emphasized. Accordingly, the word שמר refers to the commandments that will be given only in the following chapters. The introductory speech, therefore, is to be understood as the first part of a framework whose counterpart is to be found in the final ceremony in 24:3-8, where the word ברית plays a major role.

There can be no doubt that the first part of the Sinai story is aimed at the covenant ceremony in chap. 24. There is also a specific relation between chap. 19 and chap. 24. According to 19:6 the whole people of

---

4. This is also true for the chronological framework, including the *tôlĕdôt*-formulas. The still-unsolved question of the composition of the flood story I must leave aside in this context.

Israel shall be a "kingdom of priests," and it looks like a demonstration of that notion when in 24:5 precisely the "young men of the Israelites" (נערי בני ישראל) are sent to serve as priests offering the sacrifices. Afterward, a number of "the elders of Israel" (זקני ישראל) accompany Moses in the ascent to the mountain. The whole story comes to an end with the blood ceremony and the solemn establishing of the covenant.

But actually the story continues. While Moses is on top of the mountain in order to receive the blueprints of the sanctuary that should be erected, and finally also the tablets with the divine commandments (24:12—31:18), the people commit the sin with the golden calf (32:1-6). Everything seems to be finished. The covenant is broken, which Moses demonstrates by breaking the tablets (v. 19). Even the existence of the people is at stake when God declares that he has determined to annihilate them (v. 10). Only after Moses' intercession does God finally change his mind and agree to reestablish the covenant. This is reported in chap. 34 where, again, the word běrît has a central function. First, in v. 10 God declares that he will establish a(nother) covenant: הנה אנכי כרת ברית, "Behold, I make a covenant." And after the renewed declaration of the divine commandments, God (re)establishes the covenant (v. 27) on the basis of the "words of the covenant" (דברי הברית, v. 28).

Of course, a number of diachronic problems remain. Nevertheless, the meaning of the composition we have before us is clear: the first covenant is broken on Israel's part; God determines to destroy the people; Moses intervenes; and finally the covenant is established again. In this sequence of events, there is a striking parallelism with the primeval history. In both cases the original gift of God (creation/covenant) is counteracted by human sin; in both cases God determines to destroy the responsible human community (humanity/Israel); in both cases the future depends on one man (Noah/Moses);[5] and in both cases the covenant is finally (re)established.

One particular detail makes the parallelism even more obvious. Above I discussed the explicit repetition of God's assessment of sinful human nature before the establishment of the covenant (Gen. 8:21). We find the same kind of repetition in the Sinai story. As a reason for his determination to destroy the people, God calls them a "stiff-necked people" (Exod. 32:9). The same expression is used, this time in Moses' words, immediately before God's announcement of the reestablishing of the covenant:

---

5. The differences in the respective roles of Noah and Moses are obvious, according to the different contexts; but with regard to the structure of both texts, in my view the parallelism is clearly visible.

"If I have gained your favor, O Lord, then may the Lord go in our midst, although it is a stiff-necked people, and pardon our iniquity and our sin, and take us as your own possession" (34:9; cf. also 33:4, 5). And God answers: "Behold, I make a covenant' (v. 10). Like human nature in the primeval history, Israel's nature has not changed. But in spite of that, God decides to reestablish the covenant.

Just as humanity no longer lives within the original creation, but in a restored one whose existence is guaranteed by God's grace, so also Israel no longer lives within the first covenant, but in a reestablished one guaranteed by God's grace. Both humanity and Israel are sinful, and remain sinful. Humanity's sin severely endangered the existence of the creation; Israel's sin endangered God's covenant with Israel. But both times God decides not to annihilate humanity or Israel but to grant them a continued existence guaranteed by his covenant. In this (second) covenant the sinfulness of humanity or Israel is, so to speak, taken for granted. In other words, humanity's or Israel's sin no longer can endanger the very existence of the creation or the covenant because God himself guarantees its continuation, despite human sin, because of his grace.

In the particular case of God's covenant with Israel, Israel can break the covenant, and will break it many times, as the Hebrew Bible tells us. Nevertheless, the covenant itself will never be broken because God has promised to keep it.[6] Here the biblical terminology is of major significance. We have already noted the importance of the word שָׁמַר, "to keep." Israel is admonished again and again to keep the covenant, but for his part, God will keep it. In the Hebrew Bible several times he is called שֹׁמֵר־הַבְּרִית, "the one who keeps the covenant."[7] This is a sort of epithet that characterizes God's nature and behavior toward his people.

III

The result of our observations is twofold. First, we have seen the parallel structure of the primeval history and the Sinai story. Second, we have recognized the importance of the notion of *bĕrît* in both contexts. Now the question arises whether and how the use of the term *bĕrît* in the rest of the books of Genesis and Exodus can be related to these two key texts. In other words, is there a consistent use of the word *bĕrît?*

---

6. This is true for the Hebrew Bible in general, where it is never said that God has broken or ever will break his covenant, no matter how often Israel might break it.

7. This expression always appears within the formula שֹׁמֵר הַבְּרִית וְהַחֶסֶד (Deut. 7:9; 1 Kings 8:23 [=2 Chron. 6:14]; Dan. 7:9; Neh. 1:5; 9:32; cf. Deut. 7:12).

In the patriarchal story the word *bĕrît* appears for the first time in Gen. 15:18-21. The chapter contains a narrative explication of God's promise to Abraham to give him offspring and the land. This is summarized in the solemn establishing of a *bĕrît* whose content is explicitly formulated: "To your descendants I give the land," followed by a detailed description of the extent of the land and an enumeration of its present inhabitants. Here again God gives the covenant. There is no mention of anything Abraham has to do on his part.

The same promise is repeated in Genesis 17, where the word *bĕrît* appears no fewer than thirteen times.[8] First, in vv. 1-8 the same twofold content of *bĕrît* is explicated that we saw in chap. 15: God will make Abraham "the father of a multitude of nations" (vv. 4-6)—and in addition to that will be the God of Abraham and his descendants (vv. 7, 8b); and he will give them the land (v. 8a). (To the second part I will return below.)

In the book of Exodus there are several references to this *bĕrît*. In 2:24 it is said that "God remembered his covenant with Abraham, with Isaac, and with Jacob" (... ויזכר אלהים את־בריתו). This is the point at which God is going to send Moses to liberate Israel from Egyptian slavery. In 6:2-8 the reference to God's covenant with the fathers is repeated in the framework of God's solemn self-revelation to Moses. In an elaborate sentence (vv. 4-5) God recalls that he has established his covenant with the fathers (אתם הקמתי את־בריתי) "to give them the land of Canaan," and continues by saying that he has heard the groaning of the people of Israel, and has "remembered" his covenant (ואזכר את־בריתי).

In the Sinai story we find two explicit references to God's promise to the fathers to give them the land, the first in Moses' words reminding God of his promise (Exod. 32:13), the second in God's own words sending Moses to lead the people into the promised land (33:1-3). In neither case does the word *bĕrît* appear; instead the verb נשבע, "to swear," is used.[9] But then, in chap. 34, the announcement of the reestablishing of the *bĕrît* (v. 10) is followed by a list of peoples God will expel before Israel (v. 11), like the lists mentioned in both Gen. 15:19-20 and Exod. 33:2.[10] Here we

---

8. According to B. Jacob (*Das erste Buch der Tora: Genesis* [Berlin, 1934; reprint, New York: Ktav, n.d.], 431), this is already mentioned by R. Ishmael in *m. Ned.* 3:11, where all thirteen occurrences of *bĕrît* are related to circumcision (ברית מילה).

9. As for the diachronic aspects, see n. 11 below.

10. According to Exod. 33:2, God's messenger (or angel) shall expel these peoples; cf. also 23:20-33. In the latter case the Israelites are warned not to make a *bĕrît* with these peoples (v. 32); the same is said in 34:12, 15; cf. also Deut. 7:1-2. The interrelation between God's covenant with Israel and the warning not to make a covenant with foreign nations deserves further attention.

have before us a distinct semantic field that is connected with, but not limited to, the use of the word *bĕrît*.[11]

I now return to the second part of Genesis 17, the covenant of circumcision, the בְּרִית מִילָה. The structure of chap. 17 is significant: God begins to speak, and twice the sentence is opened by אֲנִי, the divine "I" (vv. 1, 4). The next divine speech turns to Abraham and begins: וְאַתָּה, "and you" (or "as for you"), and continues: אֶת־בְּרִיתִי חִשְׁמֹר, "my covenant you shall keep" (v. 9). It is, of course, the same covenant. But there is an element of human response which belongs indispensably to that covenant. This response shall be "a sign of the covenant" (אוֹת בְּרִית, v. 11) that indicates that this particular human being belongs to the people which has received God's covenant. In this case, in contrast to Genesis 9, the sign has to be performed by the human beings who thereby acknowledge themselves to be God's partners in his covenant.

There is still one more text to be included. In Exod. 31:12-17, again, a "sign of the covenant" is mentioned, namely, the Sabbath. This day, as the seventh day of the week, is related to the seventh day of the week of creation, when God rested from his creative work. Therefore, the Israelites shall rest on this day. But why is this called a *bĕrît?* First it is called a sign (אוֹת, v. 13). The terminology clearly corresponds to that of Genesis 9: "between me and you throughout your generations" (בֵּינִי וּבֵינֵיכֶם לְדֹרֹתֵיכֶם; cf. Gen. 9:12). But in the case of the Sabbath, the sign has to be performed by human beings, as has the sign of circumcision (Genesis 17). Thus, there is a double relationship, to chap. 9 as well as to chap. 17. In the latter, we find the expression בְּרִית עוֹלָם, "an everlasting covenant," twice—first used for the covenant given by God (v. 7), and second for the covenant to be performed by Abraham and his descendants as a human response (v. 13). The same expression, בְּרִית עוֹלָם, is used for the Sabbath in Exod. 31:16, that is, for the covenant to be performed by the Israelites. Is it also to be understood as a human response? If so, where is the first part to be found, the divine covenant to which the Sabbath corresponds? In my view the answer is clear: the covenant of the Sabbath responds to the covenant given to Noah (Genesis 9). There

---

11. As for the diachronic aspects, it is obvious that some of the texts quoted are related to the "Deuteronomistic" tradition (Genesis 15 and Exodus 32–34), whereas others belong to the "Priestly" texts (Genesis 17; Exodus 2 and 6). Yet it is interesting to see how in the final composition these two groups are related to each other, or even intertwined. From a compositional point of view, in Genesis 15 one might see a "Deuteronomistic" point of reference for the mentioning of God's promise to the fathers in Exodus 32–34. In this case, unlike in Exodus 32–34, the word *bĕrît* is explicitly used for God's promise to give the land to Abraham's descendants.

also we find the expression עולם ברית עולם (v. 16; cf. v. 12: לדרת עולם).
Thus, God's everlasting covenant given to the world and humanity finds
its human response in the Sabbath, which is called "an everlasting covenant" as well. The explicit reference in Exodus 31 is to Genesis 1, to
creation itself. But there the expression *běrît* is not used. Creation can
only be called a *běrît* from the point of view of its restoration after the
flood.

IV

To summarize: the primeval history in Genesis 1–11 and the Sinai story
in Exodus 19–34 show a parallel structure. In both cases the first gift
of God (creation/covenant) is endangered by human sin and threatened
with destruction because of God's wrath. In both cases God changes
his mind because of (the intervention of) one man (Noah/Moses). In
both cases God promises not to bring destruction again (on humanity/on
Israel), and in order to confirm that he (re)establishes his covenant (*běrît*).
Now neither humanity nor Israel lives in the original situation of creation
or covenant, but in a restored one, which is spoiled by human sin but
whose continuous existence, nevertheless, is guaranteed by the *běrît* God
himself has established.

The use of the word *běrît* in other texts between these two key stories shows a network of references and interrelations whereby human
involvement in the covenant as a response to God's gift is emphasized in
different ways: circumcision is the first "sign of covenant" as a response
to God's promise to Abraham (Genesis 17). Obedience to the commandments is Israel's response to God's guidance and gift of the covenant
(Exod. 19:4-6; 24:3-8), and the Sabbath as a "sign" of the "everlasting
covenant" (31:12-17) links Israel's religious life to the first covenant by
which God restored the creation once and for all (Genesis 9).

CHAPTER 12

The Birth of the Deliverer:
"The Childhood of Samuel"
Story in Its
Literary Framework

In the last ten or twenty years, new questions have come up for discussion in exegetical work on the Old Testament. Some of these new
approaches come from "outside," from other disciplines—from literary
studies especially, but from anthropology and sociology too.[1] There are
already many connecting threads between these disciplines themselves,
and in the process of their reception and application to biblical studies these mutual links are actually accentuated. Combined with these
approaches are others which come more from "inside"—canon criticism, for example. But these "inside" approaches also have a share in
the mutual relations between the other disciplines I have mentioned.

It is not my intention in this essay to enter into a discussion about
methodological principles. I should like rather to discuss the way an individual text, which itself already has a number of different strata, is
interwoven into its wider context, and what this means for its interpretation; and for this purpose I shall take an example chosen almost at
random. I am here starting from the final form of the text, in its immediate and its wider context, but at the same time I shall keep in mind the
fact that the present text probably has a more or less long, and a more
or less complex, history behind it.[2] The hermeneutical questions which
emerge from the interaction between these two aspects will be our main
concern here.

1. See here, for example, R. C. Culley, "Exploring New Directions," in D. A. Knight
and G. M. Tucker, eds., *The Hebrew Bible and Its Modern Interpreters* (Chico, Calif.:
Scholars Press, 1985), 167–200; also chapter 3 below.
2. I see this approach in the wider context of "canon criticism," in which very different
emphases have developed and are still developing. See here G. T. Sheppard, "Canon
Criticism," in *ABD* 1 (New York: Doubleday, 1992).

I

Hugo Gressmann headed his interpretation of 1 Samuel 1–3: "The Childhood Idyll of Samuel."[3] In this "story about the childhood of the later renowned priest Samuel" "interest is concentrated wholly on the life of an individual and the people who come into contact with him."[4] The term "idyll" was already used by Wellhausen[5] and has since been taken up by other commentators as well as Gressmann (W. Nowack, H. W. Hertzberg).

Of course the interpreters are aware that the story is now part of a larger complex, in which it has been given a more than idyllic significance. But this change of significance is generally assumed to have taken place only at a later level, or stage, in the redaction process, whereas the story itself is viewed as if it were untouched by this later intervention. And here, generally speaking, only the elements that point ahead are noticed, whereas the connections with what has gone before receive little attention. In the rest of this essay I should like to consider the way this unit of text is interwoven both with what goes before and with what comes afterward.

The story tells that a certain man[6] had two wives. One of them had children, the other had none. For the reader of this story in its "canonical" context[7] (or for the listener to it), this is a "signal."[8] It inevitably calls to mind the fortunes of the matriarchs—first and foremost the fortunes of Jacob's two wives, Leah and Rachel, whose destinies were shaped

3. H. Gressmann, *Die älteste Geschichtsschreibung und Prophetie Israels (von Samuel bis Amos und Hosea),* SAT 2/1 (Göttingen, 1921), 1ff.

4. Ibid., 5.

5. J. Wellhausen, *Die Composition des Hexateuchs und der historischen Bücher des Alten Testaments* (3d ed. Berlin, 1899, 4th ed. 1964), 238 n. 1: "In chaps. 4–6 we have history, in chaps. 1–3 an idyll full of significance."

6. Elkanah's genealogy undoubtedly had some special significance for author and readers/listeners, but we are no longer able to discover what it was. The explanation of the curious form of the place name *hārāmatajim* is disputed.

7. Here I am taking up the term "canonical" form of the text, which Brevard Childs especially brought into the discussion. I am using the term to designate the "final form" of the text as we have it, the intention of which I am trying to discover. Questions about the theological "relevance" of the final form of the text (which Childs raised and which have since been hotly discussed) are not under discussion here. Cf. especially B. S. Childs, *Introduction to the Old Testament as Scripture* (Philadelphia: Fortress Press; London: SCM Press, 1979) and the subsequent discussion in *JSOT* 16 (1980); also J. Barr, *Holy Scripture: Canon, Authority, Criticism* (Philadelphia: Westminster Press; Oxford: Clarendon Press, 1983).

8. I am using this expression as a summary term for "keywords" in the text which draw listeners' attention to something particular, or point them to something special, and which are intended to signalize something. This includes *Leitworte,* in Martin Buber's sense, but what is meant goes further than that.

by the same situation and its problems (Gen. 29:31ff.).[9] But we are told that the other matriarchs as well, Sarah and Rebekah, were also initially childless (Genesis 16ff.; 25:21). The story of Samson's birth too (Judges 13) belongs to the whole complex of what is being called to mind here.

But this now also awakens the expectation that this childlessness will be ended as the story goes on (for that, after all, is the only reason why it is mentioned at all)—and that the expected birth is more than merely a personal event for Hannah herself. But this means that in its canonical context the story from its very first sentences onward is anything but a family idyll—quite apart from the question of whether it ever was one, at some earlier stage.[10]

On the contrary, readers[11] now know—or will at least suspect—that the birth which can be expected in the course of the narrative is going to have some special importance. But they already know more even than that. For if they are not reading this story as a timeless idyll, this also means that they will understand it in its narrative context. And it is immediately preceded by the final sentence in the book of Judges: "In those days there was no king in Israel; every man did what was right in his own eyes" (Judg. 21:25). According to the context of the book of Judges, it is perfectly clear that this final comment is meant in a negative, pejorative sense. The fact that the people did whatever seemed good to them was an expression of license; and when this is set over against the lack of a king as ordering power, it is simply another way of saying: anarchy ruled. This becomes very much clearer still when we relate this conclusion of the book of Judges to the account at the beginning of the book. There we are told that after the death of Joshua, who had succeeded Moses, the people of Israel's first great leader, a generation grew up "who did not know YHWH or the work which he had done for Israel. And the people of Israel did what was evil in the sight of YHWH" (Judg. 2:10b, 11). The formulations are exactly parallel: "Every man did what was

---

9. K. Budde writes here: "Elkanah suffers the fate of the patriarch Jacob" (KHC 8:3). But Elkanah's fate is *not* the subject here, not even in the "patriarchal" context of the Old Testament. Budde's remark says very much more about the interpreter's context than it does about the text.

10. It is clear that this approach also implies critical questions to form criticism in the classical form in which Hermann Gunkel initiated it. Cf. here the concluding paragraphs in the present essay.

11. Even in the final stage of the text we probably have to do not only with readers, but above all with listeners to stories that were read aloud—or perhaps even recited from memory. But for simplicity's sake, in what follows I shall confine myself to the word "readers," especially since we are after all also concerned about our own understanding as readers of the text.

right in his own eyes" (אִישׁ הַיָּשָׁר בְּעֵינָיו יַעֲשֶׂה) is the precise counterpart to "The people of Israel did what was evil in the sight of YHWH"
(וַיַּעֲשׂוּ בְנֵי־יִשְׂרָאֵל אֶת־הָרַע בְּעֵינֵי יהוה). So readers of the last sentence
in the book of Judges (which they have already met word for word in
17:6) already know how they are supposed to interpret it: that what was
"right" in the eyes of the kingless Israelites was "wrong" in the sight
of YHWH. The readers of the story of Elkanah and his two wives have
just read these sentences,[12] and they must therefore now expect that the
impending birth will have something to do with this godless anarchy. So
it is surely not by chance when Elkanah makes a pilgrimage to Shiloh
(v. 3). He does this regularly (מִיָּמִים יָמִימָה), according to v. 7 "year for
year," which no doubt means once every year. The occasion of his pilgrimage is not mentioned—perhaps it was one of the three great yearly
feast days. Moreover, "Why Elkanah should have gone to Shiloh particularly, and not to other equally renowned sanctuaries, such as Bethel,
Mizpah, or Shechem, some of which may well have been nearer his own
home, is not discussed."[13] But the fact that Shiloh was not an arbitrarily
chosen place of pilgrimage is immediately signalized. The purpose of
his pilgrimage was "to pray and to sacrifice to YHWH Sabaoth." This is
already an indirect reference to the ark, which then stood in Shiloh (3:3),
and with which the name YHWH Sabaoth (יהוה צְבָאוֹת) was firmly associated (we need only look at 2 Sam. 6:2).[14] This particular name for
God is not used without deliberate intention: that already emerges from
the fact that here the name YHWH Sabaoth is used for the very first time
in the Old Testament. And this also makes it evident that the story has
now passed beyond the limits of Elkanah's private family life. Later on
Hannah also uses this name for God in her prayer, which on the face of it
is concerned only with the entirely personal problem of her childlessness
(v. 11); and in promising that her prayer will be answered, Eli talks about
"the God of Israel" (v. 17).

In v. 3b the names of Eli's two sons, Hophni and Phinehas, are mentioned almost by the way and without any detectable significance for the
immediate context. The reader will remember later that they have been
mentioned, when the account tells that in their behavior they typify the

---

12. Cf. J. A. Soggin, *Judges: A Commentary*, trans. from Italian by J. Bowden (London:
SCM Press; Philadelphia: Westminster Press, 1982), 305: "Thus the book of Judges ends,
as it were, in suspense. It is clear that according to its present, final structure, it has to
be continued elsewhere, because its narrative now forms part of a wider context, that of
the Deuteronomic history."

13. H. W. Hertzberg, *Die Samuelbücher*, ATD 10 (Göttingen, 1956), 13.

14. From when this association dated is irrelevant for our present context.

general downfall of the priestly house of Shiloh, and with that the downfall of Israel in general (2:12ff., 22ff.; 3:13b). This also shows that here
two narrative motifs are intertwined—the theme of Samuel's beginnings,
and the theme of Eli and his sons, or the end of the house of Eli, which
also means the end of an epoch.[15] The beginning of what is new is set
over against the downfall of the old.

II

Many different signals have therefore now been given, showing that
something must and will happen to change Israel's calamitous situation.
In the story itself, interest now becomes increasingly concentrated on
Samuel. After his birth, his mother herself does her part in seeing to it
that her own fortunes recede into the background in favor of the fortunes
of the son for whom she had prayed and who had then been promised her
(1:24-28). She gives back to God—and for life—the son for whom she
had entreated (the Hebrew wordplay on שָׁאַלְתִּי and הִשְׁאִלְתִּי in vv. 27f.
can hardly be rendered in translation). The phraseology "no razor shall
touch his head" (v. 11b) is reminiscent of a Nazarite oath. But this is as
a rule restricted to a certain period of time (cf. Numbers 6). So when
Samuel is consecrated for life, it shows that this is something special.
     But before the story continues, Hannah prays once more. The intro-
ductory וַתִּתְפַּלֵּל in 2:1 corresponds to the same word in 1:10. But there
her prayer was complaint and plea. Here it is thanksgiving for the hearing
of her prayer, joined with the fulfillment of her vow. The two correspond,
in their liturgical function too. True, in 1:11 it was only a simple prose
prayer, but it is nevertheless followed by the priestly "oracle of assurance
that the prayer will be answered."[16] In 2:1-10 the prayer is a "psalm,"
which here takes on the function of the prayer of thanksgiving after help
has been experienced.[17]

15. According to what has been said hitherto, however, it seems to me questionable
whether these were originally two independent stories, which were linked together only
at a "secondary" stage. Cf. here the reflections at the end of the present essay.
16. J. Begrich ("Das priesterliche Heilsorakel," ZAW 52 [1934]: 81–91 [= his Gesammelte Studien zum Alten Testament, TBü 21 (Munich, 1964), 217–31]) convincingly
worked out the thesis that complaint/plea and the promise that the prayer will be granted
belong together.
17. On this "liturgical connection" of the psalm with its context see G. C. Macholz
("Untersuchungen zur Geschichte der Samuelüberlieferungen," [Diss., Heidelberg, 1966],
65), who gives convincing reasons for dissenting from the view of many interpreters that
the psalm was "inserted later." The precise definition of the psalm's genre is disputed.
H. Gunkel and J. Begrich (Einleitung in die Psalmen [Göttingen, 1933]) talk on the one

The psalm now goes far beyond the framework of Hannah's individual biography.[18] We find the link in v. 5 especially: "The barren bears seven." But in the context, emphasis is on the psalm's assertion of the fundamental changes which God can bring about, this leading over to the prayer that God will give his king strength and "exalt the horn of his anointed one" (v. 10). The keywords "king" and "anointed one" (מָשִׁיחַ) again call to mind the wider narrative context, and point both forward and backward. Looking to the past, the reader is reminded that lack of a king was the essential reason for the general chaos—so the hope for a new beginning is bound up with the expectation of a king, an "anointed" one. Looking ahead, the passage already anticipates what Samuel will do: he will anoint the king (or the two kings, the first of them being a failure). For this he will fill his "horn" with oil (but only in David's case [1 Sam. 16:1], not in the case of Saul [10:1]!).

But the psalm in 1 Sam. 2:1-10 also forms a bridge linking the beginning of the books of Samuel and their end—that is, the "psalms" in 2 Samuel 22 and 23:1-4. In both the early and the final psalms God is called the "rock" (1 Sam. 2:2; 2 Sam. 22:3 and frequently; 23:3); his epiphany is described in similar terms (1 Sam. 2:10; 2 Sam. 22:8ff.); the theme of raising up and casting down, killing and making alive, occurs in both places (1 Sam. 2:6-8; 2 Sam. 22:17-20, 28); and in both places the psalms conclude by talking about God's blessing and help for the king and "anointed one" (מָשִׁיחַ: 1 Sam. 2:10b; 2 Sam. 22:51). In 2 Samuel 22 David's name is mentioned in this connection; it is not yet known to 1 Samuel 2.[19] Hannah's prayer therefore acts as a prelude to the royal history which, in its talk about "the anointed one,"

hand about "Hannah's song of thanksgiving" (p. 5), but then list the text under "Hymns and Fragments Related to This Genre" (p. 32). C. Westermann mentions it under the genre "Descriptive Psalm of Praise" (*Praise and Lament in the Psalms,* trans. K. R. Crim and R. N. Soulen [Edinburgh: T. & T. Clark, 1981]; translation originally published as *Praise of God in the Psalms* [Atlanta: John Knox Press; London: Epworth Press, 1966]). According to F. Crüsemann, however (*Studien zur Formgeschichte von Hymnus und Danklied in Israel,* WMANT 32 [Neukirchen-Vluyn, 1969], 295ff.), this is the "hymn of an individual."

18. According to Jewish tradition, Hannah is one of the seven women prophets in the Hebrew Bible: Sarah, Miriam, Deborah, Hannah, Abigail (1 Samuel 25), Huldah (2 Kings 22), and Esther. Like others of these women prophets, Hannah is not explicitly called a "prophetess," but she "prays with the spirit of prophecy" (Targum), was filled with the "holy spirit" (Abrabanel). Cf. here R. Gradwohl, *Bibelauslegung aus jüdischen Quellen* (Stuttgart, 1987), 2:87.

19. On these relationships between the psalmlike fragments at the beginning and at the end of the history of David, see especially R. A. Carlson, *David: The Chosen King* (Stockholm, 1964), passim.

in the tradition of the Psalms especially (cf. Ps. 2:2), has "messianic" features.[20]

III

The expectations linked with Samuel are gathered together at the end of chap. 3. Eli offers a pointer to the wider context in which the events are meant to be understood: the Israelites had done "what was evil in the sight of YHWH" (Judg. 2:11), and now YHWH himself will do "what seems good to him" (1 Sam. 3:18). This means initially that YHWH "was with Samuel" (ויהוה היה עמו, v. 19). This finds visible expression in the fact that he "let none of his words [spoken to Samuel] fall to the ground." Because of this, "all Israel from Dan to Beersheba knew that Samuel was confirmed as being YHWH's prophet" (v. 20).

Here a number of keywords turn up again to set this text in relation to its wider context. To say that God let none of his words fall to the ground is a reminder of the corresponding statements at the end of the book of Joshua (Josh. 21:45; 23:14). But a difference can immediately be detected. The words which Joshua was talking about were addressed to Israel (21:45, אל־בית ישראל; 23:14, עליכם). In the case of Samuel, on the other hand, the assertion refers to the words that have been spoken to him himself. Moreover, Samuel, unlike Joshua, is explicitly called נביא, nabi or prophet. So for him, when the divine word comes true, this signifies an endorsement in the sense of Deut. 18:22.[21] In addition, the use of the phrase . . . נאמן לנביא sounds like an echo of Num. 12:7, where Moses is distinguished from other prophets by saying that הוא נאמן בכל־ביתי. In the case of Samuel we are told that "all Israel from Dan to Beersheba" recognized that he had been installed as prophet.

Samuel therefore belongs to the tradition of Moses, who was the first of the prophets. But he is not a second Moses. The fact that he is not himself the expected new leader of the people makes this clear. He does not unite in himself the two functions of prophet and leader of the people as did Moses. Moreover he is not a prophet "like Moses" because God did not speak to him "face to face" (Deut. 34:10).[22]

---

20. See here C. Westermann, "Zur Sammlung des Psalters" (1962) (= his *Forschung am Alten Testament: Gesammelte Studien,* TBü 24 [Munich, 1964], 336–43); G. T. Sheppard, *Wisdom as a Hermeneutical Construct* (Berlin and New York: de Gruyter, 1980), 136–44.

21. Thus Hertzberg, *Samuelbücher,* 229.

22. In Jer. 15:1 Moses and Samuel are mentioned side by side—according to the con-

And yet when he is entrusted with the prophetic office this means a turn of events and a new beginning. For the "prophetic" thing about Samuel is first and foremost his direct reception of God's word. The divine words that are communicated to him are concerned primarily with the installation or rejection of the king who, the context tells us, is now to be expected (1 Samuel 8ff.; 16:1-13). In this way Samuel is Moses' successor in his "prophetic" function. But it is precisely this which enables him to install a political and military leader according to God's charge. In this way the two functions which were united in the person of Moses are certainly separated; but at the same time they are still linked with one another by way of the "prophetic" installation of the king.[23]

IV

I shall break off there. My purpose was to show the complex threads which link the "childhood of Samuel" story with its immediate and its wider context. This now raises the hermeneutical question: Under what aspect do we wish to read the existing text? Today we find a whole series of methodological approaches in which the diachronic question about a possible prehistory behind the present text is not asked at all—or is not asked any longer. Over against this, a "canon-critical" approach as I understand it is very much aware of the diachronic dimension of the text as we have it today. But it differs from the analytical and literary treatment (which is dominant in the German-speaking scholarly tradition particularly) because it does not believe that its function is to work out and reconstruct earlier stages of the text; it views the text in its present, given form as the real object of interpretation.[24]

From this aspect, the question about independent earlier narrative stages of the present text diminishes in importance. The form-critical approach, which was handled in so masterly a fashion by Hermann Gunkel and—particularly where narrative texts are concerned—by Hugo Gressmann, brought us a wealth of important insights about the narrative

text—as potential intercessors; where Samuel is concerned, we should think especially of 1 Samuel 7.

23. On this division of functions and the relationship between king and prophet that results from it, cf. R. Rendtorff, "Erwägungen zur Frühgeschichte des Prophetentums in Israel," *ZTK* 59 (1962): 165–77, esp. 164 (= *Gesammelte Studien zum Alten Testament,* TBü 57 [Munich, 1975], 220–42, esp. 239).

24. Cf. here also chapter 5 above, with the quotation cited there on p. 51 from Childs, *Introduction,* p. 76: "The depth dimension aids in understanding the interpreted text, and does not function independently of it."

structures of Old Testament texts. In this way it acted as an essential counterweight to the purely literary analysis pursued by the Wellhausen school, since it tried much more emphatically to understand the texts in the light of their own self-understanding and their original *Sitz im Leben,* or real-life situation.[25] But at the same time, because it concentrated on "the smallest units," form criticism, even more than literary criticism, furthered inattention to the complexes in which the texts stand now. From the viewpoint of form criticism, these complexes were bound to appear as "later" and "secondary."

In this approach a distinction emerged, simply of its own accord, between the "original" narrators or authors and the later, secondary revisers, editors, and so forth. It was in the nature of things that this should go hand in hand with a scale of value judgments according to which the older stages were as a general rule viewed as the more genuine expressions of Israelite national and religious traditions, whereas the later stages were seen rather as the work of literary compilers or as the result of religiously conditioned revisions and changes.

The approach by way of canon criticism, in contrast, means first of all a change of direction in the line of sight. Since the main interest is concentrated on the text in its now existing form, the wider complexes take on greater importance, whereas the earlier units of transmitted tradition which may underlie them appear essentially as the material with which the authors of the present text worked, and out of which they shaped their "compositions." But hand in hand with this goes a change in the value judgments described earlier. Interest is no longer concentrated first and foremost on the "original," often "folk," utterances. The main attention is directed rather to the consciously formative attempts to grasp and present larger historical and theological complexes.

The way in which these two methods are related to one another is something we shall have to think about further—and shall undoubtedly have to dispute about too. Rudolf Smend has raised the interesting and fruitful question about "theology *in* the Old Testament."[26] At various points in the Old Testament he finds a cohesive theological reflection

25. The reason why they entered into an association with classical literary criticism, although they actually rather presented an alternative to it, was the scholarly consensus existing at the time (the "paradigm" in Thomas S. Kuhn's sense; see his book *The Structure of Scientific Revolutions* [Chicago: Univ. of Chicago Press, 1962; 2d enlarged ed. 1970]).

26. R. Smend, "Theologie im Alten Testament," in *Verifikationen: Festschrift für G. Ebeling* (Tübingen, 1982), 11–26 (= his *Die Mitte des Alten Testaments: Gesammelte Studien,* BEvT 99 [Munich, 1986], 1:104–17, from which the quotations have been taken).

which can "with great caution" be termed theology. But "historically [it is] a relatively late product." At the same time, however, Smend also observes that, compared with Wellhausen, a not inconsiderable change has taken place. "Wellhausen took possession of the pre-theological half of the Old Testament, which was more for him than the whole, by separating out and 'reducing to its proper place' the theological half. But as we see today,[27] this place must be considerably expanded." That is to say, the share of "theology" in the existing text of the Old Testament is very much greater than people often used to think.

At the same time, Smend still clings to the distinction between "Israelite" and "Jewish" which de Wette had already initiated.[28] "The Old Testament is even less an 'Israelite' book, and even more a 'Jewish' one, than Wellhausen assumed, let alone the scholars who preceded and succeeded him." Here it would be important for us now to arrive at agreement as to whether this terminological distinction between what is preexilic Israelite, and what is exilic and postexilic Jewish, should be preserved—and above all, whether we are prepared to take over together with the distinction the value judgments which Wellhausen associated with it, and which he expressed in such forceful terms. This question is especially important because Smend goes on: "But all the more do we have good reason to pay proper regard to [the Old Testament's] 'Israelite' components, especially its prophetic ones, and to do them the justice which Wellhausen and Duhm fought for, and won for them."[29] Does this mean that the justice due to the "Israelite" components must be secured against the "Jewish" ones? And bound up with this is still another question—the question as to what rating is to be given to the distinction between "Israelite" and "Jewish" in the language of Christian theology; for that is where the distinction arose, and it is only there that it is used in this way.

These questions go beyond the scope of what we have considered here. But the fact that they arise almost of themselves does show that the questions bound up with the discussion about the "canon-critical" interpretation of the Old Testament have far-reaching theological impli-

27. This refers to the immediately preceding remark "that the redaction-history research into the Old Testament shows itself to be to an ever-increasing extent a product of exilic and postexilic work" (ibid., 117).

28. De Wette distinguished between "Hebraism" and "Judaism"; see here R. Smend, *Wilhelm Martin Leberecht de Wettes Arbeit am Alten und am Neuen Testament* (Basel, 1958).

29. All quotations from Smend, "Theologie im Alten Testament," 116f.

cations.[30] At the same time, it should be remembered here that every other methodological approach to the Old Testament also has its own theological presuppositions and consequences, even if in many cases these are tacit assumptions, and perhaps unconscious.

30. See n. 7 above.

CHAPTER 13

The Composition of the
Book of Isaiah

The question about the composition of the book of Isaiah in the form in which we now have it is not one of the generally recognized subjects of Old Testament studies. Scholars generally content themselves with saying that the separation of chaps. 40 to 56 is one of the fundamental insights of research, and they then frequently go on to treat the different parts individually (1–39, 40–55 and 56–66), sometimes even in separate chapters.[1] In recent years, however, an increasing number of exegetes have come to feel that this is unsatisfactory. They accept that the question about the intention of the text in its final, present form is a legitimate one,[2] or even themselves seek for answers.[3]

In the course of this development an interesting change has emerged in the question asked. Mowinckel strongly emphasized the inward cohesion of the three parts of the book of Isaiah by assuming the existence of an

1. This is true, for example, of O. Kaiser, *Introduction to the Old Testament,* trans. J. Sturdy (Oxford: Blackwell; Minneapolis: Augsburg Publishing House, 1975); J. A. Soggin, *Introduction to the Old Testament,* trans. from Italian by J. Bowden (London: SCM Press; Philadelphia: Westminster Press, 1976); W. H. Schmidt, *Einführung in das Alte Testament,* 2d ed. (Berlin and New York, 1982).

2. Thus, for example, R. Smend, *Die Entstehung des Alten Testaments,* 2d ed. (Stuttgart, 1981), 144; R. E. Clements, *Isaiah 1–39* (Grand Rapids: Eerdmans; London: Marshall, Morgan & Scott, 1980), 2.

3. E.g., S. Mowinckel, *Prophecy and Tradition* (Oslo, 1946); L. J. Liebreich, "The Compilation of the Book of Isaiah," *JQR,* n.s., 46 (1955–56): 259–77; 47 (1956–57): 114–38; J. Schreiner, "Das Buch jesajanischer Schule," in J. Schreiner, ed., *Wort und Botschaft* (Würzburg, 1967); J. Becker, *Isaias—der Prophet und sein Buch* (Stuttgart, 1968); R. Lack, *La Symbolique du Livre d'Isaïe* (Rome, 1973).

"Isaiah school," to which Deutero-Isaiah (the author of chaps. 40–55) belonged, chaps. 56–66 being written by a group of Deutero-Isaiah's pupils.[4] In this analysis he explicitly declared that the question about the *literary* development of the present book was less important; it played no part in his viewpoint, which was orientated toward "tradition history."[5] But in some more recent studies it is precisely the intention behind the final literary form of the book which is the subject of investigation.

I

The contributions made by R. F. Melugin and P. R. Ackroyd seem to me particularly important and fruitful. Both of them ask the question about the intention of the present composition of the book of Isaiah, but they do not put the question as an alternative, or in antithesis, to previous research. Instead they link up with earlier analyses, and themselves take these an essential step further. Their fundamental methodological insight is that the book of Isaiah consists of a number of part-compositions, some larger, some smaller, each of them with its own structure and function, but yet not completely independent of one another; for between them there are clearly detectable links which must be judged as indications that the book has a deliberate overall composition.

In this light, Ackroyd himself has subjected the two sections Isaiah 1–12[6] and 36–39[7] to a close scrutiny. He sees chaps. 1–12 as a highly complex and carefully thought-through composition, whose function is the "presentation" of the prophet as he is seen, and intended to be seen, from the present day in which the author and his readers were living: "Its effect is to direct the reader back from the situation in which he is confronted with the present collection to the moment of the prophet's activity." In so doing, this composition clearly shows—and particularly through the promises of salvation at the beginning (2:1-5) and at the end (chap. 12)—"the significance of this prophet, the messenger of doom, now fulfilled, as he is also presented as messenger of salvation."[8] In this

4. Mowinckel, *Prophecy and Tradition,* 67ff.

5. Similarly also J. H. Eaton, "The Origin of the Book of Isaiah," *VT* 9 (1959): 138–57; now also see his essay "The Isaiah Tradition," in *Israel's Prophetic Tradition: Essays in Honour of P. R. Ackroyd* (Cambridge: Cambridge Univ. Press, 1982), 58–76.

6. P. R. Ackroyd, "Isaiah I–XII: Presentation of a Prophet," VTSup 29 (1978): 16–48.

7. P. R. Ackroyd, "Isaiah 36–39: Structure and Function," in *Von Kanaan bis Kerala: Festschrift für J. P. M. van der Ploeg* (Neukirchen, 1982), 3–21.

8. Ackroyd, "Isaiah I–XII," 45.

approach, which tries to grasp the intention of the present textual cohesion, the question about the historicity or authenticity of the individual prophetic sayings is explicitly left open: "Whether the prophet himself or his exegetes were responsible, the prophet appears to us as a man of judgment and salvation."[9]

The section comprising chaps. 36–39 also has the function of a "presentation," according to Ackroyd, and supplements chaps. 1–12. Here Ackroyd, taking up Melugin's observations,[10] shows the special relationships between chaps. 36–39 and the section 6:1—9:6.[11] In both of them we find a direct link between narrative elements and prophetic sayings, and both are concerned with the confrontation between the prophet and a king—first Ahaz and then Hezekiah. Apart from the contrasting apposition of the two kings, the aim here is evidently to take the historical example of Jerusalem's deliverance at the time of Hezekiah to show the reliability of the divine assurance of salvation—over and beyond the prophesied exile (39:6f.).

Melugin has made chaps. 40–55 the starting point of his observations about the composition of the book of Isaiah. He too has first of all investigated the structure and composition of this major complex within the book, and has as a result arrived at important new insights into the inner structure of this collection. He has taken as starting point J. Begrich's form-critical approach[12] though complementing it through the findings of J. Muilenburg (with whose methodological procedure he is not, however, otherwise in agreement).[13] It emerges that the individual units which can be determined by way of form criticism have been fused together into small or more extensive compositions which have a particular "kerygmatic" intention: "Isaiah 40–55, then, is a collection of originally independent units, but the arrangement is kerygmatic."[14] An essential foundational element in this "kerygmatic" arrangement of what were originally the smallest units, is the putting together of judgment speeches and promises of salvation into quite small compositions. Otherwise too, the whole collection chaps. 40–55 is dominated by a de-

9. Ibid.
10. R. F. Melugin, *The Formation of Isaiah 40–55* (Berlin and New York: de Gruyter, 1976), 82ff. and 177f.
11. Ackroyd, "Isaiah 36–39," 16ff.
12. J. Begrich, *Studien zu Deuterojesaja* (Stuttgart, 1938; reprinted Munich, 1963).
13. J. Muilenburg, *The Book of Isaiah: Chapters 40–66, IB* 5 (New York and Nashville: Abingdon, 1956), 381–773.
14. Melugin, *Formation of Isaiah 40–55,* 175.

liberately conceived, pronounced contrast—a viewpoint which T. N. D.
Mettinger has brought out even more strongly.[15]

II

Melugin's observations about the interrelations between Isaiah 40–55
and the other parts of the book are of special interest, however. He sees
the study of these interrelations as an essential aspect of his work, or
its necessary development: "Although chapters 40–55 manifest a literary integrity of their own within the Book of Isaiah, the fact remains
that these chapters are somehow related to the whole of Isaiah. Thus our
understanding of the kerygmatic significance of chapters 40–55 will remain incomplete until their theological relationship with the entire book
is explored."[16] Ackroyd has assented to this approach and has taken it
up himself, seeing one aspect of his investigation of Isaiah 36–39 as "to
give more ground for Melugin's claim."[17]

Melugin first sees in the final words of Isaiah 39 a clear pointer to the
intended sequel.[18] The Babylonian exile had already been announced in
Hezekiah's time (39:6f.), but it had been delayed. Here Melugin points to
the correspondence between the assertion in 39:6 that nothing will be left
(יותר) and the beginning of the book: "If YHWH Sabaoth had not left us a
remnant [הותיר]" (1:9). This observation acquires its special weight from
the fact that there is also a correlation between the beginning of chap. 40
and chap. 1, by way of the word עון, "guilt." "Woe to the sinful nation, a
people laden with guilt [עון; RSV 'iniquity']" (1:4)—"Speak to the hearts
of Jerusalem and cry to her that her time of service is ended, that her
guilt [עון] is pardoned" (40:2). We might add that in both cases the root
חטא appears parallel to the word עון (1:4 חֹטֵא; 40:2 חַטֹּאתֶיהָ). In my
view Melugin has lighted upon an important clue here. The deliberate
recapitulation of a certain word or a certain phrase can be a "signal"
indicating that there is a connection between the texts in question—a
connection to which the reader's attention is to be drawn. Let us follow
up this question.

Isaiah 40 begins with the words: "Comfort, comfort my people [נחמו
נחמו עמי]." For the reader of the book of Isaiah in its present form, the

15. T. N. D. Mettinger, "Die Ebed-Jahwe-Lieder. Ein fragwürdiges Axiom," *ASTI* 11
(1978): 68–76.
16. Melugin, *Formation of Isaiah 40–55*, 176.
17. Ackroyd, "Isaiah 36–39," 21.
18. Melugin, *Formation of Isaiah 40–55*, 177.

cry is not wholly unexpected. At the close of the first major section, chaps. 1–12, there is a psalm (chap. 12) which clearly has the function of concluding this section.[19] Here we read in v. 1: "I will give thanks to thee, YHWH; yes thou wast angry with me, but let thy anger be turned away, that thou mayst comfort me [ותנחמני]."[20] The fact that at this particular point the psalm contains deliberate and significant evocations of Deutero-Isaiah becomes clear from the immediately succeeding "Behold, God is my salvation [הנה אל ישועתי, v. 2]," where the word ישועה clearly evokes the language of Deutero-Isaiah (see n. 55 below). Thus the hopeful plea "that thou mayst comfort me" points forward to the cry of the divine voice, "Comfort, comfort my people." This cry is taken up again in 51:12: "I, I am he that comforts you [אנכי אנכי הוא מנחמכם]." Here it is God himself who comforts; and he contrasts himself with the mortal human beings whom Zion ought not to fear, because they are like "grass" (חציר)—a further evocation of 40:1ff. (cf. vv. 6–8). But the line that is drawn from chap. 12 by way of chap. 40 to chap. 51 is not yet at an end. In 66:13—right at the end of the book—we read once more in the divine address: "As one whom his mother comforts, so I will comfort you [כן אנכי אנחמכם]"; here too the emphatic addition of the אנכי to the verb and the assonance of the suffix form suggest that this is a deliberate recapitulation of what has been said in 51:12.[21]

Thus the proclamation of the divine "comforting" spans all three parts of the book of Isaiah, and in each of them it has been given a prominent position: in 12:1, at the end of the great "presentation" of the prophet, as hopeful vista looking toward future salvation; in 40:1, as emphatic, encouraging announcement at the beginning of the great collection of assurances of salvation; in 51:12, at the peak of this collection, as presentative utterance of the God who creates salvation; and in 66:13, as stressed but now futurist reiteration of this utterance. (On "Trito-Isaiah" see the following paragraph.) In addition we find the "comfort" theme on still other occasions in another characteristic use. In 49:13, 51:3, and 52:9, all of them hymnic pieces,[22] we find "Yes, YHWH has comforted

---

19. See Ackroyd, "Isaiah I–XII," 36ff.

20. Many exegetes call the text in question and emend it to וַתְּנַחֲמֵנִי; cf. the discussion on this passage in H. Wildberger, *Isaiah 1–12*, trans. T. H. Trapp (Minneapolis: Fortress Press, 1991). But in the framework of the composition of the book of Isaiah, the Masoretic reading is convincing.

21. The fresh green (דשא) with which those addressed are compared in 66:14 is contrasted with the withering grass (חציר, 51:12).

22. For the function of the hymns see now T. N. D. Mettinger, *A Farewell to the Servant Songs: A Critical Examination of an Exegetical Axiom* (Lund, 1983), 18ff.

his people" (כי־נחם יהוה עמו, 49:13: 52:9) or "Yes, YHWH has comforted Zion, he has comforted all her ruins" (twice נחם, 51:3). (Here the
place of the hymns in the composition of Isaiah 40–55 must be pondered
in more detail, if we are to understand why this theme is taken up here.)
Finally, the same motif turns up yet again at a central point in chaps. 56–
66. In 61:2, the one whom YHWH has anointed says (speaking in the
first person) that one of his functions is "to comfort all who mourn" (לנחם
כל־אבלים).

Another thread connects chap. 1 with chap. 35. It has often been
pointed out that chap. 35 shows many evocations of Deutero-Isaiah, to
the point of actual word-for-word quotations.[23] There can also hardly be
any doubt that in the composition of the first main section of the book of
Isaiah chap. 35 occupies an important place, whether as the original close
of the collection in chaps. 1–35 (as is generally assumed), or whether in
connection with chaps. 36–39, which Ackroyd thinks are not merely a
later addition to chaps. 1–35, but are linked in content with these earlier chapters in the framework of the composition.[24] Here, in 35:2, we
now find the saying: "They themselves shall see the glory of YHWH
[המה יראו כבוד־יהוה]"[25]—a clear evocation of 40:5: "The glory of
YHWH [כבוד יהוה] shall be revealed and all flesh together shall see
it [וראו]." Here too other threads provide a connection both with what
has gone before and with what comes afterward. It will surely be permissible to assume that there is a connection with Isaiah's great Temple
vision in chap. 6, in which the seraphim cry: "Holy, holy, holy is YHWH
Sabaoth, what fills the earth is his glory [כבודו]" (v. 3). The idea that
what takes place in the Temple on Zion has a significance for all the na-

23. For the discussion see Wildberger (*Isaiah 1–12*) on this passage. But in my view
Wildberger puts the discussion on the wrong track by asking whether "Deutero-Isaiah"
is "the author" of this passage.

24. Ackroyd, "Isaiah 36–39," 14ff.

25. Who is meant with the המה in 35:2 is disputed. Is it the desert that will see YHWH's
kabod or is it the Israelites, who in vv. 9f. are called the redeemed and liberated?
Among more recent scholars, Wildberger (*Isaiah 1–12*) in discussing this passage, and
also O. Kaiser (*Isaiah 13–39: A Commentary*, trans. R. A. Wilson [London: SCM Press;
Philadelphia: Westminster Press, 1974; 2d ed., London, 1980]) opt for the latter view,
in my opinion rightly. Clements (*Isaiah 1–39*) prefers the former interpretation. The
question is not unimportant for the understanding of chap. 35 and its function within the
composition of the book of Isaiah. Clements sees in the taking over of this statement from
40:3, 5 "a great shift of emphasis from a historical event, interpreted as a manifestation
of God, to a change in the natural order as bringing about such a revelation." Kaiser,
on the other hand, writes: "The now despondent Jews, who are doubting God's power
and its final revelation, are none the less to see what is promised to all human beings in
40:5." In the first case, therefore, chap. 35 is interpreted in an apocalyptic sense, in the
second it refers rather to the Israel of the present.

tions can also be found in 2:2-5, so that a conscious relationship between
the utterances in chaps. 6 and 40 of the book seems quite possible.[26] The
same thread is prolonged into the third part of the book. In 59:19 we
find: "They shall fear[27] the name of YHWH from the west, and in the
east his glory [כבודו]." Immediately afterward, after the new beginning
in 60:1, Zion is addressed: "Arise, shine; for your light is coming, and
the glory of YHWH [כבוד יהוה] is rising upon you." And again in v. 2:
"YHWH is arising upon you, and his glory appears upon you." Here this
statement about the appearance on Zion of the divine *kabod* (translated
"glory") really is linked with the statement about the pilgrimage of the
nations (v. 2b)—that is to say, the lines of Isaiah 6 and Isaiah 2 converge.
Finally, this theme is taken up once more right at the end of the book. According to 66:18, YHWH will bring together "all nations and all tongues
and they shall come and see my glory [כבודי]."

Chapters 40 and 35 are additionally related through the demand:
"Say [sing./plu. אמרו/אמרי] . . . Behold your God [הנה אלהיכם]!" (40:9;
35:4). The parallelism is plain; and yet the difference is worth noting too.
In 35:4 the call is addressed to the despondent, for whom God's coming
is something that is still in the future, whereas in 40:9 it goes out from
Zion to the cities of Judah—that is to say, here God's arrival in Jerusalem
is viewed as an already existing reality. The same cry in amended form
appears in 62:11 too: "Say [אמרו] to the daughter of Zion, Behold, your
salvation [ישעך] is coming!" That this is intended to be an evocation of
chap. 40 is quite clearly shown by the way the verse goes on: "His re-
ward is with him and his recompense before him" (62:11b = 40:10b). We
shall come back to the modification of the content later. The first thing
that is important for our present question is that here again an important
element from chap. 40 finds its resonance in both the first and the third
part of the book of Isaiah. Perhaps we might also see 12:2 in the same
context: "Behold, God is my salvation [הנה אל ישועתי]."[28] Finally, we
could draw on a number of passages in which the הנה ("behold") in the

---

26. Melugin, *Formation of Isaiah 40–55*, 83f., and Ackroyd, "Isaiah 36–39," 5f., have
drawn attention to the relations between chap. 40 and chap. 6.

27. Many scholars have emended the reading וייראו to וְיִרְאוּ, "they will see"; but in my
view this is arbitrary and unjustified. In 59:15ff. talk about YHWH's *kabod* has rather
been put in a different context, in which the point is the manifestation of YHWH's power
over against his enemies.

28. The context, esp. v. 2b, would suggest the rendering as nominal sentence: "God *is*
my salvation." At the same time, however, the echo of 40:9 is undoubtedly intentional,
and this would be brought out by the translation, "Behold, the God of my salvation." The
Hebrew wording is open for both renderings, and this is probably intentional. One might
also add 25:9 to the passages mentioned above: הנה אלהינו.

divine address has been changed to הנני (58:9; 65:1), even if here the context is a different one. Verse 1 of chap. 65 could then throw light on the third passage in the book in which הנני is used in the absolute.[29] In 52:6 we read: "It is I who speak: here am I."[30] This is immediately preceded by: "Therefore my people shall know my name." In 65:1 the two elements of this verse are linked: "I said, 'Here am I, here am I,' to a nation that did not call on my name."

We already mentioned Melugin's pointer to the significance of the word עון for the link between chap. 40 and chap. 1. Here the antithetical comparison is clearly evident. The assertion that the guilt has been canceled (40:2) is contrasted with the "woe" to the people burdened with guilt (1:4). We have also already mentioned the parallelism of עון and the root חטא in the two passages. Within the complex 1–39, there are several utterances which have the same tenor as 1:4: "Woe to those who draw guilt [עון] with cords of falsehood, who draw sin [חטאה] as with cart ropes" (5:18); "Surely this guilt [עון] will not be forgiven you till you die" (22:14); "Therefore this guilt [עון] shall be to you like a break in a high wall... " (30:13).[31] But besides these passages there are others in chaps. 1–39 too which talk about the forgiveness of sins: "Therefore by this the guilt [עון] of Jacob will be expiated, and this is the full fruit of the removal of his sin [חטאה]" (27:9); "The people who dwell there [that is, on Zion] are forgiven their guilt [עון]" (33:24). The wording of the first of these two passages shows a striking parallelism to the saying that is addressed to the prophet in 6:7, after one of the seraphs has touched his lips with a glowing coal from the altar: "Your guilt [עון] is taken away and your sin [חטאת] is forgiven"; in both cases the verbs סור and כפר (pu.) are used, though assigned chiastically to the objects עון and חטאת.[32] But apart from this last question (which will be taken up again later) we again see here initially a piece of redactional work, which in 1–39 already puts the proclamation of salvation parallel to the proclamation of doom.

Within the complex chaps. 40–55, there are several mentions of Israel's earlier sins which have now been set aside: "You have given me work with your sins [חטאות], you have given me trouble with your iniq-

29. Otherwise we generally meet הנני followed by a participle: 13:7; 37:7; 38:8; 43:19; 65:17, 18; 66:12 (questionable are 28:16; 29:14; 38:5).
30. It is interesting that in v. 7 a hymnic fragment follows, which contains immediate echoes of 40:9ff.
31. חטאה also in 3:9.
32. Is it just by chance that 27:9 talks about the altar like 6:6f.?

uities [עונות].” But the passage goes on: “I, I am He who blots out your transgressions [פשעים] for my own sake, and I will not remember your sins [חטאות]” (43:24f.).[33] And 50:1: “Behold, for your iniquities [עונות] you were sold, and for your transgressions [פשעים] your mother was put away.” Apart from that, this whole group of ideas then plays a central part in chap. 53: the Servant of God carries the sins (עונות) for others (vv. 5, 6, 11); the word עונות is used, parallel to פשעים (v. 5., also in v. 8, the verb פשע in addition in v. 12); in v. 12 חטא is used. Under this aspect, the question about the relationship between chap. 53 and chap. 40 would require an investigation of its own.

In the complex 56–66, chap. 59 is again dominated by this theme.[34] First of all in the accusation: “It is your iniquities [עונות] that have made a separation between you and your God, for your hands are defiled with blood and your fingers with guilt [עון]” (vv. 2, 3a); then in the confession: “Yes, many are our transgressions [פשעים] before thee, and our sins [חטאות] testify against us;[35] yes, our transgressions [פשעים] are with us, and we know our iniquities [עונות]” (v. 12); finally in the assurance: “He comes for Zion as Redeemer, and for those in Jacob who turn from transgression [פשע]” (v. 20). The same theme turns up once again in chap. 64 in the confession of sin (v. 5 חטא, vv. 6f. twice עון) and in the plea: “Be not exceeding angry, YHWH, and remember not guilt [עון] for ever” (v. 9). But this catchword from chap. 40, unlike the other theme about the comforting, finds no echo in the final chapter of the book.

Let us try to arrive at a preliminary summing up. Evident links can be detected between the introductory chapter of the second part of the book of Isaiah, chap. 40, and the other two parts. But the points of reference in the other parts are not always the same. In the case of the keyword “comfort,” with which the second part of the book begins, the point of reference is the psalm in chap. 12, with which the first major collection, chaps. 1–12, concludes. The talk about comforting is developed at various points in chaps. 40–54, and is taken up again in chaps. 56–66 too, particularly emphatically in the final chapter, 66. At the announcement of the coming of YHWH’s glory (כבוד), the point of reference is to be found in chap. 35, a chapter which equally clearly has a concluding function and is very close to the language of Deutero-Isaiah in general. This theme too is taken up again in the third part, once more with particular

---

33. Cf. the similar formulation in 44:22, although there עון is missing.

34. Cf. also 57:17. פשע and חטאות are also mentioned in 58:1, in 57:4 only פשע.

35. The tension in the Masoretic text between the plural nominative form and the singular verb cannot be eliminated.

emphasis in the final chapter. There is also a correspondence between chaps. 40 and 35 in the proclamation "Behold your God," whereas here, in the third part, obvious evocations are certainly present, but in modi- fied form. The saying about "guilt" (עָוֹן) shows that there is a relationship between chap. 40 and chap. 1; the function of this first chapter as an in- troductory summing up has long been recognized.[36] But in this case the relationship is a relationship of antithesis: in chap. 1 the word "guilt" is used in indictment, in chap. 40 in connection with the promise of for- giveness. And here it is now important that in the first part there are not merely further accusations; there is a promise of forgiveness too. The fact that this promise appears at the close of chap. 33 throws light on the function of this chapter in the composition of the book. Conversely, it emerges that as far as the second part is concerned, this theme is by no means exhausted with the announcement of forgiveness in chap. 40; on the contrary, the problem of guilt is once again forcefully treated, espe- cially in chap. 53. And in the third part there is no assertion about the forgiveness of guilt as unequivocal as the assertion in chap. 40. Here the subject rather remains open.

The central themes of chap. 40 are therefore all to be found in the first and third parts of the book as well. The recognizable relationships show clearly that here, at least in some cases, these are links that have been deliberately forged in order to connect the three parts. In the context of the question about the composition of chaps. 1–39 and the position of these chapters in the composition of the book as a whole, it is worth noting that the points of reference to chap. 40 are to be found in at least three different chapters: in the introductory chap. 1; in chap. 12, which closes the first major complex, 1–12; and in chap. 35, which has the function of concluding the first part (though probably not without compositional relationships to chaps. 36–39)[37] The end of chap. 33 suggests that this chapter too has a particular function within the composition of the book of Isaiah as a whole.

III

Between the three parts of the book of Isaiah, however, there are also thematic and theological relationships which go far beyond individual

36. See here G. Fohrer, "Jesaja 1 als Zusammenfassung der Verkündigung Jesajas," *ZAW* 74 (1962): 251–68 (=his *Studien zur alttestamentlichen Prophetie, 1949–65* [Berlin, 1967], 148–66).
37. Cf. Ackroyd, "Isaiah 36–39," 8.

passages. This may be said first of all of the theme Zion/Jerusalem, which is one of the dominant motifs in all three parts. This being so, it is not surprising that it is to be found in all the chapters which we have already seen form the pivots of the compositional relations within the book. In chap. 1 the theme is sounded in 1:8: "The daughter of Zion is left like a booth in a vineyard, like a lodge in a cucumber field"; here and in v. 9, it is Jerusalem's preservation from final destruction that is the subject. In vv. 21-26 (27) the point is the inner constitution of the city, which is once again to become what it once was, the "fortress of righteousness" and "the faithful city." Finally, in 2:1-5[38] a third aspect emerges: the End-time vision of a pilgrimage of the nations to Zion, from whence YHWH's Torah goes out to all nations, leading them to end all wars. It is a far-reaching group of topics which the catchword Zion/Jerusalem covers here; and in the course of the exposition a link simultaneously emerges between the proclamation of judgment and the proclamation of salvation—the link which is so characteristic of the picture of Isaiah presented in the book in its present form.[39]

The next unit, 2:6—4:6,[40] contains the same theme, again in a tension-laden antithesis between indictment and a message of salvation: Jerusalem's "supports" will be removed (3:1), so that she stumbles and falls (3:8); the "daughters of Zion" have proclaimed to them the divine punishment for their arrogance (3:16ff.), but those that are left are then promised salvation and protection for themselves and Zion (4:2-6); here the words נותר and סכה from chap. 1 are picked up once more. In the following unit 6:1—9:6, chap. 7 particularly deals again with the question about the preservation of Jerusalem. In 10:5-34, in a complex collection, there is talk of Assyrian attacks which threaten Jerusalem (vv. 10f., 32); but the city is also promised YHWH's help against the aggressor (vv. 12, 24).[41] Finally, the whole complex concludes with the psalm in chap. 12, which leads up to the final verse, reminiscent of Deutero-Isaiah: "Shout and sing for joy, O inhabitant of Zion! Yes, great in your midst is the Holy One of Israel!" (v. 6). So the whole unit chaps. 1–12 is encircled by

---

38. The passage 2:1-5 forms the conclusion of the composition unit 1:2—2:4(5); cf. P. R. Ackroyd, "A Note on Isaiah 2,1," *ZAW* 75 (1963): 320f.; also his "Isaiah I–XII," 35 and 42.

39. Ackroyd, "Isaiah I–XII," passim.

40. In the division of the units I am following Ackroyd, ibid., 35f. and 42ff.

41. In discussing this passage, O. Kaiser (*Isaiah 1–12*) supposes that the section 10:24-26 was written for the first time for the present context; that would be in line with the trend of the collection chaps. 1–12 as a whole.

the theme Zion/Jerusalem. Its whole tenor is marked by the assurances of salvation in 2:2-5, 4:2-6, and chap. 12.

In the following chapters, the theme of Zion/Jerusalem is never developed in any detail; but it is constantly present, so to speak. For on the one hand Jerusalem is frequently assumed to be the arena of events, even if it is not explicitly mentioned; and on the other hand utterances about Zion or Jerusalem turn up again and again, sometimes quite abruptly and out of the blue. For example, we are told several times that YHWH dwells on Zion or is present there (18:7; 24:23; cf. 31:9; also 8:18b); that there he fights against enemies (31:4; 34:8; cf. 29:8); that he sets a foundation stone on Zion (28:16); that he fills it with justice and righteousness (33:5; cf. 1:27); that the wretched among his people will there find refuge (14:32); that the homecomers will worship him there (27:13); and that there the people can live in quietness (30:19; 33:20). Only once do we find a saying directed against the sinners on Zion (33:14). The whole comes to a conclusion in the psalm in chap. 35, which again (like chap. 12) takes up this theme in its last verse (v. 10), this time with an even clearer evocation of Deutero-Isaiah, in the form of a word-for-word quotation from 51:11.

In chaps. 36–39—if we except some mentions in the narrative (36:2) and the mockery of the Assyrians (36:20; 37:10)—the Zion/Jerusalem motif turns up only in the poetic section 37:22-32, where the "virgin daughter of Zion" mocks the Assyrians (v. 22). We otherwise encounter Zion in this personified form solely in chaps. 40–55 (see below). Verse 32 runs: "Yes, out of Jerusalem shall go forth a remnant, and out of Mount Zion a band of fugitives," and this is followed by the phrase: "The zeal of YHWH Sabaoth will do this"—a phrase which occurs only in one other passage in the whole of the Old Testament, in 9:7.

There is no need to demonstrate in detail the central role played by the theme Zion/Jerusalem in the second part of the book of Isaiah. The prologue (40:1-11) takes the form of an address to Jerusalem (v. 2) or Zion (v. 9). Here a characteristic feature already emerges: the marked personification of Jerusalem, which turns it into an acting, speaking, mourning or rejoicing person. This is then the case in the second part of this collection especially (chaps. 49–55), a section which one might term as a whole "the Zion-Jerusalem section."[42] In 49:14 a fairly long speech unit begins, introduced by "Zion speaks." In 51:17 and 57:1f. Jerusalem/Zion is addressed with imperatives, which are again reminiscent of 40:9, whereas

42. Thus R. F. Melugin, *Formation of Isaiah 40–55*, 78–80, following E. Hessler and C. Westermann.

in 52:7-9 the aspect of Zion/Jerusalem as city again comes to the fore—
the city to which "the messenger who brings good tidings" announces
the entry of the divine king. Chapter 54 again takes up the theme of the
barren woman from 49:14ff., although without explicitly mentioning the
name of Jerusalem or Zion. Both passages are marked here by a fluid
transition from the metaphor of Jerusalem as woman to sayings about
the city which is to be rebuilt. Apart from this, there are several proclamations of salvation for Jerusalem, and announcements of its rebuilding,
as proof of YHWH's sole power (41:27; 44:26, 28; 46:13; 51:16); we
find these in divine speeches couched in various genres,[43] and finally in
the already mentioned hymnic recapitulation of the theme of the divine
comforting in 51:3. Taken as a whole, the sayings about Zion/Jerusalem
in the second part of the book of Isaiah are extremely unified in theme;
they are directed entirely toward consolation and the assurance of divine
help for ruined and depopulated Jerusalem.

In chaps. 56–66 mentions of Zion/Jerusalem are concentrated in chaps.
60–62 and 65–66.[44] Verse 20 of chap. 59 could positively be viewed as an
overture to chap. 60: "He is coming for Zion as Redeemer" (59:20)—"for
your light is coming" (60:1). The trend of the saying is then entirely along
the lines of Deutero-Isaiah. Jerusalem is called "the city of YHWH, the
Zion of the Holy One of Israel" (60:14);[45] consolation is coming for Zion
(61:3; 66:13). In 62:1-12 we again find the transition between talk about
Zion as a woman whose forsakenness will be ended, and as a rebuilt city
into which the homecoming exiles and YHWH himself will finally enter.
In 65:18f. the rebuilding of Jerusalem is actually termed a new creation
(ברא), and this is a further development of sayings of Deutero-Isaiah in
which God's acts on behalf of Jerusalem are named side by side with his
acts in creation (see 44:24-28; 51:16). In 66:7ff. we find yet again the link
between Zion as woman and as city, this finally finding its conclusion in
the word of consolation in 66:13. The final section says that the nations
will bring the inhabitants of Jerusalem from the diaspora as offerings to
Zion (66:20; cf. 60:4).

If, starting from these observations, we try to draw conclusions about
the relationship to one another of the three parts of the book of Isaiah,
it emerges first of all that in the treatment of the theme Zion/Jerusalem

---

43. On the "juxtaposition" of text units belonging to different genres, cf. Melugin, passim.
44. Moreover in 64:9, in a communal lament, there is talk about Jerusalem's being laid
waste.
45. One can detect here an echo of 1:26. For the new naming of the city, cf. also 62:2,
4, 12.

there is no difference worth mentioning between the second and the third parts. In the second part the theme is more richly elaborated, however, so that we receive the distinct impression that here the third part is dependent on the second, and has not developed the theme independently. The first part is a very different matter! Here there are many sayings about Zion/Jerusalem which find no correspondence in the other two parts, and which are formulated in completely different language. This is especially true of the accusations and proclamations of judgment in chaps. 1–12, but it also applies to all the texts which talk about a threat to Jerusalem through war. Against the background of these individual sayings especially, it is noticeable that the general tenor of the sayings about Zion/Jerusalem in chaps. 1–12 is molded by assurances of salvation, which in each case conclude smaller individual collections, and finally the whole section too. At the same time, the promises of salvation in 2:2-5 and 4:2-6 are also independent in language and theme compared with the second (and third) part of the book. In chap. 12, on the other hand, the very verse which talks about Zion (v. 6) clearly belongs within the tradition of the second part. This is even more marked in the case of chap. 35, where the final verse (v. 12) contains a word-for-word quotation from 51:11. For the rest, chaps. 13–35 do not show any principle of composition as marked as that which we can see in chaps. 1–12; so no clear structures emerge as far as the theme Zion/Jerusalem is concerned either. But it is still remarkable that the three chapters which our investigations hitherto have shown to offer shifting points of reference to chap. 40—that is, chaps. 1, 12, and 35—all contain this theme.

Perhaps I might add one individual observation. Talk about "those who are left" or "the survivors," and about the "remnant," plays an important part in chaps. 1–12. In 4:3 the two terms are brought together: "He who is left [נשאר] on Zion and survives [נותר] in Jerusalem will be called holy." Here there is an echo of the two uses of the root יתר in 1:8f.: "The daughter of Zion survives [נותרה]," and "If YHWH Sabaoth had not left us a few survivors [הותיר] as remnant." In 7:22 we also read: "Every one that survives [נותר] in the land will eat curds and honey." A concentration of sayings with the root שאר, on the other hand, can be found in 10:20-22, which talks about "a remnant of Israel [or Jacob]" which will repent, and in 11:11-16, which says that YHWH will buy back "the remnant of his people" from the other countries (v. 11), and that he will prepare a road (מסלה), as he did once before for the deliverance from Egypt (v. 16). Here the evocation of 40:3 is clear. One has the impression that what can be detected here is redactional work on chaps. 1–12. It is also evoked in chap. 37. Hezekiah begs Isaiah to pray for "the remnant [שארית] that is still there" (v. 4), and in vv. 31f. a promise is given for the throng of fugitives that is left (נשארה), and for the remnant which will leave Jerusalem.[46] It is striking that this whole terminology in chaps. 40–55 remains almost without parallel. (Only in 46:3 is "the remnant of the house of Israel" mentioned twice.)

IV

It has often been noticed that the phrase "the Holy One of Israel" (קדוש ישראל) occurs almost exclusively in the book of Isaiah, but that there we meet it in all three parts. We now have to ask what this means for our present enquiry. In chap. 1 we meet this turn of phrase at the beginning, much emphasized, in the first of the accusations introduced by the word הוי (woe!): "They have forsaken YHWH, rejected the Holy One of Israel" (1:4b). The formulation in 5:24b is very similar, as close of a more extensive series of "woe" cries: "For they have despised the Torah of YHWH Sabaoth, and have spurned the word of the Holy One of Israel." The phrase occurs a third time in 5:19, within a "woe" cry, quoting what the mockers say: "Let the purpose of the Holy One of Israel draw near, and let it come, that we may know it!" A group of similar sayings can be found in chaps. 30–31. The mockers do not want to know anything about the Holy One of Israel (30:11) and he answers them (vv. 11, 15). In 31:1 there is again an accusation introduced by "woe!" directed against those who seek military support from Egypt but do not trust "the Holy One of Israel." Finally, in 37:23 the king of Assyria is accused of having mocked "the Holy One of Israel." These, therefore, are all accusations about disregard of the Holy One of Israel, his word and his purposes. In contrast, the saying about "the remnant of Israel" in 10:20 expects that "in that day" this remnant will rely only on the Holy One of Israel. A similar contrast to earlier behavior is brought out in 17:7, again in a saying introduced by the phrase "in that day." Finally, in 29:19, 23 too new worship of the Holy One of Israel is expected for the era of salvation that is imminent. (In v. 23 "the Holy One of Israel" is put parallel to "the God of Israel.")

All these texts, therefore, have to do with the question whether and how the people who are being talked about in each case worship "the

---

46. In Isaiah's address to Hezekiah in 39:5-7, on the other hand, it is said that everything belonging to the royal house will be taken off to Babylon and that nothing will be left (יותר, v. 6). Melugin (*Formation of Isaiah 40–55*, 177) sees in Hezekiah's final remark in v. 8 an indication that the redactor understood the preservation of Jerusalem at the time of Hezekiah as a delay of punishment until the Babylonian exile.

Holy One of Israel." In contrast, the psalm in chap. 12 strikes an entirely different note. The last verse runs: "Shout, and sing for joy, O inhabitant of Zion; yes, great in your midst is the Holy One of Israel!" (v. 6). This verse, therefore, which brings the theme Zion/Jerusalem to a conclusion in the composition chaps. 1–12 (see above), also takes up what has been said about the Holy One of Israel, and again does so in the language of Deutero-Isaiah. In this way a clear shift of emphasis emerges once again, compared with the other utterances on this theme in chaps. 1–11. It is also once more clear that the theme appears in chaps. 1 and 12, and therefore has an important function for this collection. At the same time, however, if we look at the book of Isaiah as a whole a striking difference can be seen: in chap. 40 the Holy One of Israel is not mentioned.[47] We shall have to ask later what conclusions can be drawn from this.

In chaps. 40–55 "the Holy One of Israel" is now talked about in very different terms. This is already shown first by the fact that most of the examples use the phrase as an epithet describing YHWH, and frequently as a description which YHWH applies to himself when he is the speaker. On two occasions this self-description follows an introductory "I am YHWH" (43:3, 15);[48] four times it follows the introductory formula "Thus says Yahweh"—for example in 43:14: "Thus says YHWH, your Redeemer [גֹּאֲלֵךְ], the Holy One of Israel"; 48:17 is very similar. In 49:7a the formula is split up: "Thus says YHWH, the Redeemer of Israel and his Holy One." YHWH also terms himself "your Redeemer" in 41:14. In 54:5, when he is being talked about in the third person, he is called "your Redeemer" and in 47:4 "our Redeemer." So the description of YHWH as "the Holy One of Israel" is used no less than six times in direct conjunction with the phrase "your [our] Redeemer." In addition to this are other participial (self-)descriptions: "helper" (מוֹשִׁיעַ 43:3), "Maker" (יֹצֵר 45:11, עֹשֶׂה 54:5, בּוֹרֵא 43:15, the formula here being split up), "faithful" (נֶאֱמָן 49:7b); also "your king" (43:15), "your husband" (54:5), "God of the whole earth" (54:5). Finally there are verbal expressions about "creating" (בָּרָא 41:20), "choosing" (בָּחַר 49:7) and "glorifying" (פֵּאֵר 55:5).

We therefore meet the phrase "the Holy One of Israel" in the second part of the book of Isaiah only in speeches touching on and promising salvation, but never in disputations or judgment speeches, in which it might seem to contain an element of accusation or polemic. This makes it very clear once more how different this is from the language of the

47. Once only, in 40:25, do we meet "the Holy One" (קָדוֹשׁ).
48. In 43:15 the formula has been split up for stylistic reasons.

first part. But at the same time, as far as the composition is concerned, the importance of chap. 12 once again becomes evident, which with this theme too links the first and the second parts. In the third part the phrase noticeably recedes. We meet it on the one hand in 60:9, in the form of a quotation from 55:5, and on the other hand in 60:14, where it is linked with the theme "Zion": "They shall call you the City of YHWH, the Zion of the Holy One of Israel."[49]

V

Among the important theological concepts which are to be found in all three parts of the book of Isaiah is the word צֶדֶק or צְדָקָה,[50] which is generally translated "righteousness." Here concordance findings already show at the very first glance that there is a fundamental difference in the way this word is used in the first and second parts of the book. In the first part צֶדֶק/צְדָקָה is frequently associated with מִשְׁפָּט, "justice," sometimes directly by way of ו, "and" (9:6; 33:5), but more often in the *parallelismus membrorum* (1:21, 27; 5:7, 16; 16:5; 26:9; 28:17; 32:1, 16). In the second part this link is completely missing. Instead we find here another characteristic connection between צֶדֶק/צְדָקָה and various nominative forms of the root ישׁע in the meaning "salvation," or similarly: with ישׁע 45:8; 51:5; with יְשׁוּעָה 51:6, 8; with תְּשׁוּעָה 46:13; also with שָׁלוֹם, "peace, salvation," 48:18; 54:13f.; in 45:21 God is called אֵל־צַדִּיק וּמוֹשִׁיעַ.

This varying linguistic usage suggests that the word צֶדֶק/צְדָקָה has an entirely different function in the two parts of the book. In the first part it is related for the most part to human behavior, to the creating and preserving of justice and righteousness, or their neglect. In the second part, in contrast, the word generally refers to God's acts or behavior; this is also brought out by the fact that it can be linked with suffixes related to God (41:10; 42:21; 46:13; 51:5, 6). The "righteousness" of God is here a component in his saving acts for Israel and the nations.

The beginning of the third part is now surprising. In 56:1 we read: "Thus says YHWH: Keep justice [מִשְׁפָּט] and do righteousness [צְדָקָה], for my salvation [יְשׁוּעָה] is near and my righteousness [צִדְקָה] will be revealed." Here therefore the linguistic usage of the first two parts has entered into an association: מִשְׁפָּט and צִדְקָה as a requirement to human

---

49. In 57:15 the word קָדוֹשׁ is used twice.

50. The two forms are treated together here, since no difference of meaning can be detected; see also K. Koch, "*Ṣdq.* gemeinschaftstreu/heilvoll sein," THAT 2, cols. 507–30.

beings, ישועה and צדקה as impending acts of God. Here the imminent becoming-revealed of the divine saving righteousness is the reason for the demand to human beings to bring about justice and righteousness themselves.[51] The reciprocal relationship between human and divine is צדקה, the subject of chap. 59 too. First the lack of משפט and צדקה is comprehensively deplored (vv. 9, 14; cf. v. 4); and here, in v. 11, the word משפט is already put parallel to ישועה, as an expression of hope, pointing to the acts of God. Verses 15ff. then talk about the divine intervention, צדקה and ישועה (v. 17) or the verbal ישע (hif'il; v. 16) being linked together twice. So here the stress is different from the emphasis in 56:1: God will bring about his saving righteousness himself, in order to overcome the deficiency of human righteousness.

Talk about צדקה is given a new turn in chap. 58. Israel (or "the house of Jacob," v. 1b) is first of all criticized because it claims that it implements צדקה and משפט (v. 2), although in actual fact unrighteousness and social injustice prevail (vv. 6f.). If these things are remedied, then Israel's צדקה will be like the breaking forth of light and will go before her in a triumphal procession, while YHWH's *kabod* (כבוד) will bring up the rear (v. 8). So what Israel expects of salvation is her own צדקה. This is even more marked in chaps. 60–62. In a context entirely in the tradition of Deutero-Isaiah, 60:17 already says that שלום and צדקה will be installed as custodians and overseers in Israel. Using the language of the song of thanksgiving, 61:10 expresses the expectation that Israel will be clothed with ישע and צדקה.[52] In 62:1, finally, the divine speech proclaims that Zion's צדקה and ישועה will break forth like light and that the nations will see her צדק and כבוד. So here utterances which in Deutero-Isaiah are made about YHWH are transferred to Zion: in the era of salvation, צדקה, ישועה, and כבוד will be the marks of Zion too. These expectations include the idea of the practical "doing" of righteousness: that is shown by the statement in 60:21: "Your people shall consist wholly of the righteous [צדיקים]."[53]

In this way statements about the human and the divine צדקה bring out still another aspect of the relationships of the three parts of the book of Isaiah. The first and second parts of the book differ fundamentally in their use of language: we find the link between צדקה and משפט only in the first part, where it is related to the practical performance of justice

---

51. Cf. here F. Crüsemann, "Jahwes Gerechtigkeit (ṣᵉdāqā/ṣädäq) im Alten Testament," *EvT* 36 (1976): 427–50, esp. 446–47.

52. In v. 11 the image changes: YHWH will let צדקה sprout.

53. צדיק also in 57:1 (twice).

and righteousness; in the second part, in contrast, the link between צדקה and ישׁועה (or related words) is dominant, as a statement about the divine saving acts which are imminent. In the third part, in the very first verse (56:1) both ways of talking about צדקה are programmatically linked with one another. As the text goes on, talk about the "doing" or "not-doing" of righteousness retains an importance of its own.[54] But parallel to this, things that are said about YHWH in the second part are transferred to Israel or Zion in the form of eschatological promises. It is noticeable that in this case, unlike the terms and themes we have discussed hitherto, the linguistic usage of the second part has found no admission into the first. It is true that the word ישׁועה is used in chap. 12, and indeed is much emphasized there (vv. 2f.);[55] but neither there nor anywhere else has it been linked with the word צדקה.

VI

Our observations have shown that there are many different mutual relationships between the three parts of the book of Isaiah. These relations vary greatly in kind and can be found on very different levels. Let us, in closing, try to classify them somewhat more precisely, and to indicate some initial conclusions about questions of the composition history of the book of Isaiah.

We may begin once more with chap. 12. Here, the way the keyword "comfort" is taken up in v. 1 shows that there is a direct reference to the beginning of the second part of the book in 40:1. It is significant in this connection that we do not otherwise meet this use of the word נחם in chaps. 1–12 at all.[56] Here it therefore clearly has the function of linking the collection 1–12 with chaps. 40ff. It is also important that the word "comfort" exercises this connecting function for the third part too, and that there it appears, stressed, in the final chapter (66:13). In 12:2f. one of the central words in Deutero-Isaiah's language is taken up, with the triple use of the word ישׁועה—again without any support from the language otherwise used in chaps. 1–12.[57] Things are somewhat

---

54. Cf. 57:1, 12, 64:5f. In 53:1 the צדקה is also talked about as proof of YHWH's power, parallel to the verbal ישׁע (hif'il).

55. Ackroyd ("Isaiah I–XII," 38) points out that here there is apparently a play on the prophet Isaiah's name.

56. In 1:24 the pi'el of נחם is used with the meaning "to revenge oneself"; in 22:4 Isaiah tells his fellow citizens not to comfort him.

57. Within the complex chaps. 1–12, the root ישׁע is only used at all in 12:2f. Otherwise we meet the word ישׁועה a number of times in chaps. 1–39, i.e., in 25:9; 26:1, 18; 33:2,

different if we look at 12:6. Here too the relations to the second part are obvious; the beginning is reminiscent of 54:1. The way of speaking about "the Holy One of Israel" again corresponds to the language of the second part; but here the phrase is used in clear contrast to other uses of "the Holy One of Israel" in 1–39. So here a new term is not being introduced, but an expression already used in chaps. 1–12 (or chaps. 1–39) is being employed in a different sense, thus again forming a bridge to the second part. In this case no significant relation to the third part can be detected.

Similar observations can be made in chap. 35. Here, first of all, v. 2 picks up from 40:5 sayings about the seeing of YHWH's כבוד. The announcement "Behold your God" in 35:4 is also clearly taken over from 40:9. In the first case the question is: How is the relation to the utterance about YHWH's כבוד in 6:3 to be interpreted?[58] In the second case, no direct relationships within chaps. 1–39 can be detected; but the statement "Behold, God is my salvation!" or "Behold, the God of my salvation!" (see n. 28 above) in 12:2 could be moved into proximity with 35:4, so that there would be a tie-up between chap. 12 and chap. 35. Finally, the last verse of chap. 35 (v. 10) talks emphatically about the blessed future of Zion (with a quotation from 51:11); here there is a striking parallel to chap. 12, where this also happens in the last verse (v. 6). In chap. 35 talk about "the Holy One of Israel" is missing, however.

Chapters 12 and 35 therefore evidently have the function of establishing a connection between the first and the second (or also the third) part of the book. In the case of chap. 12 it would seem obvious here to think initially of a link between chaps. 1–12 and chaps. 40ff., whereas the function of chap. 35 is probably related rather to the wider context of this chapter (see n. 37 above). Another, different kind of relation to chaps. 40ff. can be seen in chap. 1. Here talk about Israel's guilt in 1:4 corresponds to the announcement in 40:2 that this guilt has been abolished. But the relationship is an antithetical one: in 1:4 the reproach of guilt is made with great harshness—in 40:2 the abolition of guilt is proclaimed consolingly. In addition, talk about Israel's guilt in 1:4 is connected with similar accusations in chaps. 1–39. In 1:8, the theme of "Zion" is sounded; here it is striking that in the context of an indictment there is talk about the preservation of "the daughter of Zion," and that this is even accentuated by v. 9. Here a trend can be detected within the

---

6; also ישע in 17:10. In all these cases dependence on the language of chaps. 40–55 can be detected.

58. In 4:5 we also meet the word *kabod,* in a salvation oracle, and in 24:23 too.

collection chaps. 1–12, which finds expression particularly in the sayings about salvation for Zion in 2:2-5, 4:2-6, and chap. 12.

Here, therefore, we can perceive two quite different ways in which relationships are established between the first part of the book and the second. On the one hand terms and phrases which do not occur in the first part itself are taken over from the second part ("comfort," 12:1, "salvation," 12:2f., "Behold, your God!" 35:4). On the other, themes and ideas which are used in different ways in the two parts are related to each other; it may be that the usage of the second part is introduced into the first on one single occasion ("the Holy One of Israel" in 12:6); or it may be that an explicit antithesis remains ("guilt" in 1:4 and 40:2). In some cases this classification proves too rough—too wide-meshed—because elements characteristic of the second part also turn up in scattered cases in the first (YHWH's *kabod* in 35:2 and already in 6:3; salvation for Zion in 12:6, 35:10 and already in 2:2-5, 4:2-6 and frequently). This shows that the connections that have been shown between the second part and chaps. 1, 12, and 35 are not isolated links, but have to be seen in the context of a more radical theological redaction of the first part.

The relationships of the third part to the two previous parts have already been mentioned at various points. Thus the saying about "comforting" runs through all three parts and appears, in emphatic form, in the last chapter of the third part (66:13). Talk about YHWH's *kabod* also links all three parts and is again given marked emphasis in the final chapter of the third part (66:18). The announcement "Behold, your God!" appears in the third part, in 62:11, in the modified form "Behold, your salvation comes!," the continuation being a quotation from 40:10, which makes the relationship clear. In other cases the relationships between the second and third parts have no recognizable connection with those between the first part and the second. This applies particularly to the theme "righteousness" (צדקה). Here the way the language is used in the first part is quite different from the way it is used in the second, and there is no sign that any attempt has been made to smooth out the differences or mediate between them. But the third part has a character of its own through the very fact that it takes up the language of the other two parts, linking it together in a new way (56:1 and frequently). In this connection the theme "Zion" too is developed in a new manner, for here sayings about the saving righteousness of YHWH and his *kabod* are transferred to Zion (62:1f.).

VII

It would be premature to deduce from these initial and in part highly provisional observations an overall concept about the composition of the book of Isaiah. For that, much more penetrating investigations are required. But, in closing, an attempt should nevertheless be made to indicate some aspects of the composition history.

First of all, it has been shown, in my view, that the second part of the book, chaps. 40–55, occupies a dominant position in the book as a whole. Both in the first and in the third part it is clearly evident that the compositional work takes its bearings from the second part, either drawing on it directly or orientating its own utterances toward it. This is confirmed by the insight (acquired independently of this postulate) that chaps. 40–55 present a unified and self-contained unit.[59] Consequently it would seem reasonable to assume that chaps. 40–55 form the heart of the present composition and that the two other parts have been shaped and edited in its light, and point toward it.

But here very different stages of redaction and composition can be perceived, and the relation of these stages to each other still requires further clarification. In some cases all three parts are spanned by a single great arch (e.g., "comfort," YHWH's *kabod*) although here the keywords in question have not penetrated the substance of the first part. Conversely, in the case of the phrase "the Holy One of Israel," a tense reciprocal relationship between the first and second parts can be seen; but this phrase plays hardly any role in the third part. The theme of "Zion," again, has its clear function in each of the three parts, and in some way forms the strongest link binding the three together.

Yet it is precisely the "Zion" theme which makes it plain that it is not sufficient merely to pay attention to the total composition of the book. For here even within chaps. 1–12 we can already detect redactional and compositional work which continually sets proclamations of salvation over against accusations and announcements of judgment to Jerusalem.[60] The other more considerable units within chaps. 1–39 also clearly display their own compositional structures, which still require further investigation.[61] And here it must then be asked how the compo-

---

59. Thus, following Melugin and Mettinger, also already R. Rendtorff, *Das Alte Testament. Eine Einführung* (Neukirchen, 1983), 204ff.; Eng. trans., *The Old Testament: An Introduction* (Philadelphia: Fortress Press; London: SCM Press, 1986); cf. now also Mettinger, *Farewell to the Servant Songs.*

60. Cf. here Ackroyd, "Isaiah I–XII," passim.

61. On chaps. 36–39 and their relationships to other parts of the book of Isaiah, see

sitional work on these units is related to the composition of the book as a whole. For example, is chap. 12 in its function as conclusion of the collection chaps. 1–12 related to the book as a whole from the very outset—and that means to chaps. 40–55 as well? A similar question can be asked about chap. 35. This inevitably leads to the further question whether there was ever an independent collection comprising the greater parts of chaps. 1–39, or whether the development of the present collection chaps. 1–39 has to be conceived in correlation to the composition of the book as a whole.

Where the third part is concerned, the same questions have to be asked. Here, however, the point of departure is a different one, since we have to assume from the outset that the authors and/or redactors of this part already had chaps. 40–55 in front of them as a self-contained unit. But the beginning in 56:1 shows quite clearly that independent material was also available to them, in which they found צדקה used in a different way from the way it is used in chaps. 40–55. Indeed they apparently saw one of their most important tasks as being to link these different traditions. And here we have to assume that this particular theme above all played an important part for them in their own time. For the complaint about the disregard of justice and righteousness, and the demand that this state of affairs should be changed, was undoubtedly for them a highly topical and concrete problem. Thus they saw themselves in a situation in which the traditions which had been transmitted to them under the name of Isaiah again acquired for them a direct significance for the present. At the same time, however, in the traditions passed down to them from the exilic "Deutero-Isaiah" they had in front of them a completely different view of צדקה, which in their own difficult contemporary situation opened up a vista toward the future in which the insufficiencies of human righteousness would be overcome through the saving acts of God.

As far as the book as a whole is concerned, finally, the question arises: How are the editors of the first and the third parts related to one another? Here too we shall certainly not be able to give any simplistic answer. But nevertheless, in my own view much speaks in favor of the postulate that the people who were responsible for the final form of the third part also

---

Ackroyd, "Isaiah 36–39." But other sections also require a new investigation in the light of the now different question—for example the so-called "Isaiah apocalypse," chaps. 24–27, but also what is known as the "Assyrian cycle," chaps. 28–30. I suspect also that in the light of this question new viewpoints about the relation to the book of Isaiah as a whole of the "sayings against the foreign nations" in chaps. 13–23 could emerge.

had a share in the composition of the book as a whole, in its final form. For chaps. 56–66 are so strongly determined by their relations to the two other parts that it seems to me hardly conceivable that this third part ever had an independent existence.[62]

62. Consequently the questions about the redaction and composition history of Isaiah 56–66 must be considered afresh. Here we shall be able to take up the observations of K. Pauritsch, *Die neue Gemeinde: Gott sammelt Ausgestossene und Arme (Jesaja 56–66)* (Rome, 1971); E. Sehmsdorf, "Studien zur Redaktionsgeschichte von Jesaja 56–66," *ZAW* 84 (1972): 517–61, 562–76, and others. I have already given a brief outline of the ideas put forward here in my book *Das Alte Testament,* 210ff.

CHAPTER 14

Isaiah 6 in the Framework of the
Composition of the Book

I

The interpretation of the book of Isaiah is in a state of flux. In this respect it shares in the general movement which has made itself felt in Old Testament exegesis for the last ten years or more. And here we have to say about Isaiah what we have to say of Old Testament exegesis as a whole: that the large measure of methodological consensus which used to prevail among most Old Testament scholars—internationally at that—has given way to a diversity of methods such as has never hitherto existed since the beginnings of international critical Old Testament scholarship. Nowadays, we see not only the further development and further differentiation of previous methods of interpretation; we can see a wide variety of new methodological approaches too.[1] Some of them are still at the experimental stage, which is in the nature of things. We cannot expect that methods which, in some cases, have been practiced for over a century, will be replaced at the first attempt by conclusive and polished alternative models.

In my own view, one special problem about this development is the fact that the right to practice different and, it may be, alternative methods is not accepted by certain representatives on both sides—"both sides" meaning the people who cling to the previous methods, and the others

Lecture delivered at the Colloquium Biblicum Lovaniense in 1987.

1. A good survey may be found in J. Barton, *Reading the Old Testament: Method in Biblical Study* (London: Darton, Longman & Todd, 1984).

who pursue the new methodological paths. Occasionally the consequent disputes positively take on the character of religious wars. We can see this, for example, in the discussion between James Barr and Brevard Childs.[2] It is obvious that this cannot further the common interests of those who are engaged in scholarly work on the Old Testament.

Above all, this situation also raises the question about continuity in Old Testament scholarship. New approaches not infrequently tend to pay little attention to the link with previous work; they may even ignore the connection altogether. This danger seems to me to exist today especially among certain proponents of a purely literary way of looking at the Old Testament, who take their bearings much less from previous Old Testament research than from modern literary studies, especially as these are pursued in France and the English-speaking countries. Many of these interpreters are by their own admission not interested in a continuity of Old Testament interpretation.

This does not apply in the same degree, basically speaking, to the "canon-critical" approach developed by Childs, James Sanders, and others. It is true that here interest is essentially concentrated on the Old Testament text in its final form. But there is undoubtedly an awareness that this form of the text can be the result of a considerable history, and that where many texts are concerned, this is in fact the case. And it is not in principle denied that insight into this earlier history can possibly be important for the understanding and appropriate interpretation of the text. The essential difference, as I see it, is the priority of the interest in each case: whether concern is directed primarily to an analysis of the text and the reconstruction of its earlier stages (and even, if possible, of an "original" text), or whether the main interest is directed to the interpretation of the text as it now stands, in awareness of its possibly complex prehistory.[3]

Both approaches have, in my view, their own justification, and this justification should not be denied by either side. Perhaps a monistic method dominated Old Testament scholarship for too long, especially in Europe, so that we have first to learn once more that other questions and other methodological approaches can be viewed as possible and legitimate. This would undoubtedly be of benefit to international Old Testament scholarship. Moreover, in the practical exercise of exege-

---

2. See above all J. Barr, *Holy Scripture: Canon, Authority, Criticism* (Oxford: Oxford Univ. Press; Philadelphia: Westminster Press, 1983), in dispute with B. S. Childs, *Introduction to the Old Testament as Scripture* (Philadelphia: Fortress Press; London: SCM Press, 1979).

3. On this whole subject see chapter 3 above.

sis there are frequently more reciprocal connections than a first glance might suggest.

II

During the last ten years, the interpretation of the book of Isaiah has undergone radical changes. I may mention two above all which are especially momentous.

1. Skepticism about Isaianic authorship has grown very considerably. This trend can be seen in its extremest form in Otto Kaiser, who thinks that it is no longer possible to discover any "genuine" Isaianic sayings at all, and who also considers that the earliest written collection of sayings associated with the name of Isaiah dates back only to the sixth or fifth century B.C.E.[4] So here the interpreter is dealing almost exclusively with later, essentially literary work.

2. The question about overriding redactional or compositional links within the book of Isaiah has come to be asked with increasing frequency. This question is not in principle new, but since the mid-1960s it has taken on fresh impetus.[5] Here too the main inquiry is directed to the literary work which has lent the texts their present form.

It is in fact astonishing that between these two approaches there have up to now been hardly any interconnections. This, in my view, brings to light a fundamental hermeneutical problem. In his interpretation, Kaiser proceeds largely from the individual pericopes, and this means that, in spite of a fundamental change in the presuppositions, he still adheres to the classic form-critical notion about "smallest units," even though it is really no longer possible to talk about a genuine *Sitz im Leben* for prophetic sayings. According to his view, in the further history of the text we can then see many different hands at work—editors, redactors, and so forth, whose activity can be detected in the detail of the texts, but hardly in a more comprehensive, overall concept. The contrasting suggestions

---

4. O. Kaiser, *Das Buch des Propheten Jesaja, Kap. 1–12,* ATD 17, 5th ed. (Göttingen, 1981); Eng. trans., *Isaiah 1–12: A Commentary,* trans. R. M. Wilson (London: SCM Press, 1972).

5. The following especially must be mentioned here: R. F. Melugin, *The Formation of Isaiah 40–55* (Berlin and New York: de Gruyter, 1976), esp. 177f.; P. R. Ackroyd, "Isaiah I–XII: Presentation of a Prophet," VTSup 29 (1978): 16-48; also his "Isaiah 36–39: Structure and Function," in *Von Kanaan bis Kerala: Festschrift für J. P. M. Ploeg* (Neukirchen, 1982), 3–21; see also chapter 13 above; O. H. Steck, *Bereitete Heimkehr: Jesaja 35 als redaktionelle Brücke zwischen dem Ersten und dem Zweiten Jesaja,* SBS 121 (Stuttgart 1985); also his "Tritojesaja im Jesajabuch," in J. Vermeylen, ed., *The Book of Isaiah,* BETL 81 (Louvain, 1989).

of Melugin and Ackroyd, who try to show that an overriding concept of this kind can be shown, are not noticeably taken into account in Kaiser's work at all.

Insofar the work of Odil H. Steck on Isaiah 35[6] takes up an intermediate methodological position which is deserving of attention. On the one hand he has firmly, and in my view convincingly, raised the question about the connection between the three main parts of the book of Isaiah (which in more modern exegetical tradition have as a rule been treated completely separately). Here Steck has worked out the view that chap. 35 is a "bridge," created specially for this purpose between First and Second Isaiah (p. 59), and he has simultaneously linked this position with the question about a "Greater Isaiah redaction." On the other hand, he adheres to a viewpoint based on literary criticism which often goes very much into detail and which in many respects is methodologically close to Kaiser's way of working.

III

In what follows I should like to try to put a question to the texts which is more strongly directed to their wider contexts. In so doing I am developing the approaches of my earlier essay on the composition of the book of Isaiah.[7] Here I should like deliberately to avoid confining myself to those texts which are more or less obviously written with a view to the composition, or which recent discussion has shown to have this purpose—chaps. 12 and 35 for example, but also chaps. 1 and 33. I should like rather to take up hints which suggest that "central" texts, which we cannot simply put down to "editing," also show many relationships to other passages in the book which can hardly be fortuitous and unintentional.

This applies particularly to Isaiah 6. As Steck has shown, this chapter is "not a text that can be isolated."[8] It is "open in a forward direction," as Kaiser puts it,[9] referring to Steck. But what is its context? The "memoir" (6:1—8:18 or 9:6)? Can that be "isolated" either? And how are we to assess the relations to other parts of the book of Isaiah—to Deutero- and Trito-Isaiah too?

---

6. See the previous note.
7. See chapter 13 above; also n. 5 above.
8. O. H. Steck, "Bemerkungen zu Jesaja 6," *BZ* NF 16 (1972): 188–206, esp. 203.
9. Kaiser, *Jesaja,* 122 n. 13.

I should like to begin with the question: What is Isaiah 6 open *for?* In what direction does it point? This question really means essentially: What is the aim of the divine commission to harden the hearts of the people? The exegetes are largely at one in saying that no explicit answer to this question can be found in the immediate or wider context of "Proto-Isaiah" (chaps. 1–39).[10] Must the answer be deduced indirectly from these chapters, or perhaps from the more immediate context of the "memoir"? Or is it a question of the "documentation of an act of Yahweh's which will qualify the future but has still to be implemented"?[11]

Is the answer then perhaps to be found in the word of hope in 8:17 (Kaiser)?[12] If one looks at the concordance, it emerges that the phrase about God's hiding his face (פָּנִים הַסְתִּיר) which is used in 8:17 occurs again as an utterance about God's attitude to Israel only in 54:8—that is to say, in the second, "consoling" part of the book, Isaiah 40–55. (It can also be found once more in the historical retrospect in 64:6.) So here the gaze travels into the future, beyond 8:17, to the time after the judgment has been executed, in which the salvation that is imminent is announced and with it the end of the time when God hides his face.

Let us now return to the charge to harden the hearts of the people. It is characterized by a particular semantic field: שָׁמַע/רָאָה and the corresponding בִּין/יָדַע (6:9b, 10b); in addition the statement about the hardening is expounded further in v. 10a: the heart of the people will become "fat," that is to say insensitive and hence unrecipient, and in the same way their ears will also become "heavy" and their eyes will be closed.

It should be noticed first of all that the paired words יָדַע/בִּין already occur in the introductory verses of the book of Isaiah (1:3). There Israel's behavior is placed in a double antithesis: the heavens *hear,* the ox and the ass *know,* but Israel neither knows nor understands. Here the context also makes it plain that this has something to do with Israel's sin (v. 4), and that the consequence is going to be punishment (vv. 5-7). Insofar chap. 1 already puts into the reader's hand an aid to understanding which later makes the charge in chap. 6 to harden the hearts of the people comprehensible; for without its there being explicitly stated, the reader already knows that this lack of understanding, which is now laid upon Israel as

10. Cf. J. M. Schmidt, "Gedanken zum Verstockungsauftrag Jesajas (Is. VI)," *VT* 21 (1971): 68–90; R. Kilian, "Der Verstockungsauftrag Jesajas," in H.-J. Fabry, ed., *Bausteine Biblischer Theologie: Festschrift für G. J. Botterweck,* BBB 50 (Bonn, 1977), 209–55.
11. Steck, "Bemerkungen zu Jesaja 6," 204.
12. Kaiser, *Jesaja,* 122.

doom, has its roots in Israel's own sin. This connection is then also made plain because in order that Isaiah himself may be equipped for the charge to proclaim, he is freed from his sin (עָוֹן/חַטָּאת; 6:7), which he bears as member of the sinful people (גּוֹי חֹטֵא עַם כֶּבֶד עָוֹן, 1:4).

Israel's heart is hardened until this state of things is explicitly ended, an end quite emphatically announced in 41:20. God will transform the desert into fruitful land in order to make Israel's way back possible (vv. 17-19), so that Israel may *see and know* (לְמַעַן יִרְאוּ וְיֵדְעוּ). This is the counter-image to the statement in 6:10b: "So that it does not see . . . and know [פֶּן־יִרְאֶה . . . וּלְבָבוֹ יָבִין]." At the same time this announcement does not mean that knowledge is now already full and complete. Israel has still not freed herself from her self-made gods; the people still know and understand nothing (לֹא יָדְעוּ וְלֹא יָבִינוּ), because their eyes are closed so that they cannot see, and their hearts are therefore still unperceptive (44:18, cf. v. 19).

At other points in Isaiah 40–55 (42:16, 18f.; 43:8) the metaphorical talk about the blind and the dumb is taken up again, although here there is no explicit mention of understanding and knowing. R. Clements has pointed to the obvious connection between these passages and the charge to harden hearts in Isaiah 6.[13]

Parallel to this, readers can pursue the other train of thought, since they know the connection between lack of understanding and sin. In several eschatological sections the abolition of sin is already announced even in Isaiah 1–39. According to 27:9 the purification of Israel from her sins and guilt will be brought about through the annihilation of foreign altars. Here the terminology shows striking similarity to the wording of 6:7.[14] In 33:24, the announcement of the return to Zion closes with the sentence: "The people who dwell there are forgiven their sin."[15]

This theme is then taken up preeminently in chaps. 40–55. As early as 40:2 the "cast back" to 1:4 is evident. The גּוֹי חֹטֵא עַם כֶּבֶד עָוֹן is told that its עָוֹן is forgiven and its חַטָּאת have been discharged.[16] In 43:22ff. Israel's sacrificial cult is contrasted with her sin—in striking similarity to the sequence in chap. 1, where the criticism of sacrifice follows directly on the reproach of sin. But although Israel has given God labor and trouble with her sins, he will now "wipe them away" so that they will

---

13. R. E. Clements, "Beyond Tradition-History: Deutero-Isaianic Development of First Isaiah's Themes," *JSOT* 31 (1985): 95–113, esp. 101–4.

14. See here chapter 13 above.

15. The German translation can hardly render the compressed Hebrew sentence: נְשׂא עָוֹן.

16. See here chapter 13 above.

no longer be remembered. In 50:1 too it is stated in retrospect that Israel had been sold because of her sins and her trespasses.

Here 44:22 is again interesting. At the end of a major section which concludes with the hymn in 44:23,[17] the statement that God will wipe away the sins of his "servant" Israel is repeated, and then follows the demand: "Return to me [אלי שובה] for I redeem you." In 6:10 it is explicitly stated that the hardening of heart is also intended to prevent conversion (ושב ... פן). This impediment has now been abolished. Israel can repent.

This leads to yet another aspect. The succeeding ורפא לו in 6:10 also finds its correspondence in chaps. 40–55—in 53:5. Whereas in 6:10 the not-being-healed is a consequence of the not-being-able-to-repent, in 53:5 it is said that through the suffering of "the Servant of God" the collective who is speaking will be healed (נרפא־לנו).[18] In other passages too, in what is said about the Servant of God there are repeated echoes of Isaiah 6. Thus the Servant is to open blind eyes (42:7 [and free the ישבי חשך, cf. 9:1]). He himself was blind and deaf, so that God poured out his wrathful judgment on him (42:19-25); but then God opened his ears so that he can now speak to others too (50:4f.) and so that the people who dwell in darkness may hear his voice and through it find new trust in God (v. 10).

IV

A further point which makes the openness of Isaiah 6 especially evident is the question: "How long, O Lord?" and the answer which the prophet is thereupon given (v. 11): depopulated cities, empty houses, fields that are laid waste (שממה)—that is going to be the situation. This announcement is nothing new for readers of the book of Isaiah. The devastation of the country has been already heralded in 1:7, and here the word שממה, in which 6:11 culminates, is actually found twice. It then recurs in chaps. 40–55. The rebuilding and the repopulating of Jerusalem are among the central themes in chaps. 49ff. particularly. And here the connection with the terminology of 6:11 is obvious.[19] Thus in 49:17ff. the rebuilding of Jerusalem is announced, and its new inhabitants will stream

17. On the hymns in Isaiah 40–55 see now F. Matheus, "Form und Funktion der Hymnen in Jesaja 40–55" (Diss., Heidelberg, 1986).

18. In 57:18f. the talk about saving is taken a step further: God himself heals (רפא is used twice) and comforts (נחם; cf. 12:1 and 40:1) and creates peace (שלום). On נחם cf. chapter 13 above.

19. Kaiser (*Jesaja*, 134 n. 85) offers only evidence from Jeremiah and Deuteronomy 28, but does not point to parallels in the book of Isaiah.

in, so that its ruins and waste places (שְׁמְמֹתַיִךְ) become too narrow. Similarly, in 54:1-3 the new inhabitants of Jerusalem are called "children of the desolate" (בְּנֵי־שׁוֹמֵמָה, v. 1),[20] and the resettled cities are described as עָרִים נְשַׁמּוֹת (v. 3). Finally, this is again endorsed with great emphasis in 62:4: "You shall no longer be termed 'Forsaken,' and your land shall no more be termed 'Desolate' [שְׁמָמָה]."

Here it is quite evident that Isaiah 6 does not merely look forward (or backward, as the case may be) to the destruction of Jerusalem and the Babylonian exile, but that actually within the book of Isaiah itself it is aligned toward the continuation in chaps. 40ff. Readers who still remember the "How long?" of chap. 6 will recognize the connection. At the same time they will be able to perceive the red thread which runs from the first chapter of the book by way of the announcement of the hardening of heart in chap. 6 to the announcements of salvation in chaps. 40ff.

V

Melugin and Ackroyd have drawn attention to the obvious parallelism in the presentation of the heavenly scenes in Isaiah 6 and Isaiah 40.[21] Both texts begin with a vision (6:1-3) or audition (40:1-2). Then, in each passage, a heavenly voice (קוֹל) is twice mentioned, the first time with the addition (ה)קוֹרֵא (6:4 and 40:3), the second time with אָמַר (6:8 and 40:6). The second, "speaking" voice in each case involves a direct or indirect address to the prophet: in 6:8 with the question, "Whom shall I send?" which according to the context is aimed at the prophet; in 40:6 with the imperative "Cry!" which evokes the prophet's counterquestion: "What shall I cry?"[22] In 6:8 the voice is explicitly called *adonai*'s voice, which is understandable according to the context, since the prophet has previously seen the *adonai* on his throne (v. 1). In 40:6 the voice is left without any further definition. The fact that it is a divine voice emerges from the context. But whether YHWH himself or a heavenly herald is speaking remains open. In chap. 40, when the voice that cries is mentioned in v. 3, it would now seem obvious to think of the same voice as the one in v. 6.

20. The expression here is equivocal. According to 2 Sam. 13:20, Tamar lived as שְׁמָמָה in the house of her brother Absalom, that is to say, according to the context: without a husband or children. Correspondingly in Isa. 62:4 the earlier description שְׁמָמָה is contrasted with the new one.

21. Melugin, *Formation of Isaiah 40–55*, 83–84; Ackroyd, "Isaiah 36–39," 5–6.

22. Whether וַאֹמַר should be read as third person, as in the Masoretic text, or as first person, following 1QIs[a] (and the Septuagint), does not affect this interpretation of the text.

Before it gives the prophet any charge, it first of all cries to the world, requiring nature to make preparation for the return of the exiles. When all this has happened—or through this event itself—the divine *kabod* will become visible (v. 5). But what about the voice that "cries" in 6:4? Most exegetes think that the expression הקורא applies to the seraphs, and often also translate it as a plural.[23] But it is often asked too whether it is not YHWH himself who is to be understood as the one who calls here.[24] In that case the one from whom the "voice" proceeds would be the same both here and in Isaiah 40, and this would correspond to the parallelism in the buildup of the two heavenly scenes.

Both texts talk about the divine *kabod* (6:3; 40:5). In Isaiah 6 this is striking, because this word is not otherwise part of the vocabulary of Isaiah 1–39.[25] But the position and function of the *kabod* is different in the two texts: 6:3 talks about it in the heavenly world, in the seraphs' song of praise,[26] whereas in 40:5 it is to be visible for "all flesh." Accordingly in 6:3 the divine *kabod* is mentioned in the context of the introductory vision, whereas in 40:5, in contrast, it belongs to the utterance of the "crying voice." In this sense we see here a shift between the two heavenly scenes.

How ought we to assess the obvious parallelism between these two texts? Two "classic" answers present themselves first of all. On the one hand it could be assumed that one text is dependent on the other, in the literary sense. If Isaiah 6 is taken to be Isaianic, this would mean that the emphasized beginning of Deutero-Isaiah is dependent, in the literary sense, on the Isaiah text. This would have far-reaching consequences for the interpretation of Deutero-Isaiah. Alternatively, one might think of a common "copy." But how should its genre be defined? As a "call account"? K. Elliger, who does in fact see Isaiah 40 as reflecting

---

23. As Rashi already did incidentally: קול המלאכים הקוראים, and also Ibn Ezra: קול ההמון הקורא.
24. Thus, for example, explicitly A. Dillmann in his comment on this passage, appealing to H. Ewald, and thus too now also Ackroyd, "Isaiah 36–39," 5 n. 7: "It is when God speaks, at the sound of his thunder (cf. also Ezek. 1), that there is a shattering effect."
25. In 35:2 the reference to 40:5 is clear (cf. Steck, *Bereitete Heimkehr,* 15). H. Wildberger in his commentary *Isaiah 1–12,* trans. T. H. Trapp (Minneapolis: Fortress Press, 1991) presumes this too for the difficult passage 24:32.
26. Cf. here Ps. 19:1 and R. Rendtorff, "Die Offenbarungsvorstellungen im Alten Israel," in W. Pannenberg, ed., *Offenbarung als Geschichte,* 5th ed. (Göttingen, 1982), 21–41, esp. 28–29 (= R. Rendtorff, *Gesammelte Studien zum Alten Testament* [Munich, 1975], 35–59, esp. 46–47); Eng. trans., "The Concept of Revelation in Ancient Israel," in W. Pannenberg, ed., *Revelation as History,* trans. D. Granskou and E. Quinn (New York: Macmillan, 1968; London: Collier-Macmillan, 1969).

"Deutero-Isaiah's call experience,"[27] denies that there is a connection in actual genre between this and other prophetic call accounts. It would therefore seem plausible here too to put the question in the light of the composition. For the two texts mark two corresponding fundamental aspects of the book of Isaiah: the climax of the announcement of judgment, whose inescapability is expressed in the statements about the hardening of the people's hearts in Isa. 6:8ff., and the beginning of the announcement of salvation, in which it is explicitly stated that now sin has been canceled (40:2). The two aspects are therefore related.

It is obvious that without the preceding judgment the announcement of salvation has no function. But conversely, we saw in connection with the statement about the hardening of hearts in Isa. 6:8ff. that its annulment is found for the first time only in Isa. 40ff. So in the same sense the first part of chap. 6 could also be formulated with an eye to chap. 40 and in mutual relationship to that chapter.[28]

VI

Where the composition is concerned, therefore, both from a literary point of view and in substance, Isaiah 6 is mutually related in many ways to a number of texts in Isa. 40ff.; and in these cases it is only in their mutual relationships that the two respective texts can be fully understood. To show this was the primary purpose of this essay. At the present stage of the discussion, I have deliberately avoided raising the diachronic questions about the genesis of this composition, the age of the texts and traditions, their literary dependencies, and so forth. It seems to me more important first to keep one's gaze free for observations on the synchronic level of the present text, without simultaneously making the attempt in each case to answer the questions that arise on the diachronic level, with their hitherto customary formulations—formulations, that is, which belong largely to the aspect of literary criticism.

Two things, it seems to me, may already count as certain. On the one hand observations about compositional connections on the synchronic level open up many different insights into the intention of the text, insights which were not brought to light by earlier questions. They are also generally speaking entirely verifiable—in many cases with the help of a

---

27. K. Elliger, *Deuterojesaja*, BKAT 11/1 (Neukirchen-Vluyn, 1978), 10.

28. One might consider whether Isa. 1:2, the cry to heaven and earth, should also be seen in this context. In this case too (as already in earlier observations) the bridge would stretch from chap. 1 by way of chap. 6 to Deutero-Isaiah.

concordance—provided that the interpreter is prepared not to let clear observations be obscured by preconceived ideas about possible diachronic processes in the genesis of the text. But on the other hand the diachronic questions themselves (whose justification in principle we also explicitly recognized in section 1) will change too through observations of this kind. For it is now no longer possible to apply the traditional methods unaltered; these themselves will have to be reexamined, and if necessary modified, in the light of new observations.

Old Testament scholarship is at present going through a stage of "crisis," in the sense of Thomas S. Kuhn's conception in *The Structure of Scientific Revolutions.*[29] Kuhn has also convincingly described the varying reactions to such a crisis, once it begins to show itself. If we follow his analysis, we must expect that, for a longer or shorter period, some Old Testament scholars will not recognize the symptoms of crisis at all, or will not be prepared to recognize them. Instead they will expect that solutions to the problems can be found through an even more rigorous and even more precise application of the old methods. So in the near future we have to reckon with an increasing pluralism of methods, rather than with a unification of the questions asked. But this will not necessarily be detrimental to Old Testament scholarship.

29. T. S. Kuhn, *The Structure of Scientific Revolutions* (Chicago: Univ. of Chicago Press, 1962; 2d enlarged ed. 1970), esp. chaps. 7 and 8.

CHAPTER 15

Isaiah 56:1 as a Key to
the Formation of the
Book of Isaiah

I

In recent years the formation of the book of Isaiah has become a frequently discussed topic. My first question is: Why? Are there specific reasons for this present and increasing interest in the formation of this particular book? Of course the answer will differ, according to the interests of the scholar concerned. I hope that in the next few years we shall have an opportunity to study the current state of Isaianic scholarship in more detail, but at the moment I should like to restrict myself to the reasons determining my own approach to this question. I should like to term my approach "canonical-critical." By using this term I should like to indicate my closeness to one of the most recent essays on the topic, written by Christopher Seitz: "Isaiah 1–66: Making Sense of the Whole."[1] He too begins his article by defining his approach as "canonical-critical," giving some reasons which I need not repeat here. I should only like to indicate a certain continuity.

My next question is then: Why, as a scholar motivated by a canonical-critical approach, am I interested in the formation of this particular book? As I thought about this question, I came to the conclusion that, next to the Pentateuch, the book of Isaiah is the most challenging subject against

Paper read in English at the SBL meeting in Anaheim in 1989. The text has undergone some stylistic revision.

1. C. R. Seitz, "Isaiah 1–66: Making Sense of the Whole," in C. R. Seitz, ed., *Reading and Preaching the Book of Isaiah* (Philadelphia: Fortress Press, 1988), 105–26.

which to test the consequences of a changing approach to Old Testament books. On the one hand, there is almost undisputed agreement among Old Testament scholars about the tripartite structure of the book. At the present stage of Old Testament scholarship this agreement seems to be much greater than agreement about the structure of the Pentateuch. On the other hand, from a canonical-critical point of view our aim is to find a way of access to an understanding of the book as a whole.

But what does that mean: the book as a whole? It is easier to say what it does not mean. It does not imply that we should simply ignore the many indications of the book's complex structure. On the contrary, our task will be, not to ignore those indications but to try to understand them— not by dividing the book into multiple layers and sources, but not either by making a simple distinction between "original" and "redactional" elements. At the moment we do not yet have an elaborated methodological approach, and certainly not one that has already achieved any degree of consensus. We are rather at the experimental stage. What I should like to do, therefore, is simply to put forward some observations and reflections for discussion.

II

Let us start with some remarks about the book's tripartite structure. It is important to realize that "the literary boundaries between 1, 2, and 3 Isaiah are not marked in any special way."[2] It was evidently not the intention of the author(s) of the book in its present form to make the reader feel at certain particular points a transition to something different or new. Opinions can differ about the degree to which the reader becomes aware of a change at all. My own impression is that it is in a sense easier to define the end of something than the new beginning. For instance, chaps. 36–39 are a unit without any parallel within the book, and there has recently been a very interesting debate about their exact function in the book.[3] But it is only through the existence of these chapters that the transition to chap. 40 becomes noticeable. If chap. 40 were to follow immediately on chap. 35 it would not be a transition to "a new tone and emphasis."[4] More or less the same thing seems to be true of chaps. 55 and 56. Chapter 55 contains clear elements of a summary, leading to a

2. Ibid., 109.
3. Ibid., 110ff., with footnotes.
4. Ibid., 109.

certain climax. Chapter 56 itself, however, does not seemingly announce anything particularly new.

But let us go a little more deeply into the matter. Isaiah 56:1 reads, in the Revised Standard Version:

> Thus says the Lord:
> "Keep justice [מִשְׁפָּט] and do righteousness [צְדָקָה],
> for soon my salvation [יְשׁוּעָתִי] will come,
> and my deliverance [וְצִדְקָתִי] be revealed."

Our first observation about this verse is a double one: the word צְדָקָה appears twice—and it seems to be difficult to translate the word in the same way in both cases. In the first instance the RSV renders it by "righteousness," in the second by "deliverance." The Septuagint already felt this problem, translating צְדָקָה first by δικαιοσύνη and then by ἔλεος. (The Vulgate, on the other hand, had no problem, rendering צְדָקָה both times by *iustitia,* just as Luther did with his *Gerechtigkeit.*)

In fact the word is used in two quite different contexts in the two halves of the verse. The first time the phrase is introduced by an imperative, addressed to the listeners or readers: שִׁמְרוּ . . . וַעֲשׂוּ ("keep . . . and do!"); the second time it announces what God himself is going to do: to bring forth his salvation and let his צְדָקָה be revealed. In both cases צְדָקָה is used in parallelism with another word: the first time with מִשְׁפָּט ("justice"), the second time with יְשׁוּעָה ("salvation"). If we check the use of the word צְדָקָה in the book of Isaiah,[5] we find a definite distribution of these two word pairs. The combination צְדָקָה and מִשְׁפָּט occurs frequently in chaps. 1–39, but not a single time in chaps. 40–55. Instead, in chaps. 40–55 we several times find the combination between צְדָקָה and יְשׁוּעָה, or between the related words תְּשׁוּעָה and יֵשַׁע, a combination which never appears at all in chaps. 1–39. This means that in the book of Isaiah we find two different concepts of צְדָקָה. The one, dominant in chaps. 1–39, relates צְדָקָה to מִשְׁפָּט, thereby emphasizing the righteousness which has to be kept and done. The other, specific to chaps. 40–55, speaks of God's own צְדָקָה, whose coming is announced and whose character will be יְשׁוּעָה, salvation.

Both these aspects now appear side by side in 56:1. At no earlier point in the book of Isaiah do we find a verse or even a paragraph in which these two different aspects of צְדָקָה are combined in this way. Consequently it is not only the translators who, as I have shown, had problems with this verse; many commentators also feel that the verse says something new

---

5. See chapter 13 above, esp. pp. 162ff.

and unexpected. We may suppose that the same was true for the original readers of the book.

In addition, it is the first time in the whole book of Isaiah that we find the imperatives שמרו משפט and עשו צדקה. Both are frequent in other biblical books,[6] but they are completely missing in the book of Isaiah up to this point. I believe that even such a quite minor element of linguistic usage is of some importance at such a turning point.[7]

III

Now, two things are evident in the framework of our discussion about the composition of the book of Isaiah. First, Isa. 56:1 is the deliberate beginning of something new. Second, the author of this verse is fully conscious of the fact that in the texts up to this point two different concepts of צדקה have appeared, concepts which he is combining in this verse for the first time.

If these observations are accepted, the consequence would again be a double one. First, the third part of the book of Isaiah must be seen as something different from parts 1 and 2. Second, this third part can never have existed independently of the preceding two parts, in whatever specific form these parts may have existed.

This last question has to be pursued further. In what form did these two parts exist, before chaps. 55–66 came into existence? Were chaps. 56–66 added to the more or less complete parts 1 and 2? The answer clearly has to be "no."[8] But this answer must be differentiated with regard to the two preceding parts. Where part 2 is concerned (chaps. 40–55), I feel that these chapters are homogeneous to such a degree that they have to be taken as a more or less deliberately shaped literary unit—which of course does not exclude minor additions and changes. (I may leave on one side for the moment the question of how this unit is related to chaps. 1–39.) In the case of chaps. 1–39, however, things are obviously different. "The whole notion of Second and Third Isaiah depends in no small part on there being a clear First Isaiah. Such an Isaiah is not to be

---

6. Particularly so in the book of Ezekiel.

7. One might also mention the use of the word אשרי, "blessed," in v. 2. This word appears only three times in the book of Isaiah, always in the same context as צדקה and/or משפט (cf. 30:18 and 32:20).

8. R. Rendtorff, *The Old Testament: An Introduction,* trans. John Bowden (Philadelphia: Fortress Press; London: SCM Press, 1986), 200.

found. Isaiah 1–39 is an extremely complex collection of material, with a diverse background."[9]

I believe that the majority of Old Testament scholars would agree with the last statement, namely that Isaiah 1–39 is a "complex collection of material, with a diverse background." But what does that mean for the question of the book of Isaiah as a whole? I would like to expand the just cited thesis to cover the so-called Trito-Isaiah too: a Trito-Isaiah is not to be found, neither as a prophetic person nor as an independent literary unit. In recent years Odil Steck has published some notable pieces of work denying the literary existence of Trito-Isaiah.[10] His last essay begins with an appeal that we should stop talking about "Trito-Isaiah" and study this complex third part in the framework of the book of Isaiah as a whole. It would go beyond the framework of this paper to discuss Steck's method and theses in detail. He is working in the context of the traditional *Literarkritik,* which I should not like to follow. But nevertheless, he is always looking for the relation between chaps. 56–66 and the preceding parts of the book of Isaiah.

Let us come back to 56:1. Steck agrees with my thesis[11] that this verse is intended to establish a deliberate continuity with the other two parts of the book, including the different use of צדקה. He sees this as the third and last stage of the redaction which he finds in chaps. 56–66. Whether we accept this analysis or not, it is important that at this point— and even earlier—Steck talks about a *Grossjesaja,* a "Greater Isaiah," which in general comprises the three parts of the book as we now have them before us. And his main thesis is that major parts of chaps. 56–66 (without chaps. 60–62, which in his view had already been linked with chaps. 40–55 even earlier) could only have come into existence, at least in their present form, at the "Greater Isaiah" stage.

IV

In a highly skillful way, Steck relates 56:1 to the last two verses of chap. 55. In these verses Israel is still in Babylon, and is just preparing to depart: "For you shall go out in joy, and be led forth in peace," and so forth (vv. 12f.). But then, in 56:1, the people addressed are obviously

9. Seitz, "Isaiah 1–66," 111.

10. O. H. Steck, *Bereitete Heimkehr: Jesaja 35 als redaktionelle Brücke zwischen dem Ersten und dem Zweiten Jesaja,* SBS 121 (Stuttgart, 1985), 68ff.; also his "Tritojesaja im Jesajabuch," in J. Vermeylen, ed., *The Book of Isaiah,* BETL 81 (Louvain, 1989), 361–406.

11. See nn. 5 and 8 above.

back in the land, being admonished to keep justice and do righteousness. However, as we have already mentioned, the basic precondition for this admonition is the fact that God's righteousness and salvation are about to come. This immediate link becomes much more evident and striking if we read continuously from chap. 55 to chap. 56. Now the addressees have arrived at this turning point, back in the land, and back in the present situation.

But if we read the whole in the framework of "Greater Isaiah," the addressees of chap. 56 are the same as those of earlier chapters. Let us go back to earlier parts of the book in order to see what the consequences of such a reading might be.

In the very first chapter of the book,[12] צדקה or צדק and משפט are already central terms in the divine word about Jerusalem (vv. 21-28). The city that had once been full of משפט ("justice") and in which צדק ("righteousness") had lodged, God will now restore, so that it may be called עיר הצדק, "city of righteousness"; the whole saying concludes with the solemn declaration: "Zion shall be redeemed by משפט and her repatriates by צדקה" (v. 27). If we look back at these words from the standpoint of chap. 56, this is an extremely interesting text: God himself will be the one to restore צדק in Jerusalem, and finally to redeem her and her inhabitants by משפט and צדקה. The text does not explicitly say that the people should now keep and do justice and righteousness, even though this is clearly meant. But God's help in attaining this goal is the most important element. The people are called שָׁבֶיהָ, those who are returning to her, her repatriates.[13] The readers of 56:1 could immediately feel that with this they themselves were meant. And they are now admonished to keep justice and to do righteousness.

But let me turn things the other way around. The two above-mentioned postulates were that neither an independent First Isaiah nor an independent Third Isaiah can be found; but these theses have to be related to one another: this means that in the framework of "Greater Isaiah" the author of 1:21ff. could have meant precisely this group of addressees who, according to 56:1, had now arrived in the country as repatriates from Babylon. For it is these very people who are the present readers of the book, since it is obvious that the whole book in its present form is addressed to postexilic Israel. And if there is no independent First Isaiah, then it will always be permissible, and even necessary, to ask whether a

---

12. On the comprehensive function of chap. 1, cf. also Seitz, "Isaiah 1–66," 112ff.
13. LXX and other commentaries.

particular text in the first part of the book—and of course in the second part also—was deliberately written for this community of repatriates.

Of course this cannot be true of every text. On the contrary, that would ruin my thesis. The observation of two different uses of צדקה in different parts of the book, and their deliberate combination in 56:1, presupposes the existence of two different traditions older than the composition of 56:1. But I believe that in many cases the diachronic question becomes irrelevant as soon as we read the texts in the context of the "Greater Isaiah."

With regard to chap. 1 let me add one minor detail: in 1:28 the word about Zion ends with a condemnation of those who even after its restoration are still going to remain in rebellion against God. The word פֹּשְׁעִים ("the rebellious ones") appears again in the last verse of the book (66:24). Even in the last days, the community which comes to worship God every month and every week will see the dead bodies of those פֹּשְׁעִים, or "rebels," outside the city. But in the central or second part of the book too this group is addressed, namely in chap. 46, in the judgment over the idols. Verse 8 says that the פֹּשְׁעִים will remember the fate of the idols and call it to mind. Finally, the end of this chapter sounds like a pointer to 56:1:

> Hearken to me, you stubborn of heart,
> you who are far from righteousness [צדקה]:[14]
> I bring near my deliverance [קרבתי צדקתי],
> it is not far off,
> and my salvation [תשועתי] will not tarry;
> I will put salvation on Zion,
> for Israel my glory. (vv. 12f.)

Here we have entered part 2, which speaks about תשועה in direct relation to צדקה.

Let me mention one or two more texts. Chapter 32 is dominated by the word צדק. At the beginning it talks about the king who will rule in righteousness (v. 1), and at the end there is a whole sequence of צדקה and משפט. After v. 15 has announced the pouring out of "the spirit from on high" which will make the wilderness a fruitful field, the following verses read:

> Then justice will dwell in the wilderness,
> and righteousness abide in the fruitful field.

---

14. RSV reads "deliverance." But that is impossible here.

> And the effect of righteousness will be peace,
> and the result of righteousness, quietness and trust for ever. (vv. 16f.)[15]

It might be asked what kind of justice and righteousness is meant here. I think it comes close to that of chap. 1. It is the righteousness which people have to *do,* but God gives them the chance to do it, through the outpouring of his spirit.

So we could set these texts along a single line which leads to chap. 56; but nevertheless, the different way צדקה is used in chaps. 40–55 is always evident. Let me quote just one text from the second part of the book, 45:8. We find it in the oracle addressed to Cyrus, where in v. 5 one of the great self-praisings of God in chaps. 40–55 begins:

> I am the Lord, and there is no other,
> besides me there is no God.

People in all parts of the world are to know that he has created everything, light and darkness, salvation and disaster. Then the text goes on:

> Shower, O heavens, from above,
> and let the skies rain down righteousness [צדק];
> let the earth open, that salvation [ישע] may sprout forth,
> and let it cause righteousness [צדקה] to spring up also;
> I, the Lord, have created it.

Here it is the צדק itself that comes from heaven, accompanied by salvation (ישע), and God himself creates it.

So we have something like a network of texts spread over the whole book which talk about צדקה in its different aspects. Looked at in the light of 56:1, as well as from the aspect of chap. 1, it is clear that this is one of the key concepts in the "Greater Isaiah." At different central points it is related to Zion. Let me add just one example from the third part of the book, 62:1f.:

15. In the last verse of the chapter the word אשרי, "happy," appears:

> Happy are you who sow beside all waters,
> Who let the feet of the ox and the ass range free. (v. 20)

The third occurrence is in chap. 30. Verse 18 marks the turning point from accusation and judgment to the announcement of salvation:

> Therefore the Lord waits to be gracious to you;
> therefore he exalts himself to show mercy to you.
> For the Lord is a God of justice;
> blessed are all those who wait for him.

The reason for God's desire to be gracious and merciful is that he is "a God of justice" (משפט).

> For Zion's sake I will not keep silent,
> and for Jerusalem's sake I will not rest,
> until her righteousness [צֶדֶק]¹⁶ goes forth as brightness,
> and her salvation [יְשׁוּעָה] as a burning torch.
> The nations shall see your righteousness [צֶדֶק],
> and all the kings your glory;
> and you shall be called by a new name
> which the mouth of the Lord will give.

This new name is not identical with the restored name of chap. 1, where Jerusalem is once more named עִיר הַצֶּדֶק, "city of righteousness," and קִרְיָה נֶאֱמָנָה, "faithful city." Now a new name is announced to her which is coined mainly over against the two negative attributes:

> You shall no more be termed Forsaken,
> and your land shall no more be termed Desolate;
> but you shall be called חֶפְצִי־בָהּ ["my delight is in her"],
> and your land "married,"
> for the Lord delights in you,
> and your land shall be married.

This last text shows clearly that, notwithstanding its central role, the concept of צְדָקָה is not the sole, and not the final, concept in the book of Isaiah. Surprisingly, it is missing at certain points. For instance, in chap. 12, whose central function is absolutely clear,¹⁷ we find an extensive use of יְשׁוּעָה (v. 2 twice, v. 3), but the word צְדָקָה is lacking. Later, in the last chapters of the book, neither צְדָקָה nor יְשׁוּעָה/יְשׁוּעָה תְּשׁוּעָה appear any longer. Here other concepts are dominant—for instance the concept of God's glory (כָּבוֹד) or of the name—both the name of God and the name of the community which is addressed, whose descendants and name are to remain like the new heavens and the new earth (66:18).

These last remarks are mainly intended to make us conscious of the fact that we are still at the beginning, in reading the book of Isaiah as a whole. But I believe that in recent years we have taken some very important steps. I hope that we shall soon be able to summarize our insights and to develop some methodological criteria for further research.

---

16. RSV reads "vindication."

17. See especially P. R. Ackroyd, "Isaiah I–XII: Presentation of a Prophet," VTSup 29 (1978): 16–48, esp. 34ff. (= his *Studies in the Religious Tradition of the Old Testament* [1987], 79–104, esp. 94ff.).

CHAPTER 16

Ezekiel 20 and 36:16ff. in
the Framework of the
Composition of the Book

Attention has often already been drawn to the relationships between the first main part of the book of Ezekiel (chaps. 1–24) and the third main section (chaps. 33–48).[1] I should like to go into this question in rather more detail here. The hermeneutical presupposition for this is the method of "holistic interpretation" which has been described and used by M. Greenberg in particular.[2] This method stands in a close mutual relationship to the "close reading" through which we can discover indications of deliberate compositional shapings in the text.[3]

A first clear pointer—a "signal," as it were—to the relationships between the first and third parts can be found at the end of God's first address to the prophet (2:1-5): "Whether they hear or refuse to hear, they will know that there has been a prophet among them" (v. 5). When are they to know this, and how? The answer is found at the close of the first chapter of the third part (chap. 33): "When this comes—they will know that a prophet has been among them" (v. 33). Greenberg makes this connection clear by translating 2:5: "And they . . . shall (yet) realize that a

---

1. See here also R. Rendtorff, *Das Alte Testament: Eine Einführung,* 3d ed. (Neukirchen, 1988), 221ff.; Eng. trans., *The Old Testament: An Introduction* (Philadelphia: Fortress Press; London: SCM Press, 1986).

2. M. Greenberg, *Ezekiel 1–20,* AB 22 (Garden City, N.Y.: Doubleday, 1983).

3. See here S. Talmon and M. Fishbane, "The Structuring of Biblical Books. Studies in the Book of Ezekiel," *ASTI* 10 (1976): 129–53; M. Fishbane, *Text and Texture: Close Readings of Selected Biblical Texts* (New York: Schocken Books, 1979); on the problems in general also M. Weiss, *The Bible from Within* (Jerusalem, 1984).

prophet was among them"; and in his interpretation he adds: "When the doom you foretell comes (cf. 33, 33)."[4]

Another plain indication of the connection is to be found in the statement about Ezekiel's dumbness. This is imposed on him directly after the introductory charge, with the word וַנֶּאֱלַמְתָּ (3:26); and its later ending is announced by אֶפְתַּח אֶת־פִּיךָ (v. 27); in the last verse of the first part (24:27), this pronouncement is repeated word for word, and in the first chapter of the third part the dumbness is indeed ended (33:21f.), again with the same words.

There can be no doubt that these three texts are deliberately and explicitly related to one another. What is especially important here is above all that in the first part of the book an announcement is made ("I will open your mouth," 3:27, cf. 24:27) which is fulfilled only in the third part ("he opened my mouth," 33:22). There is therefore a clear and deliberate trend leading from the first to the third part.[5]

In this connection it is also important to notice that the decisive turning point is the fall of Jerusalem, or the news of its fall. So it is not enough to relate the two parts of the book to each other under the aspect: "proclamation of doom" and "proclamation of salvation." One must add: before the fall of Jerusalem, or afterward, as the case may be. This is not merely a date; it is the decisive turn of events, not only in the prophet's proclamation, but above all in God's own acts and in his relationship to Israel.

This is also brought out in another explicit link between the two parts. In the vision about the destruction of Jerusalem in chaps. 8–11, YHWH's *kabod* ("glory") departs from the Temple and by so doing releases it for destruction (11:23). In the great concluding vision in chaps. 40–48 the *kabod* returns to the Temple once more (43:1ff.). Here there is an explicit reference to the earlier vision in chaps. 8–11 as well as to the one in chap. 1 (43:3). With this a new era of salvation begins, *after* judgment has been executed.[6]

The same division of the story into two different epochs can now also be found in chap. 20 on the one hand, and in 36:16ff. on the other. In 20:5-26 the beginning of God's history with Israel is described in three

---

4. Greenberg, *Ezekiel 1–20*, 66.

5. The inner structure of chaps. 2f. and chap. 33 and their relation to one another are topics that still require thorough investigation.

6. Further obvious relationships exist between the two sayings about "the mountains of Israel" in chaps. 6 and 36. The striking and frequently reiterated word "bones" (עֲצָמִים) in the song about Jerusalem, 24:1-14, could be a play on the restoration to life of the "dry bones" (עֲצָמוֹת) in chap. 37.

stages: the generation of slaves in Egypt (vv. 5-10); the same generation
in the wilderness (vv. 11-17); the second generation in the wilderness
(vv. 18-26). Three times we hear: "Then I thought I would pour out
my wrath upon them" (ואמר לשפך חמתי עליהם, vv. 8, 13, 21). But
God does not do it. Israel lives under the proclamation of judgment but
this is not yet implemented. It is only in 36:18 that we then read in
the same words: "So I poured out my wrath upon them" (ואשפך חמתי
עליהם). The announcement of dispersion (להפיץ אתם בגוים ולזרוח
אותם בארצות, 20:23) is now endorsed in the same words as having been
executed (ואפיץ אתם בגוים ויזרו בארצות, 36:19).

The reason why God has not acted hitherto is stated three times in
chap. 20, with the same wording in each case: "I acted for the sake of my
name, that it should not be profaned in the sight of the nations" (vv. 9, 14,
22). Now, after he has scattered Israel among the nations, they do indeed
profane his name there (36:20). So God acts again, in order to sanctify
his holy name once more, after it has been profaned (vv. 20-23).[7]

The reason why God is angry with Israel is her pollution through
"idols." The first directive which God gave Israel in Egypt was: "Do
not defile yourselves with the idols of Egypt!" (20:7; cf. v. 18). But they
have continually offended against this commandment; consequently God
himself made them impure through their idolatrous cult (v. 26). Greenberg stresses that none of the other historical reviews (chaps. 16; 23)
puts the cultic aspect so exclusively at the center, leaving the political
one entirely on one side. It is precisely this cultic aspect that 36:16ff.
picks up. Here it is then said that the people have polluted the land
(v. 17). This too is a consistent development of chap. 20, because there
the promised land, in contrast to other countries, plays a central role—
again in distinction from the other historical reviews. And here the root
occupies a key position. The assurance of the deliverance from Egypt
plays a decisive part. Deliverance is promised to the Israelites (20:6:
להוציאם מארץ מצרים)—words incidentally closely modeled on Exod.
6:2-8. This promise is also the reason why God "does not pour out his
wrath," since if he were to do so, the nations would see that God does not
keep his promise and his name would consequently be profaned (v. 9).
Correspondingly, it is said that after the deliverance (v. 10) God did not
wish to profane his name before the nations before whose eyes he led
Israel out of Egypt (vv. 14, 22). This is taken up again in 36:20, but
it is now applied to the land of Israel: God's holy name is profaned
because the nations say: "These are YHWH's people and yet they had

7. Cf. here also 20:39 and 44.

to go out of his land" (יצֹא). For this reason God will sanctify himself before the eyes of the nations by bringing back Israel again into its land.

Because Israel had polluted the land, the Israelites' return to their land will be bound up with their purification from the impurity brought about by their idolatry (36:25). And finally God will give them a new heart and a new spirit, so that they may keep his commandments and live in the land which God gave to their fathers—"and you shall be my people, and I will be your God" (v. 28). The "covenant formula" expresses the fact that the road God has traveled with Israel, which began with its election in Egypt and the promise of the land (20:5f.), is finally arriving at its goal. The central point at issue in the mutual relationship between God and Israel, both here and in the other passages where this formula is used, is again the purification from the false cult (cf. 11:20; 14:11; 37:23, 27, and the respective contexts).

The section 36:16ff. can in my view only be understood as a deliberate continuation and development of chap. 20. Between the two lies the decisive event: God has poured out his wrath over Jerusalem. Judgment has been executed and now a new epoch is beginning. To be more precise: it has already begun, for in 36:21 the turn of events is indicated through the impf. cons.: קדשׁי על־שׁם לֹ ואחמל ("But I had concern for my holy name"). The era of redemptive action has already begun.

These observations are of great importance for an understanding of the composition of the book of Ezekiel. They show that here not only have texts been gathered together under particular aspects, but that certain texts have been formulated with an eye to the compositional context— and vice versa: that a text such as chap. 20 is open for a necessary continuation, and is therefore not self-contained.

But the section 36:16ff. does not merely pick up chap. 20 once more. The mention of the "covenant formula" in v. 28 has already directed our gaze toward the end of the vision in chaps. 8–11. There too we also hear the same, or very similar, formulations about the gathering in from the diaspora, the bringing back into the land, the laying aside of idols, the new heart and new spirit, and finally the keeping of the commandments, the covenant formula standing at the end (11:17-20). Here the fundamental importance of the caesura brought about by the destruction of Jerusalem is once again made plain. What is proclaimed at the end of the vision for the era after the destruction is now taken up once more, after the judgment imposed on Jerusalem has become a reality.

Still other connections can undoubtedly be traced. Here my initial purpose was to draw attention to the importance of the composition for an understanding of the book of Ezekiel. In closing, let me try to indicate a few conclusions.

1. The question about the composition changes the meaning of the form-critical viewpoint. Form criticism is still, in my view, an indispensable exegetical instrument. But today I would no longer concede to it the unreserved importance which it has hitherto enjoyed in the "school" from which I come. It can easily lead to the isolating of individual text units from one another and over against one another, the consequence being an atomization of the text. Form criticism should therefore always be supplemented, and if need be also corrected, by an inquiry into the position and function of the individual text or speech units in their immediate and wider context.

As far as the prophetic books are concerned, this question is especially important, because ever since Gunkel we have been accustomed to ask in each given case about the individual, original prophetic saying. It is on this that the questions about the historical situation, the *Sitz im Leben,* depend—and of course the question of "authenticity" as well. From a strict form-critical standpoint, the question about the context and, especially, the composition only comes afterward; it is, that is to say, a "secondary" question. If it now emerges that texts have actually been formulated with an eye to a wider context, the questions put to them are bound to change. Thus the section Ezek. 36:16-28 (or 16-32) can undoubtedly be set apart form critically; yet if our observations are correct, this section never existed independently at all. But if it was shaped with a view to as wide a context as I have tried to show, this will then surely hardly be a saying spoken by the prophet; it is not, that is to say, a "prophetic saying" in the strict form-critical sense, but is a component belonging to the genre "prophetic book."

2. The ideas put forward hitherto show that the relationship of every individual section of text to its more immediate and its wider context must be examined; and also that the question about this relationship will receive varying answers. We should, I believe, proceed from a consistent "holistic" approach inasmuch as we reckon with the fact that the position of every individual section of text in its more immediate and wider context is intentional and has a point. We shall not succeed in all cases in detecting and understanding the intention of the composition. But this does not mean that the method as such is confuted. The difficulty should only stimulate us to further intensive study.

It does thereby emerge, however, that many units of text had a history behind them before they became components in the present composition, and that this prehistory differs from case to case. Here, then, we are faced with the exegetical and hermeneutical question of how we wish to deal with the earlier stages of the transmitted tradition, and how we should view the relations of the "original" "smallest units" to the present total context.

This brings me to the question about the "final canonical form." I neither can nor will enter here into the extensive and sometimes fierce discussion which is being carried on, in the English-speaking world particularly, and which has been evoked above all by Brevard Childs's concept. This discussion is waged by some authors as if it were a religious war—I am thinking here of James Barr in particular. I must admit that my sympathies are on the side of Childs, and that apart from some dogmatic-sounding formulations I believe that the method he has adopted is a promising one. As far as the prophetic books are concerned, Peter Ackroyd's work on the book of Isaiah also seems to me a pioneer approach. In the work of these scholars particularly, I see a useful combination of insights into the earlier history of the texts and the question about what they want to say in their present composition. The book of Ezekiel too will in my view be most appropriately treated if we see it as the "presentation of a prophet" and if instead of trying to break down its final form, we ask what its message to the reader is.

CHAPTER 17

What Is New in the
New Covenant?

What is new in the new covenant? For a Christian to ask this question in connection with Jeremiah 31 is something quite different from what it could be for a Jewish interpreter of the Bible. The Christian interpreter cannot avoid having in mind the whole Christian tradition, in which the notion of a "new covenant" is of crucial importance. So his or her task is a double one: to read in as unbiased a way as possible what the Hebrew Bible says about the new covenant; and to try to find an appropriate explication of the Christian understanding of the new covenant.

The second task—the Christian understanding of the new covenant—has several different aspects. I should like to name three of them: first, the interpretation of the New Testament passages which deal with the new covenant; second, a critical evaluation of the Christian tradition of "old" and "new" covenants; third, the attempt to formulate a new understanding of the Christian notion of the "new covenant" which is free from any anti-Jewish implication.

It is obvious that it would be impossible to deal adequately with all these aspects in the framework of this paper. But I am in a fortunate position, because my paper is only one of a series. Moshe Greenberg has already dealt profoundly with the concept of the new covenant in the sayings of Jeremiah. Tonight Zwi Werblowsky will explain Paul's approach to the covenant with Jews and Gentiles. And tomorrow

Lecture held in English at the symposium "People and Covenant" in Jerusalem, 1988. Small stylistic changes have been made in this printed text, but the lecture character has been preserved.

Friedrich-Wilhelm Marquardt will give an outline of a Christian theology of covenant. So I can restrict myself to some reflections on the interrelations between the different aspects of the problem.

I

Let me begin with some remarks about Jeremiah's message of a new covenant. I have found it interesting to read this chapter or chapters (Jeremiah 30, or 30 and 31) together with Christian students. For them, it is always a great surprise to find that what is new in this covenant is not a change of content, but that it is the same Torah which is at the center of the new covenant as was at the center of the former one, and that the same promise is given to Israel and Judah: that the Lord will be their God and that they shall be his people. For Christian readers, it is an important discovery to understand that Jeremiah does not envisage a new covenant without Torah, without the "burden of the law," as some Christians would like to put it; but that what he has in mind is a covenant in which the Torah is even more firmly anchored, and in which the observation of the Torah is guaranteed by God himself. In addition, Christian readers have to realize that in Jeremiah's words God is promising what Deuteronomy had already said: that "the word is very near you; it is in your mouth and in your heart, so that you can do it" (Deut. 30:14). That means that there is no prophetic contradiction, let alone rebellion, against the law, and no vision of a future without a Torah that has to be observed and fulfilled.

This means that one way of interpretation, often employed by Christian theologians, is actually unusable, for simple exegetical reasons: it is impossible to play the prophets off against the law, and to link the gospel directly to the prophets, in order in this way to bridge the dark period of postexilic, law-dependent Judaism, by linking one "peak" with another—the prophets with Jesus. From such a point of departure, Jeremiah is often interpreted as saying that the "old covenant" has failed, so that a new covenant has to be given; for otherwise Israel would be lost, being without any covenant with God at all.

Let me mention just one prominent and fairly recent example of this kind of Christian use of Jeremiah's words, which is closely linked with the topic of our meeting here today. At the famous Rhineland Synod in 1980, Hans Walter Wolff gave an exegesis of Jer. 31:31-34. According to his interpretation, Jeremiah's distinction between old and new clearly includes a "no" to the old. Verse 32, "my covenant which they broke," he understands to mean: "They have destroyed it, abolished it, made it invalid." But this is in clear contradiction to what the whole Hebrew Bible says, namely that the validity of the covenant does not depend on the behavior of the people, however bad it might be, but that God himself guarantees the covenant's continuance. As one of the preconditions for the new covenant, Wolff stressed in particular the last verse of the paragraph: "For I will forgive their iniquity, and I will remember their sin no more" (v. 34b). For him it is clear that this happened only in Jesus, never before. So he says: "This was not mentioned among the foundations of the old covenant." Unfortunately even this is simply wrong. In the record of the giving of the covenant on Mount Sinai, it is said that after the sin with the golden calf, Moses prayed to God: "Pardon our iniquity and our sin, and take us for thy inheritance" (Exod. 34:9). And God immediately answered: "Behold, I make a covenant," renewed the covenant, and wrote the broken tablets anew. Here the forgiving of the sins is *the* basis for the renewal of the covenant, and thereby the basis of the covenant with which Israel has lived ever since. So even at the particular point where Christian interpreters wish to link the prophetic text to the New Testament (in order to show that Jeremiah is announcing something that goes beyond the Old Testament and finds its fulfillment only in the New) they make a fundamental exegetical mistake which actually withdraws the basis of their argumentation. One might almost say, turning Paul's words the other way around, that when they are reading the Old Testament, a veil lies over the minds of many Christian interpreters, so that they are unable to understand what they are reading.

This is just one example of a traditional Christian way of using the Hebrew Bible: not to read it in its entirety, but to select single passages or even verses, and to interpret them in an eclectic manner. There are several reasons for this behavior. First of all, Christians are taught to look on the Hebrew Bible as the "Old Testament," that is, as part of the Christian Bible, without reflecting that it is also, and above all, the Jewish Bible. In our present framework, on the tenth anniversary of our program in Jerusalem, this sounds like a mere truism. But in the reality of the context we live in, most Christian theologians are not yet conscious at all that there might be a theological problem about the traditional Christian use of the Old Testament. (I must apologize for using the term "Old Testament." It is sometimes necessary, in order to describe the relation between the two parts of the Christian Bible and the Christian use of the first part. Moreover it seems to me implausible to talk about the Hebrew Bible while discussing Greek terms. So at the moment I see no alternative.)

Again only one example: recently a new edition of a well-known book appeared, Antonius Gunneweg's *Vom Verstehen des Alten Testaments,* with the subtitle *Eine Hermeneutik.* The familiar thesis of this book is that there is no legitimate theological interpretation of the Old Testament at all except the Christian one. I eagerly picked up the new edition in order to see what changes the author had made, after more than ten years of lively debate over hermeneutical questions about the understanding of the Old Testament. But there are no changes. On the contrary, in a very brief postscript, the author says that because of the kind reception accorded to the book he sees no need for changes. So this book will be sold and bought for another ten years or more, as *the* book on Old Testament hermeneutics in German; and it has also, of course, been translated into English as well.[1]

II

One of the central points in this mainstream Christian tradition is the unquestioned premise that the key to an understanding of the Old Testament is to be found only in the New. The exegetes therefore feel forced to find facts, ideas, or at least words which could serve as links between the two Testaments. For that reason, Jeremiah's word about the new covenant has a particular fascination for Christian Bible interpreters, because it is spontaneously associated with the "New Testament." In Christian ears this word has a double connotation. On the one hand it describes the book itself, the New Testament, which in the eyes of most Christians is the more important part of the two-part Bible, because it contains the specifically Christian message—the gospel. And on the other hand the word occurs in the framework of the Lord's Supper. According to the version in the Gospel of Luke, Jesus said, when giving the cup to his disciples: "This cup which is poured out for you in the new covenant in my blood..." (Luke 22:20). In the traditional German (Luther) translation, which is also used in the liturgy, these words are translated: "This cup is the new testament in my blood..." ("Dieser Kelch ist das neue Testament in meinem Blut, das for euch vergossen wird zur Vergebung der Sünden").

It is obvious how important it must be for Christian interpreters of the Old as well of the New Testament to discover what exactly the relation is between Jeremiah's announcement of the new covenant and the Christian

---

1. Eng. trans. A. Gunneweg, *Understanding the Old Testament,* trans. J. Bowden (London: SCM Press; Philadelphia: Westminster Press, 1978). The first German edition was published in 1977.

adoption of this expression. At first sight the relation seems to be very close, because Jeremiah 31 is quoted several times in the New Testament. But let us look in more detail at the meaning and relevance of those quotations.

1. First of all it must be emphasized that the use of the Greek word διαθήκη (which is the usual translation for בְּרִית in the Septuagint) is fairly marginal in the New Testament. It occurs thirty-three times, two-thirds of these occurrences being quotations from the Greek Old Testament; the rest are confined to Paul and the Letter to the Hebrews. There is no mention of διαθήκη in Jesus' own words except in the context of the Lord's Supper, to which I shall come back later. And even in Paul's writings the term is not of crucial relevance. Nevertheless, the remaining texts are interesting enough and have had considerable consequences in the history of Christian theology.

2. I do not want to say too much about Paul's use of the word "covenant" (διαθήκη) because I hope to learn much more about that from Zwi Werblowsky. So I will restrict myself to only a few remarks.

2.1 First, one of the most relevant texts where Paul talks about διαθήκη is to be found in the Letter to the Galatians. Here Paul uses the word διαθήκη first of all in the sense of a legacy, the will of a deceased person. In Gal. 3:15 he gives "a human example": that "no one annuls even a man's will, or adds to it, once it has been ratified." What he wants to demonstrate is that the promise given to Abraham and his offspring cannot be changed by anything added later, namely the law. But then he plays with the word διαθήκη, using it in the sense of בְּרִית, saying: "The law, which came four hundred and thirty years afterward, does not annul a covenant previously ratified by God, so as to make the promise void" (v. 17). And then he turns back to the metaphor of inheritance, but now using another word, κληρονομία: "For if the inheritance is by the law, it is no longer by promise; but God has granted it to Abraham by promise" (v. 18).

It is interesting, and sometimes rather frustrating, to see how modern Christian New Testament scholars deal with this text. (In the following discussion I shall mainly be quoting from Erich Grässer's book *Der Alte Bund im Neuen* [1985], though drawing on several articles by Ferdinand Hahn, Ulrich Luz, Otto Hofius, and others as well.) It is obvious that the main and comprehensive term in this text is covenant/διαθήκη. The covenant is given to Abraham by promise. This is unalterable, so the covenant God has made with Abraham remains valid throughout the centuries. In the Letter to the Romans, Paul mentions the διαθήκη as one of Israel's enduring privileges, alongside the giving of the law: "They are Israelites, and to them belong the sonship, the glory, the covenants [διαθῆκαι], the giving of the law [νομοθεσία], the worship, and the promises" (Rom. 9:4). The question is now: How are these two texts related? To my mind it is obvious that in both cases Paul is saying that the covenant has been given to Israel and that it is still valid. But this is not at all obvious to some modern Christian interpreters. They assume that Paul uses διαθήκη differently in Romans and Galatians. Whereas in Romans he uses the word indiscriminately for the covenant with Abraham and the covenant given on Sinai, according to a certain Christian interpretation he is supposed to have employed the word in a different way in Galatians, establishing an antithesis between the covenant with Abraham (which is the covenant of promise) and the Sinai covenant (which is the covenant of law). According to this interpretation these two covenants are incompatible with one another.

One problem these interpreters have with the text is that in Galatians 3 Paul used the term διαθήκη only once, namely for the covenant given to Abraham. Then he goes on to discuss the meaning and relevance of the law. But he never says what the interpreters make him say: that now Israel is under another covenant, different from the one given to Abraham. He could not have said such a thing because Abraham stands for Israel: of course for the true Israel, the Israel of promise, which here in Galatians—other than in Romans—he sets over against Israel under the law, for the purpose of criticizing certain judaizing Galatian Christians. We should not try to minimize Paul's polemic against the law, but what these interpreters do is to mix up law and covenant in such a way that not only is the usefulness and validity of the law questioned but God's covenant with Israel seems to be called in question too. But this Paul never did.

2.2 In our present framework, it is important to add that in Galatians 3 Paul never quotes, or even hints at, the new covenant of Jeremiah. The interpreters ask themselves why. Let me quote Grässer: "The 'new covenant' is no longer, and in no way, seen as the old covenant renewed, but only as the radical antithesis to the παλαιὰ διαθήκη, which actually means a contradiction no less radical than that between freedom and slavery (Gal. 4:21-31), life and death (II Cor. 3:6f)."[2] Here the interpreter has smuggled in the expression παλαιὰ διαθήκη, which occurs only once in the New Testament, in a completely different context, 2 Corinthians 3, where Paul talks about the "reading (from) the παλαιὰ διαθήκη" (v. 14), in this case referring to the written Torah. In this chapter Paul also uses

2. E. Grässer, *Der Alte Bund im Neuen* (Göttingen, 1985), 68.

the term "new covenant," saying: "God...has made us competent to be ministers of a new covenant" (v. 6). He goes on: "not in a written code but in the Spirit," adding: "for the written code kills, but the Spirit gives life." Here Paul establishes a strong antithesis between *gramma* and *pneuma,* the written, codified word and the Spirit. But he nevertheless attests that the written word, which had been "carved in letters on stone" (v. 7), had *doxa,* "splendor." And when he later on uses the term παλαιὰ διαθήκη, the old covenant, or even "Old Testament," then he does not at all say that it is outdated, let alone obsolete. Now there is a veil over the old covenant, "but when a man turns to the Lord the veil is removed" (v. 16). The antithesis between the killing *gramma* and the life-giving *pneuma* is obviously not simply identical with the difference between the old and the new covenant. I cannot discuss that in more detail here. In our present context it should only be stressed that even here Paul is not referring to the new covenant of Jeremiah 31, or quoting from this chapter. That shows that Paul uses the terminology about an old and a new covenant in different ways, but never with explicit reference to Jeremiah 31.

2.3 On one occasion, indeed, Paul does speak explicitly about two διαθῆκαι: in Galatians 4. Here again, as already in chap. 3, he plays with the different meanings of the word. He takes the story of Abraham's two sons as an allegory, explicitly using the word *allegorein* (v. 24). And then he switches from the meaning "legacy" to that of "covenant," playing another game by relating Hagar to Sinai, possibly with certain allusions to geographical facts. Thus in the allegorical context everything is turned upside down: Israel becomes Ishmael, Hagar is taken back again from the Sinai wilderness and identified with Jerusalem, and the true Jerusalem is elevated to heaven; there she is free, and Christians are her children. This is a nice allegory, sounding a bit like science fiction, but the message is clear: Christians are to feel free of the law. Unfortunately Christian interpreters seem unable to understand what an allegory is, and so try to extract from this allegory a particular kind of dogmatics, using the same mixture between "old" and "new" covenant as before, in total disregard of the fact that neither the word "new" nor the word "old" is used in this text. I think it is not worthwhile arguing about this exegetical method, since it is obviously wrong.

3.1 I must deal briefly with two further contexts in which the word διαθήκη is used in the New Testament, one of these being, as I have already mentioned, the accounts of the Lord's Supper. Here we find a very interesting combination of two Old Testament texts. Paul uses the same version as the one in Luke, which I have already quoted. In 1 Cor.

11:25, Paul quotes Jesus according to the tradition as saying: "This cup is the new covenant in my blood." Here we have a combination of Jer. 31:31 with Exod. 24:8, where the blood of the covenant (דם־הברית) is mentioned. The relation to Exodus 24 is even more evident in the versions in Mark and Matthew, where the passage reads: "This is my blood of the covenant," which, except for the word "my" (μου), is the same wording as the Septuagint version of Exod. 24:8. But interestingly enough, in the mainstream textual tradition of these versions, the word χαινή, "new," is missing. This shows that there have been different stages in the development of this combined text.

This combination means a fundamental shift compared with Jeremiah 31, because now the new covenant is related to the sacrificial covenant ceremony on Mount Sinai. Whatever idea may lie behind this combination, the combined text cannot be understood as an adoption or interpretation of Jeremiah 31. The question of the meaning of the Lord's Supper would go beyond the scope of this paper. But it is obvious that the idea of a sacrifice of atonement has a part to play in this combined text, which actually increases the distance to Jeremiah's words.

3.2 The last-mentioned threefold combination is explicitly developed in the Letter to the Hebrews, which I must finally deal with very briefly, considering particularly the reference to, or quotation from, Jeremiah 31. The standpoint from which the notion of διαθήκη is looked at is the cult, and in particular the priesthood. Jesus is the mediator of a new covenant which had become necessary because the old one had not been faultless. To prove this, the author quotes Jer. 31:31-34 in full. Obviously he is only picking up the keyword "fault" without caring about the real context of the quoted passage. And then he concludes: "In speaking of a new covenant he treats the first as obsolete. And what is becoming obsolete and growing old is ready to vanish away" (8:13). So that is that! The old covenant is finished. But again, the author is talking almost exclusively about the cultic aspect of the covenant, combining the Sinai covenant (Exodus 4) with the yom-hakkippurim (Leviticus 16). At the end of a lengthy exposition, the author sums up by quoting Jeremiah 31 again. To the final sentence: "I will remember their sins and their misdeeds no more," he adds: "Where there is forgiveness of sins, there is no longer any offering for sin" (10:18). This shows once more that the author is not at all interested in what Jeremiah says (who never mentions offerings at all), but that he is using this text in a totally different context, in order to prove his thesis that the old covenant is obsolete.

III

What the author of the Letter to the Hebrews does is not too far from what many modern Christian interpreters do. If we look back to what we have discovered by looking at some of the recent exegetical literature on the new covenant in Jeremiah, we can distinguish two different, and actually contradictory, approaches. The first one, represented by Hans Walter Wolff and others, wishes to demonstrate that Jeremiah's announcement of a new covenant has been fulfilled in Jesus Christ. For that purpose Wolff had to isolate the text in Jeremiah 31 and interpret it eclectically. The other approach, represented by Erich Grässer for example, wants to demonstrate the very contrary, namely that there is no continuity at all between the old and the new covenant. For this purpose Grässer had to do more or less the same with certain New Testament texts.

What the two have in common is the nature of their theological approach. Both of them have a certain theological, or even dogmatic, premise in mind, which they try to prove or demonstrate through certain biblical texts. Both of them share, first of all, their main conviction, namely that the old covenant to which the Hebrew (or even Greek Jewish) Bible testifies has come to an end and no longer possesses any validity. The difference between the two approaches lies in the question whether there is any continuity between the two covenants or not. The one group, to which some New Testament scholars also belong, understands the old covenant as being unfinished and open for a fulfillment which lies beyond the Old Testament. The premise for such an attitude is the basic idea of promise and fulfillment as developed by von Rad, Zimmerli, and others. These theologians have a profound appreciation of the Old Testament, but see it as still incomplete and as waiting for the final and definitive fulfillment which could only come, and has meanwhile come, through Jesus Christ. This of course implies that those who do not understand that this fulfillment has already taken place are actually blind, and have a veil over their minds, as 1 Corinthians 3 says. And these Christian theologians hope that one day all Jews will understand the true message of their own Bible as it is expounded in the New Testament.

The other group has a much less positive prejudice in favor of the Old Testament. For them there is no continuity between the old and the new covenant, so there is no actual continuity between the Old and the New Testaments either. Some of these theologians would deny this last conclusion and undertake certain dialectic attempts to avoid the either-or to which the consequences of their own approach must inevitably lead them. But their language, of which I have given some examples, is too clear for it to leave any doubt that in fact the Old Testament has been superseded by the New Testament in a way which does not allow the former to have a message of its own.

From a Jewish point of view, one could say that the difference between these two approaches is not too relevant, if it is relevant at all, because in both cases the result is the same: that only Christians have the key to the full meaning and message of the Old Testament, whether they wish to include this message in their own Christian one, or to exclude it. In a certain sense this is true. We therefore have to ask ourselves whether there could be a third way for Christians to use the Hebrew Bible which neither claims possession of it nor rejects it.

I believe that this is one of the crucial points in what we are trying to do through our program here in Jerusalem. We have to confess that we are still at the beginning. So in closing I can only attempt to indicate some of the steps we should try to take, and which we have perhaps already begun to take, in one way or another.

The first and fundamental step is to realize that the Hebrew Bible is the Jewish Bible first of all—not only that it was the Jewish Bible before it became part of the Christian Bible, but that it still is. In order that this fact may penetrate our awareness as deeply as possible, we should try to study the Hebrew Bible, at least for a while, as if there were no other, and in particular no Christian interpretation. I believe that Christians are usually too deeply entangled in their own tradition of biblical interpretation for them to be able to compare or contrast it with the Jewish interpretation without having gone through such a period in which they deliberately leave any Christian interpretation aside.

The next step would be no less fundamental: to realize that there are, and always will be, two different interpretations of the Hebrew Bible, a Jewish one and a Christian one, and that there cannot be an either-or, but that each of them has its own right, which cannot be disputed by the other tradition or community. This step will of course have far-reaching theological consequences, insofar as it includes the question about the "true" interpretation, and thereby ultimately the question of the truth in general. Since it is a biblical, Bible-based religion, Christianity cannot avoid coping with this problem, if it admits and accepts the propriety of a specifically Jewish Bible interpretation. From this aspect it becomes clear that the third way cannot be an "objective" exegesis which looks at the Hebrew Bible from a neutral point of view, but that it has to be a committed theological exegesis that faces up to the new theological problems which must inevitably arise from such a new approach.

Another step will be to reread and reexamine the New Testament against the background of a still-existing Jewish community which claims to have its own, and even its prior, right to take the Hebrew Bible as the foundation of its own religious and national identity. This will include in particular a reexamination of the traditional anti-Jewish elements. Here we have to learn to distinguish between those elements which are only the result of an anti-Jewish interpretation (and which we can more or less overcome through a new and more appropriate exegesis), and those elements in the New Testament which really are anti-Jewish. The question of how to deal with these will be one of the greatest challenges for a new thcological exegesis of the New Testament.

All this will finally lead to the theologically decisive step: the development of a new Christian theology in which the traditional antithetical relation to Judaism is replaced by a new one, in which the differences, the tensions, and even the contradictions between the two religions are not ignored or covered up, but are worked out and afterwards worked into a new theological concept. But that would go far beyond the scope of this paper, and far beyond my own theological competence. Yet I am sure that during these days we shall have the opportunity to listen to some outlines of a new concept of this kind, and to learn from each other, and with each other, what the next steps could be.

CHAPTER 18

Forty Years On: Four Decades
of Old Testament Scholarship
as I Have Experienced Them
in Heidelberg and
Elsewhere

When I pass the Theodor Heuss Bridge today, I can still see my arrival in Heidelberg in the summer of 1950, and can live it over again. I was temporally lodged in the theological "students' house" on the other side of the River Neckar, and in order to get there one had to cross the bridge on foot; for although it had been to some extent rebuilt after its destruction by German troops, it was still only a footbridge, and could not be used by wheeled transport. (It was not yet called the Theodor Heuss Bridge, incidentally, for it was only some months later that Heuss, then president of the Federal Republic, officially opened it.) That was forty years ago. Forty years are evidently a long time, not only in a person's life, but in the life of a bridge too.[1] Although there are certainly bridges that last longer than that.

As I crossed the bridge I had my completed thesis under my arm, so to speak. In our faculty, the dean's office keeps a list of the doctorates that have been conferred since 1945. On the first page you can read the following names: 1947, Hannelis Schulte; 1949, Heinz Zahrnt; 1950, Heinz Kraft (later of Kiel); Georg Kretschmar (later Munich), Rolf Rendtorff. I had come to Heidelberg in the footsteps of Gerhard von Rad, who had left Göttingen for Heidelberg the previous year. It so happened that my oral examination took place on his forty-ninth birthday, and I was his first doctoral candidate; the war had caused a good many delays. In

Farewell lecture given in the theological faculty of the University of Heidelberg, July 19, 1990.
1. The bridge is now in need of repair and is being demolished and rebuilt bit by bit.

the winter term of 1950–51 I was then given a teaching assignment for Hebrew, and in the following terms proseminars for Old Testament and *Bibelkunde*. So this summer term of 1990 also rounds off the fortieth year of my teaching career at the university. It began where it is ending: in Heidelberg.

A glance back could take in many different facets, some of them very personal: Gerhard von Rad was rather shy in his personal contacts, but in spite of that—or perhaps for that very reason—my relationship to him was an extremely personal one. Klaus Koch remembers that when we once went to see him together, he opened the door and proudly introduced us to his wife, saying: "These are the boys the Lord has given me."

But I should now like to talk particularly about the reason why Gerhard von Rad was in Heidelberg at all, and why I had followed him there. That reason was the Old Testament. In recent years I have often become conscious during my lectures—and I have often told my students so—of the fundamental changes which Old Testament scholarship has undergone during these four decades; and I am also very much aware that these changes belong within a wider context. It would burst the bounds of this single lecture if I were to try to give a comprehensive account of the history of Old Testament scholarship during this period, quite apart from its involvement in developments in theology generally, in the humanities, and not least in political life. So I am deliberately choosing a more personal aspect, and should like to talk about "Old Testament scholarship as I have experienced it."

I

Round about 1950, a new overall picture of Israel's early history consolidated in German Old Testament scholarship. This picture was made up of many elements which had already existed for some considerable time, but which now began to grow together into a whole. In Heidelberg we were able to experience this directly. In the summer term of 1950, in the Old Hall of the university, Gerhard von Rad held his inaugural lecture under the title: "The Holy War in Ancient Israel." The slim volume which resulted (published in 1951) is an important building block in this new edifice. The book begins with the following sentences:

> Work on the Old Testament today is largely determined by the question of institutions. The form-critical research initiated by Hermann Gunkel has led to sharp distinctions between quite diverse *Sitze im Leben*. These *Sitze im Leben*—each of them a focal point of public, sacral or judicial life—are

seen as the places in which tradition, formed according to precise rules, was preserved.[2]

These sentences contain in concentrated form essential elements of the program that was then beginning to take shape. It is not by chance that Hermann Gunkel is mentioned first here, even though he had died as long before as 1932, for this great Old Testament scholar had struck out new paths, especially through his intuitive grasp of literary forms and their relation to social reality; and the seed he had sown was now really beginning to spring up in all its fullness. Von Rad very consciously saw it as one of his tasks to make people generally aware of what Gunkel had initiated, and to develop it further. He occasionally remarked in his inimitable way that he had "Gunkel's blood" in his veins.

As von Rad says in this passage, Gunkel's research into literary forms led him to distinguish between completely different real-life situations, or *Sitze im Leben*. But he confined himself largely to the literary field; and above all, his literary insights did not lead him to any new recognitions about "institutions"—that is to say, about the established, institutionally manifest and tangible sectors of life which for their part provided the situations or *Sitze im Leben* for particular literary genres. It was left to the generation that followed Gunkel to develop the interplay between the recognition of genres and the reconstruction of institutions which could be assumed to be their *Sitze im Leben*.

We shall see more clearly how to "place" the year 1950 from another book published in that year: Martin Noth's *History of Israel*.[3] Here we are immediately struck by what the keyword "institution" could mean: the sacral alliance of the twelve tribes of Israel, which Noth, following Greek models, called an amphictyony, that is, "a community of those who dwell around" (p. 88). Noth had already published his theory about the amphictyony in ancient Israel in 1930. But it was only now that this institution became part of the general stock of ideas. At the same time (and that is now the really interesting thing) von Rad made it the sustainer of sacral and cultic traditions to a much greater degree than Noth himself either could do or wished to do.

The amphictyony, therefore, had now became the linchpin or cornerstone of Israel's early history. We must be clear about what it meant, to have so firmly cemented an institution in view for the early period. In his study on the Holy War, von Rad used the term "amphictyony"

---

2. G. von Rad, *Holy War in Ancient Israel*, trans. and ed. Marva J. Dawn (Grand Rapids: Eerdmans, 1990).

3. M. Noth, *History of Israel*, trans. S. Godman (London: A. & C. Black, 1958).

quite as a matter of course, but he used the adjectives "pre-" and "post-amphictyonic" too. Everything could take its bearings from this center. At the same time it also becomes evident how much interest was directed toward Israel's early history, and how much people were convinced on the basis of these constructions that they could penetrate far back into Israel's beginnings. Today, in contrast, discussion about the same texts is not a debate about whether they are pre- or postamphictyonic; it is concerned with what is pre- and what is postexilic—that is to say, with an era five hundred years later. But more of this later.

First of all a little more about the "earlier," preamphictyonic phase. Here we must mention Albrecht Alt. Martin Noth and Gerhard von Rad were both pupils and senior graduate students of Alt's, and in many ways took over and developed further what he had begun. Others of their generation also felt that they were members of this group, which we then joined in our turn, as the next generation. Von Rad liked to talk about "Alt's family clan." In 1953, at the instigation of his pupils, his widely scattered *Kleine Schriften zur Geschichte des Volkes Israel* were collected and published.[4] To pick up these two volumes is to be continually fascinated by the intuitive power and systematic sweep with which Alt developed his postulates.

The table of contents for the first volume gives us the essential keywords for the picture which Alt drew of the early period. First of all "the God of the Fathers"—that nameless God of a nomadic group who was later to become the "παιδαγωγός [the tutor or guide] leading to the greater God" (p. 62). With this the reader of the Old Testament was made at home in the period of the patriarchs, so to speak, and could then join the author in the next step to "The Settlement of the Israelites in Palestine" (essays of 1925 and 1939), which Alt saw as a peaceful settling-down, following on, or prolonging, the yearly change of pastures practiced by nomadic or seminomadic groups. This viewpoint, which Martin Noth developed, led to a conflict with the American Albright school. And in the 1950s this conflict reached its climax. The Americans reproached the Germans with failing to take sufficient account of "the archaeological evidence" and, moreover, with having a "nihilist" attitude to the texts; for in defining them by way of form criticism as aetiological sagas, they were really simply trying to prove that they were unhistorical.

This conflict (in which I myself was not directly involved) has remained so vividly in my memory because these were fundamental

---

4. See A. Alt, *Essays on Old Testament History and Religion* (a selection, in one volume), trans. R. A. Wilson (Oxford: Blackwell, 1966).

questions about the relation of the Old Testament texts to history. The aim of the exegesis practiced by Alt and his pupils was to define the texts according to their literary types (as Gunkel had taught). This kind of exegesis was now confronted by a viewpoint in which the texts were seen primarily as historical sources, the attempt being made to confirm their historical reliability by way of "external evidence." The scholars belonging to this second group thereby also represented a conservative theological position, from which the others, who belonged to the liberal tradition, were denigrated as nihilist. Incidentally this discussion showed a striking lack of symmetry, for Albright, and above all some of his pupils, felt this problem very deeply and expressed it very forcibly, whereas for Noth it was a matter of relative indifference, and it was somewhat unwillingly that he entered into the dispute.[5]

Finally, let us return for a moment to Alt's *Kleine Schriften*. Here the third, epoch-making essay in the first volume must be mentioned. It was entitled "The Origins of Israelite Law"—and at this point my own scholarly history begins to play a part. This essay was the first form-critical treatment of legal texts, to which Gunkel himself had devoted no attention. When I first tentatively raised the question of a doctorate with Gerhard von Rad (who was still in Göttingen at the time), he talked about the need to extend the same questions to the provisions of cultic law as well. He said that he did not know how one should start, but that I should have a try. So that is where I landed, and where I am still, as I brood over my Leviticus commentary.

If time allowed, I should have liked to glance at the surrounding theological scene in those years. But I must confine myself to a few pointers. The publication of Rudolf Bultmann's *Theology of the New Testament* was for us epoch-making. Between its two volumes (1949 and 1953),[6] the *Zeitschrift für Theologie und Kirche* began to appear again (1950), opening with Gerhard Ebeling's great essay "The Importance of the Historical-Critical Method for Protestant Theology and the Protestant Church." For us at that time this provided a yardstick, not least because of Ebeling's clarion call to the systematic theologians "not merely to take the results of historical-critical research into account (though even that is often sadly lacking) but to absorb the problem of the historical-critical method fully and whole-heartedly into their own approach" (p. 44).

5. Cf. above all M. Noth, "Der Beitrag der Archäologie zur Geschichte Israels," VTSup 7 (1960): 262–82 (=*Aufsätze zur biblischen Landes-und Altertumskunde* [Neukirchen-Vluyn, 1971], 1:34–51).

6. R. Bultmann, *Theology of the Old Testament,* trans. K. Grobel (New York: Scribner's, vol. 1, 1951; vol. 2, 1955; London: SCM Press, vol. 1, 1952; vol. 2, 1955).

Ebeling was then of course writing as a church historian, not as a systematic theologian. This demand of his also pinpointed a profound conflict in the Heidelberg faculty between the exegetes and historians on the one hand (especially Günter Bornkamm and Hans von Campenhausen) and the systematic theologians on the other (Peter Brunner and Edmund Schlink). We younger ones reveled in the duel.

By talking about "we younger ones" in the plural, I have already touched on another facet of the theological scene—the so-called Pannenberg group. I say so-called for two reasons. First, Wolfhart Pannenberg was the last to join the group, and he was initially accepted by us exegetes only with some reserve, simply because he was a systematic theologian, or was on the way to becoming one. Second, the bond between us could be far more accurately defined through the name of Gerhard von Rad. This fact is actually publicly documented, inasmuch as the Festschrift presented to "Gerhard von Rad, our teacher, on his 60th birthday,"[7] included contributions not only by Klaus Koch and myself but also by the non–Old Testament members of this group in its original form: that is to say, Wolfhart Pannenberg, Dietrich Rössler, and Ulrich Wilckens.

For all of us, von Rad's theological work was particularly important in one essential point. At one of our regular meetings I read a paper about the Old Testament view of history—of course entirely along the lines of the first volume of von Rad's *Theology,* which had just appeared. The subject of the following paper was supposed to be Ernst Fuchs's phrase about "Christ, the end of history." But after the discussions about von Rad, it was clear that to maintain any such interpretation of history was now no longer possible. This was in a sense the moment when the program "revelation as history" was born, and it was therefore at the same time our farewell to the theology of the Bultmann school. Out of the historicity of our existence we had turned again to history itself—and above all to the way the Bible talks about history.

This laid down the theme for the years that followed. I called my inaugural lecture in Berlin in 1959 "Old Testament Hermeneutics as a Question about History." And the word "history" turned up in many variations and combinations in the work we published during these years. In the forefront here was the phrase about "the history of tradition," which Pannenberg, the systematic theologian, and my brother Trutz had also taken over at that time. But the phrase "history of religion" also cropped up not infrequently; for Klaus Koch and I felt that von Rad's position was

---

7. R. Rendtorff and K. Koch, eds., *Studien zur Theologie der alttestamentlichen Überlieferungen* (Neukirchen-Vluyn, 1961).

in some respects too conservative, and we tried to win back the "history of religions" dimension of Old Testament religion, which at that time was still maintained almost solely by Otto Eissfeldt among German Old Testament scholars. This, apart from pleasure in the language, was not the least of the reasons for my own Ugaritic studies, which I took up in the 1950s. And when I returned to Heidelberg in 1963, my inaugural lecture was entitled "El, Ba'al and Yahweh: Some Thoughts about the Relation between the Canaanite and the Israelite Religion." This moved Hans von Campenhausen to remark that I was the young Ba'al who had infiltrated into the Heidelberg pantheon. After all, I was almost twenty-five years younger than most of the other members of the faculty at that time. Professor Gensichen was the youngest of them, and he was born in 1915.

II

At this point, in the early years of my second decade in university teaching, the erosion of the great picture of Israel's early period had quite quietly begun. In 1962 Siegfried Herrmann, one of Alt's last pupils, had dedicated an essay to Martin Noth on his sixtieth birthday called "The Rise of Israel."[8] Harmless though the title sounded, this essay was nothing less than a denial of the amphictyony hypothesis. It is true that this had already been disputed even earlier, for example by Georg Fohrer; but Herrmann was an insider—just as much Alt's pupil as Noth himself—and his arguments were drawn from Alt's own arsenal. At that time a phrase of Alt's own took on a key position: the Canaanite "crossbolt"—that is to say, the series of fortified Canaanite cities which thrust like a bolt right across the country, cities which the Israelites would not have been able to capture, and which—and this was now Herrmann's postulate—prevented the Israelite tribes from growing together more closely before the period of the monarchy. This initiated a discussion which after only a few years led to a complete collapse of the amphictyony theory, especially since even its defenders—for example Rudolf Smend—readily admitted its weaknesses. My first lectures in Heidelberg in the winter term of 1963–64 were devoted to a history of Israel, and the manuscript clearly shows that we were already moving away from the amphictyony theory.

This of course also affected the question of the Holy War, and Gerhard von Rad did not like to hear anything about this whole development. When I once began about it in conversation, he looked at me very sadly

8. *TLZ* 87 (1962): 561–74.

and said: "Can't we talk about something else?" And in the years that followed I respected his wish.

In any case, my own interests were developing in different directions during these years. In the spring of 1963 I was in Israel for the first time, with a group of theology students from Berlin. The phase that now began had for me a double history behind it. On the one hand, I had already been in the countries of the Bible once, in 1959, on a teaching course offered by the German Palestine Institute (again with Klaus Koch, incidentally), but that took me only to the Jordanian side, including the Old City of Jerusalem. Now the other side was thrown open to me too—Jewish Israel, and especially the Jewish Jerusalem. Second, in Israel I again met Jewish colleagues whom I already knew from conferences, and who met me—a German belonging to the generation of Hitler's army—with an astonishing and humbling friendliness. I should like to say this especially about Isaak Leo Seligmann, who has since died. This encounter led in 1965 to an invitation to the World Congress of Jewish Studies in Jerusalem, in which I have participated regularly ever since. The fact that no fewer than seven Jewish Old Testament scholars contributed essays to the Festschrift dedicated to me is one of the direct results of that 1963 journey.

In 1965 I was able to intensify another contact too, this time with Swedish Old Testament studies, especially the Uppsala school. I had felt for some time that in spite of certain exaggerations there were approaches there which had to be discussed. Helmer Ringgren had been visiting professor in Berlin a few years previously, and he now invited me to Uppsala. This made me compare and contrast the German tradition of literary criticism with the Swedish concept about tradition history. The lecture I gave then is the first publicly expressed doubt about literary criticism as the be-all and end-all.[9] Before the end of the 1960s, at the next World Congress of Jewish Studies in Jerusalem, I then put on record my basic rejection of the division of the sources in the Pentateuch, although this received little notice at first.

However, the same question was exercising our minds here in Heidelberg too, at that time. In 1967 Hans Walter Wolff succeeded Gerhard von Rad. His inaugural lecture in May 1968 began with the words: "The people who slew the Elohist with the stroke of a pen are still among us"; and he cast a sharp glance in my direction.[10] He did not yet suspect that I

9. R. Rendtorff, "Literarkritik und Traditionsgeschichte," *EvT* 27 (1967): 138–53.

10. H. W. Wolff, "Zur Thematik der elohistischen Fragmente im Pentateuch," *EvT* 29 (1969): 59–72 (= *Gesammelte Studien zum Alten Testament* [Munich, 1964], 402–17).

was already hatching many other ideas as well. It must then have been in the summer of 1969 that students from our seminar induced us to engage in a public disputation about the sources of the Pentateuch—in this very lecture hall. Looking back, I am continually astonished that the subject could arouse such interest at that time, when the call to revolution was already the order of the day.[11]

III

The first years of my third decade in university teaching were dominated by very different aspects. It was the era of agitation in university politics, and this was true especially of the period when I was rector, from the beginning of 1970 until the end of 1972. This is not the place to talk about that. I might at most mention that the then university press officer recollected a little while ago, in a letter, how "you led us into the mysteries of Ugaritic, while at the same time we were discussing our attitude to the forcible eviction of the Heidelberg AStA."[12] The fact that contact with Old Testament scholarship was not lost altogether during these years was due above all to the postgraduate seminar, which continued to meet regularly—and this, it must be said, could never have happened without the steady groundwork and cooperation of Konrad Rupprecht. I must also mention that on October 21, 1971, a very small group of us was able to visit Gerhard von Rad on his sick bed, and to present him with the Festschrift for his seventieth birthday, shortly before his death on October 31.

My period as rector was followed by the other extreme, as it were, for in the winter of 1973–74 I went as visiting professor to the Hebrew University in Jerusalem for several months. It was a hard winter in many ways. It was immediately after the Yom Kippur War, many students were still in the army, supplies were short, and it was a winter in which Jerusalem was submerged in snow. But it was also a time of complete concentration on intensive work on the Old Testament, both in regular teaching sessions with small groups of students, and in a postgraduate colloquium, in which I had to defend my concept of transmission history in fierce discussions. But this helped me essentially to clarify and work out my position, which I was then able to put forward for discussion for the first time in 1974, at the Congress of the International Organization

11. The late 1960s were the years of student protests in France and Germany particularly.
12. AStA=Der Allgemeine Studentenausschuss: the official student representation.

for the Study of the Old Testament in Edinburgh, and subsequently in my book *The Problem of the Process of Transmission in the Pentateuch.*[13]

I had another new experience too during these months in Jerusalem. Every Sabbath morning, after synagogue, a small group of friends and colleagues met at Moshe Greenberg's home to study a passage from the Midrash. We read *Leviticus Rabbah,* the haggadic, narrative midrash on the book of Leviticus. To be plunged like this into reading rabbinic texts (which in this group meant drawing on all the possible tools of interpretation offered by biblical, rabbinic, and modern texts) gave me my first access to this wide field. I am still only on the very fringe of that field, but at least from that point I can look in, and can profit from it for the exegesis of Old Testament texts.

While I was working on these questions, I had still no idea that the problems of the Pentateuch sources had been taken up afresh in other places too, and that the mid-1970s would mean the end of a consensus in Old Testament studies which had lasted for almost a century. Shortly before my own book came out, books by John Van Seters[14] and Hans Heinrich Schmid[15] appeared, both of which pleaded for a radical change in the dating of the earlier Pentateuch sources. This meant striking at the very heart of the concept which had been essentially built up by Julius Wellhausen. A preexilic, or even an exilic, "Yahwist" had little or nothing in common with Wellhausen's earliest source—even less, admittedly, with the great theologian of the enlightened Solomonic era put forward and so convincingly interpreted by Gerhard von Rad. Even as one of the people who was diligently involved in this demolition, I cannot think back to that great and splendid era without a degree of nostalgic melancholy. It was great above all in its impressive unity, and in the masterly interpretation offered by our teachers. It seems to me that we are still a very long way away from replacing it by anything comparable, and I sometimes ask myself if a later history of Old Testament studies will not view us primarily as the wreckers of that impressive structure.

At the same time, I must add that Gerhard von Rad had a highly developed sense of the temporal nature and the metamorphoses of methodological approaches, and frequently made this evident. When Klaus Koch once enthusiastically wanted to interpret a text in the light

---

13. R. Rendtorff, *The Problem of the Process of Transmission in the Pentateuch,* JSOTSup 89 (Sheffield, 1990; German orig. 1977).

14. J. Van Seters, *Abraham in History and Tradition* (New Haven: Yale Univ. Press, 1975).

15. H. H. Schmid, *Der sogenannte Jahwist* (Zurich, 1976).

of the Holy War, von Rad gave him a sideways glance and said: "Isn't it enough for one person to talk nonsense?" And when I read the final sentence of the ninth edition of his Genesis commentary (whose publication he did not live to see) it is as if he were handing on a torch; for there he talks about "a comprehensive new analysis of the Pentateuchal narrative material, which we urgently need."[16] That was in 1971, even before the great changes had begun to make themselves felt.

IV

In the 1970s a debate had developed in the United States about the question of the Old Testament canon. At first it hardly attracted any notice in Germany. I myself came across it in the final phase of my work on an introduction to the Old Testament, to which I had at last addressed myself.[17] (It had already been planned in the 1960s but had continually fallen victim to the circumstances and needs of the times.) The most important book in this debate was Brevard Childs's *Introduction to the Old Testament as Scripture* (1979), which drew me inescapably into the discussion.[18] I very soon had the impression that in methodological approach what this book offered was not merely a variant of previous treatments of the Bible; it was a genuine alternative. In the judgment of an American reviewer: "Over against historical critical Biblical exegesis, [Childs] has turned things upside down in a truly radical way. It is not the original form of the text that is important, . . . it is its final form."[19] The debate about this is now being vigorously pursued in the United States, and among us in Germany too the contributions of people who have become alive to it are increasing. I do not yet know what is going to be the outcome, but I do know that here a task has emerged for me myself which I have to face—and have already begun to face, to some degree.

The matter can be put quite simply: the function of scholarly theological exegesis is not to analyze the text as we have it, and then to interpret the earlier stages of the text which have been elicited. Our function is

16. I should also like here to draw attention to his essay on Exodus 1–15: "Beobachtungen zur Moseerzählung Exodus 1–14," *EvT* 31 (1971): 579–88 (= *Gesammelte Studien zum Alten Testament* [Munich, 1973], 2:189–98), which shows his discernment of new questions.

17. Published in German in 1983 (3d ed. 1988); Eng. trans., *The Old Testament: An Introduction* (Philadelphia: Fortress Press; London: SCM Press, 1986).

18. B. Childs, *Introduction to the Old Testament as Scripture* (Philadelphia: Fortress Press, 1979).

19. P. D. Miller, Jr., "Der Kanon in der gegenwärtigen amerikanischen Diskussion," *JBTh* 3 (1988): 217–39, quotation from 233.

to interpret the text itself as it stands, in its present and final form. This certainly does not mean dispensing with the question about the stages which preceded the present text. But the task has changed: the earlier, preliminary stages are *really* preliminary stages to the present text as we have it. And interpreters must face up to the tensions in the text in their interpretation, instead of getting rid of them through analysis, and then expounding their own smoother version.

Apart from this undertaking, another one has presented itself in recent years, although the two are in many ways related. I can put it in the words that head an essay written by one of the younger American Old Testament scholars: "Why Jews Are Not Interested in Biblical Theology."[20] The essay explains why Jews cannot be interested in Old Testament theology in its prevailing form, because it is a Christian discipline which as a general rule views Christian interpretation as the key to the Old Testament. And the author, Jon D. Levenson, asks whether there cannot be another theology of the Hebrew Bible—a Jewish theology, or even a joint Jewish and Christian one? The question has been raised and the discussion has begun at scattered points in recent years. I sometimes think that this could perhaps be the most important task for the years remaining to me: to make a contribution to this discussion, and to help to free the Hebrew Bible from the captivity into which it was brought when it came to be labeled merely a preliminary step, now superseded and overcome, on the way to the Christian Bible.

The Old Testament field in its theological context is at least as exciting today as it was forty years ago. I have only presented one segment, from my own very personal viewpoint. I know that even in this faculty other ways of looking at things, and other projects, are thought to be important, and that my successor, whoever he may be, will formulate the tasks ahead of him differently. As one grows older, one of the things one learns is not to think that one's own view of things is the only view possible, and yet to hold to it as being mandatory for oneself.

This faculty, in all its interesting diversity, makes this viewpoint seem entirely natural and a matter of course. As I leave the ranks of its active members I should like say: "Thank you!" In the list of its members my name will now move one page forward. I think it is valuable for readers to be presented at the beginning with the names of the people who gave the faculty its profile in past years and decades, so that these names are

---

20. J. D. Levenson, "Why Jews Are Not Interested in Biblical Theology," in J. Neusner et al., eds., *Judaic Perspectives on Ancient Israel* (Philadelphia: Fortress Press, 1987), 281–307; published in German in *EvT* 51 (1991): 402–30.

not all too quickly forgotten. But above all, let me offer my good wishes to all those who are now going to carry on the faculty's work, and to my still unknown successor. It is my hope and wish that in some way or other he too will be able to see himself as one of the successors of Gerhard von Rad.

Acknowledgments

Chapter 1, "Old Testament Theology: Some Ideas for a New Approach," was published in *Nederduitse gereformeerde teologiese tydskrif* 30 (1989) 132–142. Translated and used by permission of N. G. Kerk-Uitgewers.

Chapter 2, "Rabbinic Exegesis and the Modern Christian Bible Scholar," was originally published in *Proceedings of the Eighth World Congress of Jewish Studies* (Jerusalem: World Union of Jewish Studies, 1983) 29–36. Copyright © 1983 The Magnes Press, The Hebrew University, Jerusalem. Used by permission of the publisher.

Chapter 3, "Between Historical Criticism and Holistic Interpretation: New Trends in Old Testament Exegesis," was originally published in *Congress Volume, Jerusalem 1986*, ed. J. A. Emerton, *Vetus Testamentum* Supplement 40 (1988) 289–303. Used by permission of E. J. Brill, Leiden.

Chapter 4, "Toward a Common Jewish-Christian Reading of the Hebrew Bible," was originally published in *Hebrew Bible or Old Testament? Studying the Bible in Judaism and Christianity*, ed. Roger Brooks and John J. Collins (Notre Dame, Ind.: University of Notre Dame Press, 1990) 89–108. Copyright © 1990 University of Notre Dame Press. Used by permission of the publisher.

Chapter 5, "The Importance of the Canon for a Theology of the Old Testament," was originally published in *"Wenn nicht jetzt, wann dann?" Aufsätze für Hans-Joachim Kraus zum 65. Geburtstag*, ed. H.-G. Geyer et al. (Neukirchen-Vluyn: Neukirchener Verlag, 1983) 3–11. Used by permission of the publisher.

Chapter 6, "The Place of Prophecy in a Theology of the Old Testament," is published here for the first time in English.

Chapter 7, "The Image of Postexilic Israel in German Old Testament Scholarship from Wellhausen to von Rad," was originally published in *Sha'arei Talmon: Studies in the Bible, Qumran, and the Ancient Near East Presented to Shemaryahu Talmon*, ed. M. Fishbane and E. Tov (Winona Lake, Ind.: Eisenbrauns, 1992) 165–173. Used by permission of the publisher.

Chapter 8, "Christological Interpretation as a Way of 'Salvaging' the Old Testament? Wilhelm Vischer and Gerhard von Rad," was originally published in *Schöpfung und Befreiung: Für Claus Westermann zum 80. Geburtstag*, ed. Rainer Albertz, Friedemann W. Golka, and Jürgen Kegler, 191–203. Copyright © 1989 Calwer Verlag, Stuttgart. Translated and used by permission of the publisher.

Chapter 9, " 'Where Were You When I Laid the Foundation of the Earth?' Creation and Salvation History," was originally published in *Frieden in der Schöpfung: Das Naturveständnis protestantischer Theologie*, ed. G. Rau, A. M. Ritter, and H. Timm (Gütersloh: Gütersloher Verlagshaus Gerd Mohn, 1987) 35–57. Translated and used by permission of the publisher.

Chapter 10, "Revelation and History: Particularism and Universalism in Israel's View of Revelation," was first published in *Weltgespräch der Religionen* 7 (1981) 37–49. Translated and used by permission of Verlag Herder, Freiburg.

Chapter 11, " 'Covenant' as a Structuring Concept in Genesis and Exodus," was first published in *Journal of Biblical Literature* 108 (1989) 385–393. Used by permission of the publisher.

Chapter 12, "The Birth of the Deliverer: 'The Childhood of Samuel' Story in Its Literary Framework," is published here for the first time in English.

Chapter 13, "The Composition of the Book of Isaiah," was first published in *Vetus Testamentum* 34 (1984) 295–320. Translated and used by permission of E. J. Brill, Leiden.

Chapter 14, "Isaiah 6 in the Framework of the Composition of the Book," was first published in *Le livre d'Isaie: Les oracles et leurs relectures, unité et complexité de l'ouvrage*, ed. J. Vermeylen (Bibliotheca Ephemeridum Theologicarum Lovaniensium, 81), Leuven University Press/Uitgeverij Peeters, Leuven, 1989, 73–82. Translated and used by permission of the publisher.

Chapter 15, "Isaiah 56:1 as a Key to the Formation of the Book of Isaiah," is published here for the first time in English.

Chapter 16, "Ezekiel 20 and 36:16ff. in the Framework of the Composition of the Book," was originally published in *Ezekiel and His Book: Textual and Literary Criticism and Their Interrelation*, ed. J. Lust (Bibliotheca Ephemeridum Theologicarum Lovaniensium, 74), Leuven University Press/Uitgeverij Peeters, Leuven, 1986, 260–265. Translated and used by permission of the publisher.

Chapter 17, "What Is New in the New Covenant?" is published here for the first time in English.

Chapter 18, "Forty Years On: Four Decades of Old Testament Scholarship as I Have Experienced Them in Heidelberg and Elsewhere," is published here for the first time in English.

Index of Biblical References

Index of Names

Abramowski, R., 78, 86, 86 n. 30, 87, 90 n. 40
Ackroyd, P., 52, 64, 147–48, 149, 151, 152 n. 26, 156 n. 40, 164 n. 55, 173, 177, 178 n. 24, 195
Albertz, R., 95–96
Albright, W. F., 25–26, 210, 211
Alt, A., 25, 26, 83, 85–86, 86 n. 26, 210, 211, 213
Anderson, B. W., 52

Bacher, W., 20
Barr, J., 12 n. 26, 171, 195
Barth, K., 7, 39, 85, 94, 95
Barton, J., 28 n. 1
Bauer, G. L., 5, 38
Baumgärtel, F., 87
Begrich, J., 83, 139 n. 16, 139 n. 17, 148
Blenkinsopp, J., 47, 53, 53 n. 27, 54, 61–63, 63 n. 14, 65
Bodelschwingh, F. von, 89
Bonhoeffer, D., 90
Bornkamm, G., 212
Brunner, P., 212
Buber, M., 28 n. 2, 136 n. 8
Budde, K., 137 n. 9
Bultmann, R., 47, 87, 114, 211, 212

Calvin, J., 80, 84
Campenhausen, H. von, 212, 213
Childs, B., 12 n. 26, 36, 46, 48, 52, 126, 136 n. 7, 142 n. 24, 171, 195, 217; on the biblical theology movement, 47; on the book of Amos, 50; exegetical method of, 18–19, 51 n. 22; on Fuchs and Ebeling, 47 n. 4; as "systematic," 126 n. 3; tradition-history method and, 51
Clements, R. E., 61, 64 n. 16, 125–26, 151 n. 25, 175
Coats, G. W., 47, 49, 49 n. 11, 50–51
Crüsemann, F., 96, 140 n. 17
Cullmann, O., 46, 47

De Wette, W. M. L., 18, 66–67, 68, 69, 121, 144, 144 n. 27
Dillmann, A., 178 n. 24
Duhm, B., 57, 144

Ebeling, G., 47, 47 n. 4, 73, 73 n. 19, 74, 74 n. 23, 211–12
Eichrodt, W., 6–7, 8, 39 n. 15, 46, 58, 78 n. 6, 95
Eissfeldt, O., 6 n. 8, 213

233